Partnership Council Field Book

Strategies And Tools For Co-Creating A Healthy Work Place

Bonnie Wesorick, Laurie Shiparski,
Michelle Troseth and Kathy Wyngarden

Printed in the United States of America.
Grandville Printing Company
Grandville, Michigan

Published by:
Practice Field Publishing
600 28th St., S.W.
Grand Rapids, MI 49509
(616) 530-9206

Library of Congress Catalog Card Number: 97-069991

ISBN: 0-9648264-4-5

DEDICATION

This book is dedicated to our husbands,
our cherished partners:

David Wesorick
Michael Shiparski
Kevin Moore
Henry Wyngarden

And to those who have the
courage and persistence to
forge partnerships in the places
they live and work.

Table of Contents

Contributing Authors

Margie Bosscher, RN

Jeanette Brooks, LPN

Deb Chapman, PCA

Tracy Christopherson, RRT

Jan Falk, RN

Carol Glass, RN

Carol Gemink, RPh

Joseph Moore, MD

Marti Rheault, RN, MSN, CURN

Deb RitzHolland, RN, BSN, OCN

Jeanne Roode, RN, MSN,CNA

Kristin Root, BSW, SW

John Silowsky, RN

Darren VandeZande, RN, BSN

Marcia Veenstra, RN, BSN

Opening

This book is collective learning at its best. It has golden nuggets of creativity and wisdom from those living and working in the world of health care. As the authors of this book we have learned much about relationships and thriving in the work place. We are inspired to share the learning we have had about new ways to be together and ways to create systems to support us in our work. The success of this work can be attributed to the development and evolution of a Partnership Council (or Unit-Based Council, as it has been named in some organizations). The name has evolved to Partnership Council because the word "unit-based" did not fit organizations without walls, such as community programs and home care. As Unit-Based Councils have evolved, the word "partnership" seems fitting to describe the key reason they exist.

Partnership Councils serve as the core support for individual and group growth in numerous health care settings. They provide an infrastructure and utilize practical methods to enhance relationships, develop shared leadership, and improve outcomes for those receiving and providing health care. This book reflects our successes, setbacks, excitement, and challenges. Our intention is to portray the real experiences of those who have committed to changing their work settings.

In 1984 work began at Butterworth Hospital in Grand Rapids, Michigan to enhance relationships and care delivery in health care organizations through the use of the Clinical Practice Model (CPM). CPM is an integrated systems thinking framework that supports the emergence of a healing environment for both the person receiving care and the provider. One component of the framework is the Partnership Council infrastructure. Hundreds of other people began embarking on this same journey and there is now an ever growing CPM Associate Consortium of over 40 health care settings (See Appendix B for list). These organizations are all connected through the CPM Resource Center (CPMRC). The mission of the CPMRC is to enhance partnering relationships across the world for the generation of collective knowledge and wisdom that continually improves professional practice and community health care services.

This book reflects the wisdom of many as they developed and progressed Partnership Councils. We share the experiences of others through our Wisdom From The Field stories. These stories come from individuals working in diverse health care roles and diverse settings including the CPMRC Associate Consortium. There is wisdom from the different tracks including support staff, management/operations, direct care providers, educators/resource, and researchers. Within these tracks arc diverse disciplines representing respiratory therapy, social work, nursing, pharmacy, pastoral care, nutritional service, physical therapy, physicians, occupational therapy, speech therapy, and business/operations. There is also wisdom from those who have received health care services.

A diverse core group of contributing authors have worked over a year to create this field book and a parallel video series (see Appendix C). The members of this group were invited to be authors and participants in the video because they are living the realities of Partnership Councils. They contributed their learning and brought experiences from others which made the actual writing a unique learning experience within itself. As we gathered to produce this book and video series, more learning was generated. It was not easy to find the time and resources needed to do this work in the midst of our busy schedules. As a group we worked together in partnership, living the principles put forth in this book.

The effort seemed worth it, for during the collective process we became even more clear on what we had learned during the years of doing this work. As we contributed our individual learning and experiences, compelling collective wisdom emerged. This reinforced our belief that there is yet untapped potential, within ourselves and our work settings. As we put forth the outcomes of our work together, we hope you will reflect on the insights offered, not to merely accept them but to ask yourself, "What is my thinking and why? What really matters most for me, my colleagues and those I serve? How can I uphold what matters most?"

This is the fourth book in the Wisdom From The Field Series. We welcome back those who began the journey with either the first, second, or third book in this series: *A Journey From Old To New Thinking* (Wesorick, 1995); or *A Journey From Old To New Relationships In The Work Setting,* (Wesorick, 1996); or *Can The Human Being Thrive In The Work Place? Dialogue As A Strategy Of Hope* (Wesorick and Shiparski, 1997). Each of these books explored in depth one of the three fundamental components of a healthy work culture; new thinking, relationships, and conversations. Although we reference the health care arena, we have found the principles and situations to be universal and applicable to all work settings.

This book, along with a parallel video, will bring all three components alive by addressing the integration of each into the daily work place. It is designed for, and by, those whose legacy will be one of helping co-create healthy work relationships and, therefore, healthy work cultures. This is called a field book which means it centers on learning from the field. It does offer references that support or add clarity to this learning but it is not intended to be an exhaustive literature review of the topics. There are many tables and diagrams to use as teaching and learning tools.

For those just beginning this journey within the Wisdom From The Field Series, the following travel tips will be helpful. Please do not bring any baggage. We have found that it gets in the way, interferes with your desired pace and prevents you from going to the most exciting places along the way. Stories will be shared throughout this book to capture the wisdom from the field. It is shared to provoke your thinking and deepen your insights about the realities of creating healthy work cultures.

If you believe you see yourself or someone you know in a clinical story, realize it may not be a story about any one individual. We see ourselves and others because the stories are universal and represent realities across the practice field of life. The confidentiality of all people and practice settings is honored.

The success of this journey rests with your thinking, your wisdom. Questions will be asked with that end in mind. That is also why this book is laid out with wide margins. These margins provide a place for you to write your learning, thinking, questions, realizations, concerns, feelings, and insights.

We are not taking you on this journey, our intention is to partner and travel with you. We will share our learning and assumptions as we travel. You will probably be both comfortable and uncomfortable as you read. If you write in the margins "comfortable" and "uncomfortable" and write what is behind those feelings, your personal wisdom will emerge. That is one goal of this book.

We invite you to read the following pages that are filled with reflections of current realities, and visions for a hopeful future. After years of doing this work, we are now compelled to write about it. We are hopeful that in some way it will help others who are on the path of co-creating healthy work places. We offer this poem that reflects the essence of what we are trying to create in Partnership Councils.

Create A Place...

Create a place
where we can gather
learn our stories
be with each other.

Create a place
where ears are open
words are welcome
truths are spoken.

Create a place
where learning is constant
practice is permitted
wisdom is abundant.

Create a place
of meaning and purpose
a respite from busy
time to focus on service.

Create a place
where wholeness is nourished
Connecting in BodyMindSpirit
together we will flourish.

- Laurie Shiparski

Chapter One

A Healthy Work Place:
What is the call?

"No matter how large the corporation you work in,
it is too small for one human soul."
- David Whyte

There is a call for freedom, the freedom to express the soul in the work place. The soul is expressed in meaningful relationships. Relationships rooted in the ways of the soul are called partnerships. Partnerships join hearts, hands, and minds around a common purpose. Partnerships create the invisible field of hope, potential and discovery for the work place. Throughout the pages of this book we will share with you the lessons learned by thousands of colleagues across the continent who collectively decided to work together to create healthy work cultures. It is not another reiteration of the theory that supports a healthy culture but a book about the day-to-day work necessary to bring the soul into the work place via partnerships. The places, the infrastructures created to help with this work are called *Partnership Councils*.

The western world created a work culture where the body and mind were welcomed but the soul was insidiously ignored resulting in a two dimensional rather than three dimensional state. If one wanted to achieve real success in the work place, it was best to leave the explosion of soul at home or leave it in the parking lot outside the door. Without the soul, the mind and the body could focus more clearly on the things to be done, the work at hand, the ability to produce more efficiently and improve productivity and bottom line. Yet the soul is the essence, the spirit of life, the center of humanness, joy and creativity This book is about creating a healthy work culture, one in which the soul is honored. It is in response to the call from the many whose quality of life is influenced by the nature of their work environments.

The desire for a healthy work culture sits in the hearts of those who enter it daily. It may not be spoken out loud, but there is a longing for it. Many adults spend more waking hours in the work place than they do in their home, in the community, or in play. Consciously or unconsciously people know the impact of the work culture on their private lives. Have you ever said, "I had a bad day at work" or "I had a good day at work?" Regardless of the particular events of the day, did either influence the time you spent with your family or friends outside of work?

Have you ever left your work place tense, frustrated, feeling a lack of support or respect, or trying to understand why no one seemed to care about those things that you thought mattered most? On those days did you find yourself wondering why you picked this type of work, or if it was worth it? Have you ever felt drained or found that your frustration turned to anger? Have you ever snapped back in conversation with your loved ones because of the frustration you brought home with you? Can you recall how that influenced your relationships at home?

Conversely, can you recall a day when you left work and felt a sense of accomplishment and excitement? What was it that happened? What was the nature of the circumstances that surrounded you? For example, recall the conversations and relationships that occurred. In what way did that day at work influence the conversations and relationships with your friends and family?

If our work culture nourishes our human spirit, we will bring a nourishing energy into our home and into our relationships. If the culture is dehumanizing, impersonal, robotic, stressful, disrespectful or controlling, we will bring home the same. The work culture influences the quality of our life. So, what are the fundamental characteristics of a healthy work culture, one that welcomes the soul?

In our work with many diverse settings, people often talk about "their" culture and comment that it is different from any other place. There is often comparison of cultures and great fear of moving into a new culture. What is this invisible but very tangible force that surrounds each person who walks into the work place? What do we mean by culture? Culture is a way of being together. Quinn (1993, p. 41) defines culture as "A people enacting a story." Is it influenced by the presence of each human being? Is this invisible field nothing more than the presence of the unseen souls of the many who walk or have walked there? If so, what is it that makes one culture healthy and one culture unhealthy?

There is no one thing that "creates" a healthy work culture. It is not healthy today and unhealthy tomorrow. There is no arriving at a point and declaring "we have done it." It is not a static thing. Healthy and unhealthy cultures have a lot in common. For example, both are often very busy, and there is always much to be done. In a typical day there are unexpected events, problems, opportunities, challenges, and failures. It is not the busyness, but the way in which it is lived out.

What if the healthy culture is nothing more than the connection of the unseen souls carrying out important work, and an unhealthy culture the disconnection of the unseen souls carrying out important work? How do we connect the souls, the spirits, the being of the many who enter into the work place? Over the years, three interrelated characteristics have emerged to be fundamental in connecting souls and creating healthy work cultures:

1. Shared meaning and purpose in work,
2. Healthy relationships and,
3. Meaningful conversations.

The glue that connects these three characteristics is the spirit of continuous learning. Throughout these pages, the efforts, the tools, the strategies, and the lessons learned to strengthen all three characteristics will unfold. A brief look at each will provide a common ground and enhance the learning as it is weaved throughout the text.

Characteristic: Shared Meaning And Purpose In Work

The soul is connected to that which gives meaning and purpose to life. Shared meaning and purpose in work connects the souls of those who walk there. Roach (1997, p. 12) noted that "Our search for meaning is more than a search for individual identity; it is, rather, a search for the meaning of our personhood, our connectedness with others." Healthy work cultures honor the personhood of another and consciously connect people through shared purpose and meaning.

It is easy in a productivity and bottom line driven culture to focus only on the things to be done, the tangible. It becomes difficult to keep focused on the purpose and meaning of the work when conversations only center around tasks, rituals, initiatives, and profits. It becomes difficult to keep focused when one's accomplishments are continuously judged by the speed and the number of things or jobs finished. It can lead to depersonalization and dehumanization of the work. It is easier to focus on "doing" than it is on becoming. It is not easy to hear the whispers of the invisible voice of the soul when the loud noise of "doing" surrounds us. Because it is foreign to listen to the soul in our typical settings, it takes conscious effort.

The initial step to establish shared purpose and meaning is to uncover what each person and the group collectively believe matters most. We call this the "Core Belief Review Process." The tools and resources used in the process are presented in Chapter Eight. Table One on page 11 shows the outcomes of the process that has been carried out over the last 20 years in multiple health care settings across the continent. The Core Belief statements are the summary of the collective work of thousands of health care providers who review the beliefs every two years to assure they represent what they collectively think matters most. There are two columns in Table One on page 11 so you can compare the results of the recently completed review of the Core Beliefs (1997) with the belief statements that were written in 1995. The word changes in column two are the result of interviews with over 2,000 individuals, groups of providers, and recipients of care from the CPM Associate Consortium.

The Core Beliefs are important because once we establish shared beliefs about the mission, *we can help each other live them*. When we use the core beliefs as the center of our work, we do not impose structures, but healthy structures emerge. We at the CPMRC have formed partnerships with over 40 diverse health care settings across the continent and are continuously creating and improving our clinical systems to help us live the Core Beliefs. The words listed in Table One reflect the new level of depth and expression to which the Core Beliefs have grown and are being lived in the work place. We are collectively bridging the gap between what we believe in our hearts is important about our work and what we live everyday. We are forming partnering relationships with many colleagues to do this work, which is the second characteristic of a healthy work culture.

TABLE ONE

1995 Core Beliefs	1997 Core Beliefs
Quality emerges from an environment driven by mission, principles, and partnerships	Quality emerges in environments where individuals share mission, values, and partnerships.
Each person has the right to receive care that optimizes health which is body, mind, and spirit in balance.	Each person has the right to health care which promotes wholeness in body, mind, and spirit.
Each person is accountable to explain and provide his/her unique contribution to care.	Each person is accountable to communicate and integrate his/her contribution to care.
Health care is coordinated and delivered in partnership with the person receiving care.	Health care is planned, coordinated,and delivered in partnership with the person/family/community.
New ways of thinking are essential to continually improve health care throughout the life span.	New ways of thinking are essential to continually improve health.
Empowerment begins with each person and is enhanced by relationships and systems design.	Empowerment begins with each person and is enhanced by partnerships and systems supports.

Characteristic: Healthy Relationships

Healthy relationships create healthy work cultures. The term partnership is used to describe healthy relationships throughout this writing. This book is the fourth in a series called Wisdom From The Field. The goal of Book II, *A Journey From Old To New Relationships In The Work Setting,* (Wesorick, 1996) was to uncover the Principles of Partnership. These principles are reviewed in Table Two on pages 14 and 15. The goal of this book is to *share what we have learned about the work of living the Principles of Partnership.*

When a person lives the Principles of Partnership, respect comes alive. Have you ever been disturbed by news or a story that poignantly brought to your attention the lack of respect for another human--for example, a news program that used undercover cameras to expose the abuse of the elderly in some nursing homes, or the abuse of children in day care centers? What was it that moved you? Conversely, have you ever been touched by the great respect demonstrated by one person toward another, such as volunteers at the Special Olympics, or an elderly woman walking for two hours to be by the side of her comatose husband, or simply the placement of flowers honoring someone who has died? What was it that moved you? And what does this have to do with a book about partnerships? A lot, since it is in the extremes of human behaviors or actions that we are able to gain insight into the nature of human relationships.

In the extremes of behaviors we are able to see the importance and the outcomes of healthy and unhealthy human relationships. The examples of extremes teach us the differences between relationships that honor or dishonor others. The awareness of extremes stimulates us to ask deeper more meaningful questions, such as, "What lies beneath the behaviors that value or devalue another?" Or, "What can be done to prevent the violation of the sacredness of one's personhood?" Extremes stimulate us to ponder, *"Are we all less when another is disrespected?"* They help us realize that healthy and unhealthy relationships are a reflection of the human nature in all of us. Extremes lead us to consider the insidious factors which we experience in the day-to-day patterns of living that influence the relationships we have as humans with one another.

What does a relationship based on the Principles of Partnership look like? Have you ever walked into a room and felt the energy of creativity and innovation? Have you experienced enthusiasm, acceptance, and an invitation to discover and recognize mystery? For a moment, recall how that felt. This is what partnership feels like. What impact would a culture like this have on you?

In a healthy work place you sense the sustained intention of people to connect with one another as human beings. What is apparent is the respect for the personhood of the other, not just the task at hand. There is a sense of importance of each person's work, regardless of the role each contributes. The synchrony of action is similar to a group of musicians playing from the same sheet of music. There is no air of hierarchy, entitlement, competition or judgment--just synchrony. The interactions create new potentials. There is an invitation to question, discover and expand thinking. There is desire to listen to and acknowledge individual capacity and collective capacity. There is confidence and a sense of trust that comes from personal independence, and the understanding of collective interdependence. There is a welcoming of diversity of opinion and a hunger for continuous learning. There is an understanding that for partnering relationships to occur the third characteristic, meaningful conversation, is essential.

Characteristic: Meaningful Conversations

Meaningful conversations create meaningful relationships. One cannot exist without the other. Meaningful conversations are rooted in the Principles of Dialogue, which was the focus of Book III in the Wisdom From The Field Series: *Can the Human Being Thrive in the Work Place? Dialogue As A Strategy Of Hope,* (Wesorick and Shiparski, 1997). Table Three reviews the Principles of Dialogue.

What does a relationship look like that is developing and using the Principles of Dialogue? Think of a time at work when you felt welcomed, your perspective sought, diverse views were honored and explored, and your message was not judged but listened to deeply. For a moment, recall how that felt.

TABLE TWO

PRINCIPLES OF PARTNERSHIP

Principle of Intention: a personal choice to connect with another at a deeper level of humanness.
- Is not about doing, but becoming.
- Requires going within, so one can reach out.
- Connects at a place where purpose and meaning of life emerge.
- Connects with others, not to control, but to deepen insights into oneself and others.
- Requires vulnerability and starts with personal work of becoming a partner.

Principle of Mission: a call to live out something that matters or is meaningful.
- Centers around shared purpose, principles, and core beliefs--not position, policy/procedure, personal needs, bottom line, or power.
- Requires work of synchronizing personal and professional mission.
- Envisions work as an opportunity to make visible a person's purpose.

Principle of Equal Accountability: a relationship driven by ownership of mission, not power-over or fear.
- Holds each person to his/her choice: one is not the boss, one is not the subordinate.
- Knows competition and judgment interfere with individual and collective accountability to mission.
- Honors another's choice of role, responsibility, and contribution.
- Is accountable to support others in achieving mission.
- Is not in relationship to evaluate or judge the other's work or worth.
- Knows credibility relates to quality of work, not type of work.
- Does not feed the ego, but nourishes the spirit.

Principle of Potential: an inherent capacity within oneself and others to continuously learn, grow and create.
- Sees self and others as continuous learners with untapped potential.
- Pursues clarity on each other's role and responsibility, not to judge but to integrate and potentiate one another.
- Taps others' expertise related to mission.
- Enhances choices, options, creativity, and the imagination of others.
- Helps others recognize and tap personal wisdom.

Table Two, continued

- Seeks different perspectives but maintains common mission.
- Respects the individuality, uniqueness and diversity of self and others.
- Does not spend time molding others to be what he/she thinks they should be.
- Supports others as they evolve and change to achieve the mission.
- Explores self and others' assumptions so to deepen wisdom.
- Knows when to ask for help.
- Requires compassion and ability to learn from and see beyond vulnerability.

Principle of Balance: a harmony of relationships with self and others, necessary to achieve mission.

- Understands that personal stability deters being controlled by external forces.
- Accountable for personal balance, choice, and competency.
- Cares for self and others.
- Knows that harmony in work relationships, as the mission, is not optional.
- Addresses imbalance in work relationships.
- Helps others self-organize.
- Knows the source of energy is not in the tasks, but in the relationships.
- Works on continuous learning and shifting to improve relationships.

Principle of Trust: a sense of synchrony on important issues or things that matter.

- Starts with self, must trust self first before trusting others.
- Knows personal trustworthiness precedes a trusting relationship with another.
- Recognizes that fear is a barrier to trust.
- Values the power that is within, not outside self.
- Does not have secrets, but shares information openly.
- Does not defend thinking, but shares it.
- Does not speak for the other, but seeks to hear the voice of the other.
- Does not try to get "buy-in" but dialogues to discover what is best for shared mission.
- Does not focus on who gets to make the decision, but what is the best decision.
- Does not blame, withdraw, instill guilt, rescue, fix, criticize or perpetrate.
- Focuses on quality of time together, not amount of time.

This is how we connect when we live the Principles of Dialogue. Conversely, while speaking at a meeting have you experienced some of your colleagues having side conversations, or doing work they brought with them? Have you observed apathy or experienced the fear to speak openly? Have you felt tension, noticed blaming or felt your perspective was being judged by those in charge? For a moment recall what that was like. In what way did the experience impact you, the way you felt, the way you reacted? Did it influence your thinking, your actions, the quality of your conversation or the quality of your day?

Conversations in the work place are often determined by the underlying patterns of relationships that prevail in the culture. Table Four compares the focus which describes the behaviors between bureaucratic and hierarchical versus empowered, partnering relationships. Conversations in each culture are very different and parallel with the listed behaviors. Bureaucratic and hierarchical cultures cultivate conversations of competition, judgment, debate and control. These are very different from conversations between partners which focus on what matters most, enhancing potential and tapping into collective wisdom. Dialogue strengthens conversation skills that shift from hierarchical to partnering conversations.

It is easy to maintain what is familiar, whether good or bad. Conversations are a reflection of what is familiar, accepted, or encouraged in a culture. Just as we must continuously learn new ways to become competent in our work, so must we learn new ways to have meaningful conversations. Dialogue gives us permission to be together differently. The principles deepen the nature of our conversations, which in turn deepen our relationships and strengthens the meaning and purpose of our work place. Table Five reviews the correlations between healthy or partnering relationships and dialogue.

Response To The Call

Where do we begin in response to the call from the work place? What is the fundamental work necessary to weave shared meaning and purpose, healthy relationships and meaningful conversations into the fabric of the day? We begin by creating a place to do the work. We call this space "Partnership Councils." The following chapters discuss the structures and processes that support Partnership Councils and the outcomes of the work. The outcomes of implementing structures and processes designed to create healthy work cultures were studied in a six year pilot of CPM within multiple settings. Leadership was noted to play a major role in the successful transition from old to new thinking, practice, and relationships. A closer look at the nature of leadership necessary to initiate and sustain the work will be the focus of the next chapter.

TABLE FOUR

Comparison of the "Focus" of Hierarchical versus Partnering Relationships

OLD PARADIGM **Bureaucratic Culture** **Hierarchical Relationships** **Focus: "I"**	**NEW PARADIGM** **Empowered Culture** **Partnering Relationships** **Focus: "We"**
↓	↓
Position and Power Driven	Principle, Mission, and Vision Driven
↓	↓
Boss/Manager/Subordinate	Partnership
↓	↓
"Power-Over"	"Power Releasing"
↓	↓
Evaluate and Judge	Enhance Potential
↓	↓
Problem Focused	Opportunity Focused
↓	↓
Urgency/Crisis	What Matters Most
↓	↓
"Transactional" Relationships Task Driven Visible/Time Oriented	"Transformational" Relationships Mission Driven Invisible/Value Oriented
↓	↓
Individual Wisdom	Collective Wisdom
↓	↓
Competition/Turf	Collaboration
↓	↓
Entitlement	Alliance
↓	↓
Efficiency	Effectiveness
↓	↓
Compliance	Ownership
↓	↓
Ramification: Blame/Guilt	Ramification: Accountability

Used with permission: © Wesorick, B. (1996) <u>The Closing and Opening of a Millennium: A Journey From Old To New Relationships In The Work Setting</u>. Michigan: Practice Field Publishing.

TABLE FIVE

Dialogue Helps Create Cultures Of Partnerships

PRINCIPLES OF PARTNERSHIP	HOW DIALOGUE STRENGTHENS PARTNERSHIPS
Intention: A personal choice to connect with another at a deeper level of humanness.	Extends an invitation to connect with another in a respectful conversation which honors the Body-MindSpirit.
Mission: A call to live out something that matters or is meaningful.	Provides an opportunity to speak about, and together with others, dig deeper into those things that matter or are meaningful to each person.
Equal Accountability: A relationship driven by ownership of mission, not power-over or fear.	Creates a practice field where there is no position, role, hierarchy, judgment or competition. There is equal accountability to listen, inquire, share, and learn.
Potential: An inherent capacity within oneself and others to continually learn, grow, and create.	Provides a renewal process that honors the right of each person to speak from his/her personal wisdom. It ponders the mystery of another. It teaches others through advocacy, listening, and inquiry to tap into, and dig deeper into personal and collective wisdom. It connects diversity which unleashes and creates new thinking, uncovers new possibilities, opens new doors and unfolds new potentials and alternatives for choices.
Balance: A harmony of relationship with self and others necessary to achieve mission.	Welcomes silence which helps individuals listen to themselves, others, and then reflect. It exposes inconsistencies. It brings awareness of personal thinking which uncovers deep values—important for self balance. Personal independence precedes healthy interdependence. It helps find common understanding and creates a passion to connect in common purpose.
Trust: A sense of synchrony on important issues and things that matter.	Uncovers the truths that dissipate fear. The practice field creates a safe, respectable place that helps uncover and expose basic thinking. There is no attempt to guess or judge. It honors diversity, extremes, and seeks to connect patterns. It is easier to listen to someone's voice when one's own voice is heard. Inquiry helps break patterns of assumptions and checks into deeper meanings. Deeper, yet personal thinking seems to mirror universal truths which connect beings.

Used with permission: © Wesorick, B., Shiparski, L. (1997) Can The Human Being Thrive In The Work Place? Dialogue As A Strategy Of Hope. Michigan: Practice Field Publishing.

Chapter Two

Leadership:
What is the role of the leader in
a work setting of partnership?

"Leaders owe the organization a new reference point for what caring, purposeful, committed people can be in the institutional setting. Notice I did not say what people can do-what we can do is merely a consequence of what we can be."
- Max Depree

Leadership is one of the greatest strengths and one of the greatest barriers for the development of Partnership Councils needed to create healthy work places. Our hierarchical ways of thinking about leadership have held us back. There are different ways of thinking about leadership. This is the reason we are devoting a chapter to the clarification and exploration of new leadership that is rooted in partnership. Consider the following ways of thinking about leadership that were brought to our attention by Beth Jandemoa and Glennifer Gillespie (1997) of Collaborative Changeworks.

A traditional view of leadership is reflected in the following statements by Rost (1991, p. 180). "Leadership is great men and women with certain preferred traits influencing followers to do what the leaders wish in order to achieve group/organizational goals that reflect excellence defined as some kind of higher level effectiveness. The leader defines a process, which acts on the followers in order to produce an outcome."

This traditional view is also referred to as the "Industrial leadership paradigm which is hierarchical, individualistic, reductionistic, linear and mechanical." (Lambert, 1995, p.32) Though some continue to believe this view, it stunts the growth of councils and people in a work setting. Many well intentioned leaders operating from this perspective are unable to tap the full capacity of the people they *think* they are leading. This implies that only a few people really have the capability to lead and that the essence of leading is persuading another person. Actually, many have the ability to lead and demonstrate leadership in a culture of partnerships. If ideas and actions come from only one leader, there is limited thinking and options. Often this leader spends more time seeking support and "buy in" from their followers.

Thinking about leadership in a new and different way, Lambert (1995, p. 33) states, "Leadership is the mutual and dynamic interaction among members of an organization/community that enables them to construct meanings and behaviors that lead towards a common purpose."

This belief is more congruent with the way Partnership Councils are intended to experience leadership. It refers to leadership as building community and shared meaning. In Chapter Eight there is a more in-depth discussion around the concept of shared meaning. This view offers more capacity for leadership that is rich with diverse views and expanding choices. Leaders in the old way of thinking did not ask for help, knew the answers, and told others what to do. However, shared leadership brings forward the capacity of every member to partner and achieve the shared purpose. Table Six summarizes ten beliefs about effective leaders as they have been experienced in Partnership Councils and work settings.

Partnership Councils represent a new way of thinking about leadership. They survive and even thrive because they are a catalyst in converting hierarchical cultures into ones of partnership. The shifts in a culture moving from hierarchy to partnership were introduced earlier and provide a basis for envisioning this culture change. Further exploration of these ideas will help us develop a common ground for understanding shared leadership.

What images jump into your mind when you hear the words manager, leader, boss, subordinate, or follower? The diversity of responses is often based on past experiences. The common bureaucratic and hierarchical work cultures emerged from a boss-subordinate mind set. In this mental model the boss is the one in charge, and the subordinate does as told. The boss's thinking and goals are more important than the subordinate's. Though hierarchy is about relationships, they are relationships based on who has the most power, authority, or control. In hierarchy there is a boss with the power and a subordinate with little power.

TABLE SIX

Effective leaders in Partnership Councils and partnering cultures act from the following beliefs:

1. Leaders are needed for the transition from old to new ways of thinking and being.
2. Leaders help others lead themselves and do not guide others to think their way.
3. Leadership is assumed by each person and it rotates through everyone.
4. No position or role has higher authority; everyone brings expertise.
5. Group actions arise out of a collective purpose--not one leader's purpose.
6. The success of a leader is not how many followers he/she has but how many leaders step forward.
7. Mission, vision, core beliefs, and partnership provide foundation and direction for leaders, especially in the midst of great change.
8. Leaders are teachers and learners.
9. A leader shows accountability for his/her development by taking his/her own inward journey.
10. Leaders do not defend what they know but help others expand what they know.
11. Leaders have meaningful conversations around what matters most.

As the work place became more developed, the word "boss" began to be replaced with the word "manager." Then a major leap took place: the word manager was interchanged with the word leader. As the word leader emerged so did the word follower. There can be no leader without followers and no followers without a leader. In the old thinking it was common to believe that manager was the leader, just because of their position. The term leader became associated with position.

Although the words changed, the relationships did not change. Whether called boss, manager, or leader, bosses are bosses and followers are subordinates. The underlying difference between boss/subordinate or leader/follower is importance, power, authority, and control. Bosses, now referred to as managers or leaders, are those people listed on the organizational chart. The words subordinate and follower are of less importance. In fact, they are rarely placed on the organizational chart. Subordinates are implied at the bottom, a place with little power, authority, and/or control. At times, their importance was recognized via the term "informal leaders." These people were not included on the chart because they came from the rank and file. Yet they were known to have power or influence over others.

Some still question, "What is so wrong with using the word subordinate?" It is important in using such a word to ask ourselves if it conveys our intention. What mental model will it evoke in the others whom we call subordinate? The word usually evokes feelings of inferiority and insignificance in others. Is this what we are trying to convey?

In *The Power of Followership,* Robert Kelley (1992), explores the myths about leaders and followers. He notes that followers are the people who contribute more than 80 percent to the success of any project or organization while leaders contribute only 20 percent at best. He notes that "Leadership and followership have been stereotyped to the detriment of both." (p. 28) He wonders how and why the leadership myth of hierarchy continues. He sites that followers are people of exceptional ability who know how to lead themselves. He asks, "How did we come to see followership as the antithesis of leadership rather than followers as collaborative in effort of organizations work?" (p. 33)

Healthy relationships are about partnership, a word that has no roots in the old ways. It is not just another new word, but a whole new way of thinking. It represents the heartbeat of a healthy work culture. In partnership, one is not the boss and one is not the subordinate. One is not the leader; one is not the follower. In partnership, each person is both, that is shared leadership. For the council to be successful, both roles are needed continuously and there is equality. Equality does not mean they have the same job, the same responsibilities, the same talents. It means both roles are of equal worth, respect, and dignity. One individual is not more important than the other. They have equal accountability to the mission. A healthy work culture is about everyone. Kelley (1992, p. 24) reminded us about the roots of our country when he said, "The U.S. Constitution begins with 'We the people,' not 'We, the leaders.'" The Partnership Council is about "we the people" in shared leadership.

Leaders and followers relying on hierarchy are not at all like those in partnership. In partnership a leader is accountable to serve the group to achieve its work. The follower does the work because they know it is important. Neither demand recognition, power, authority, or control over another. Both are committed to do the work of partnership and create a healthy work culture. The outcomes of partnership are the same as the outcomes of shared leadership. These outcomes are listed in Table Seven which speak to the importance of the work on partnership.

Though the outcomes of partnering and shared leadership are desirable, it requires constant attention to develop and maintain them. During the transition from boss-subordinate roles into partnership, one challenge relates to the personal work necessary to develop the skills of partnership, which includes leadership and followership skills. Many people have not developed the skills for leading group work and connecting as partners. Learning to be partners with people previously seen as the boss, the one in charge or the person who is the informal leader, needs work. Providing opportunities to support the transition is essential. See Chapter Eight for ways to support this transition.

In trying to shift from hierarchy to partnerships, another challenge has been for people to break the patterns or responses that perpetuate the hierarchy. For example, some staff have found it easier to have managers make decisions and be the boss. This way there is someone to blame if things go wrong. At times, staff have perpetuated the hierarchy through apathy and withdrawal, or by expecting the manager to have all of the answers to fix the problems.

TABLE SEVEN

Outcomes of Partnership

The desire for partnership is an innate component of an evolving humanity.

Partnership:
- Awakens the spirit within, the inner self.
- Provokes self understanding.
- Stimulates exploration, expansion and discovery.
- Connects the spirit within self to the spirit of another.
- Instills hope, creativity and imagination.
- Explores assumptions and deepens wisdom.
- Stops defining, limiting or judging another's potential.
- Seeks the mystery and potential of another.
- Looks for and celebrates the wisdom within.
- Helps each person self organize.
- Respects the diversity within relationships and finds harmony.
- Moves beyond the images of self and others that are limiting.
- Opens the eyes of the mind to see and appreciate the wisdom of the soul.
- Strengthens compassion and motivates to take action.
- Helps one transcend vulnerability and move to a place of greater potential.
- Seeks questions that help others find answers within themselves.
- Enhances the integrity of relationships with self and others.
- Provides opportunities to make one's spirit, compassion, love and humanness visible.
- Connects one to an inner energy.
- Provides capacity for people to change the world around them in synergistic ways.
- Reminds us we are never alone.
- Is a quality of life intervention.

Used with permission:

© Wesorick, B. (1996) The Closing and Opening of a Millennium, A Journey From Old To New Relationships In The Work Setting. Michigan: Practice Field Publishing.

Some managers have responded with fear. They have asked the question, "If staff are involved in leadership, what will be left for me to do?" Managers who have cultivated shared leadership know that the role requires working very differently as compared to the work of boss. A successful strategy has been for managers to consider their present work responsibilities and ask themselves, "In what ways would my role be different if I operated from a partnership paradigm?" This requires changing systems, educating people, building relationships, and eliminating barriers to shared leadership. We refer to the role of the manager as an operations resource, or one who is expert in the operations of the department or area in which they work. More information on this role can be found in Chapter Three. There is a need for an operations resource and a practice expert as well as many others on the Partnership Council. All leaders on the council bring diverse perspectives and expertise to continuously improve our work settings.

Partnership Councils do not need a boss or a typical leader. They need partners. Because they are a group, they do need someone to help coordinate the organizational work needed by a group to do its work. We call that person the Partnership Council Coordinator (has also been called Unit-Based Council Leader or Chairperson). The Coordinator role supports the work of partnership. The person who chooses this role takes on two responsibilities that are important to a strong council: coordination of the group's work and linkage with other councils across the entity.

A question often asked in councils is, **"Where do we begin in facilitating the emergence of such leadership?"** The answer is simple. *It always begins within each one of us.* The assumption about shared leadership in the council is that everyone has a leadership role. Parker Palmer (1990, p. 7) has written about the spiritual side of leadership and tells us, "Great leadership comes from those who have made that difficult inward journey." He also says, "It is easier spending your life manipulating an institution than it is dealing with your own soul." This has been a most valuable lesson learned in Partnership Councils. As managers, educators, staff, and researchers gather they have realized that all change begins within each person. Each person has choices to make about themselves and their work cultures.

We mentioned earlier that in Partnership Councils, leadership is assumed by each person and it rotates through everyone. A metaphor that has often been used by council members is that of the geese. As geese fly in formation each of them knows their role. They know their flying efficiency increases as they maintain their alignment in flight. When the leader of the formation becomes tired or injured it falls back to make way for another goose to take the lead. This rotation continues as needed, each goose taking its turn. We have much to learn from the geese. We see in the following illustration that each of us has to first see ourself as having the potential to be a leader. This Wisdom From The Field describes how one care provider came to this realization.

Wisdom From The Field

I never saw myself as a leader until one day when a patient's daughter asked me, "You are a leader on this unit aren't you?" My first response was "I'm not the manager or director." She said, "No, I don't mean that kind of leader. I have been watching and noticing how your peers come to you for advice and how you direct all of your attention to them. You have a calming presence with them. They seem to feel at ease coming to you." I said, "Yes, I think they do see me as a leader. Maybe it is because I lead our Partnership Council here on the unit." We talked and I shared my perspectives about effective leadership. I told her I believed a leader's role was not to control but to teach others and learn from others. Good leaders know the right questions to ask so that others can realize their own potential. I went on to describe a leader as someone who helps others lead themselves, not someone who guides you to their way of thinking.

I realized that day that I had many beliefs about what made a good leader and I was living many of them. It was in my actions that this family member saw my leadership. It was not from my title. The Partnership

Council experience was helping me to uncover my abilities as a leader. That day I had made a very important discovery. Now that others saw me as a leader I could begin seeing even more potential in myself for growing as a leader.

We all have to give constant attention to our relationships, personal learning, and growth. Once we realize we have leadership potential, we begin to seek more learning experiences. Each of us must work on ourselves to cultivate our own leadership and encourage our peers to do the same. We are whole people at work and we are learning to lead using our BodyMindSpirit. This is often difficult work because we have come from cultures that still think of leadership in the old ways. Leadership training that emphasizes managing external systems without regard for this internal journey will not provide the leaders that are needed now and in the next millennium. We know that in order to lead others we must first learn to lead self.

As leaders we are constantly seeking ways to expand our views and ways to move forward in our journeys. In her book, *Leadership And The New Science*, Margaret Wheatley (1992) challenges all of us to explore our leadership potential. Her thoughts on the definition of leadership are as follows: "Leadership is context-dependent and relational among leaders and followers, with an emphasis on the concepts of community, dignity, meaning and love." She also suggests directing our energy toward co-creating vision, sharing information, working on relationships, and accepting chaos as the way to let order emerge. Wheatley's video (1993) of the same title has been used to stimulate discussion as council members gather to expand their thinking and generate collective understandings around leadership.

Another way to help us move forward as leaders has been through the use of dialogue. Dialogue is discussed in Chapters One and Six. Many have used intention, inquiry, advocacy, silence, and listening to learn about themselves and to gain understanding into the thinking of others. Dialogue also provides strategies for leaders to potentiate healthy relationships.

For us to learn more about how to take our own journey in life, it is helpful to read about the experiences of others. Leadership stories are most valuable when they are honest and from the heart. In the following stories you will see the cycles of change and learning in others. Their search for meaning and purpose in work and life is a common pattern. Both are hallmarks of personal transformation, the fundamental work of leaders.

Few have the courage to share their learning from their vulnerable place of real experience. Honesty of this nature is critical to leaders cultivating integrity and caring. The following transformational stories come from those who are living leadership in Partnership Councils. They have chosen to influence their work cultures in positive, healthy ways.

We invite you into the transformational journeys of eight people who are living the realities of the work place. In their stories they may refer to Partnership Councils as Unit-Based Councils as they are called in some settings. The Clinical Practice Model (CPM) is also referenced in some of their stories which is a framework for an integrated health care system that includes Partnership Councils as one of its components.

Transformational Stories:
1. Carol Geurink, RPh (Pharmacist)

I have been a Pharmacist for 16 years. I started when the Pharmacy staff spent all their time in the main Pharmacy Department. The only contact we had with the rest of the hospital was done over the phone. As the hospital grew, so did the Pharmacy and the value of having Pharmacists on the patient care units became apparent. All the services we provided were directed at the physician and nursing staff and we spent very little, if any, time dealing with the patients.

Over the past few years the Pharmacy tried to define what we do that directly affects the patient. We sat down and composed a Pharmacy mission statement that included all the buzz words of that time (pharmaceutical care, contributions to patient care, and positive patient outcomes). What did we do with that vision of our future? Framed it and hung it on a wall in the administrative office. We didn't set goals. We didn't develop a plan to accomplish what we had felt was so important. We just hung our mission statement up and continued with what we were currently doing.

I have worked on many different units in the hospital and have been involved in numerous committees, staff meetings, and CQI groups. I provided the services to the nursing units that I thought they needed and did not really get involved in the Partnership Council until about one and a half years ago. I had no idea what a Partnership Council was or did. I was introduced to the council by one of the nurses on an intermediate care unit. A pharmacy related issue had come up at the last council meeting and I was asked to attend their next meeting to provide information on that particular issue. I attended several more meetings to answer other pharmacy related questions and we finally decided that I should become a permanent member of the council.

I think the thing that struck me most about the Partnership Council was the diversity of the people represented on the council. Everyone's comments were important and every voice was heard. I was part of the group, not an outsider. The issues brought to the table didn't always involve pharmacy, but it gave me much insight into what was important to the unit. The Core Beliefs I learned about from the council were very similar to the pharmacy mission statement, except here, they were living it. All the decisions being made were measured against these beliefs. It was exciting to find a whole group of people who were all working together towards a common goal. I began to find myself focusing more on being part of the unit and trying to use my expertise to accomplish the goals of the Partnership Council. I found myself interacting more with patients and their families. I discovered I was learning new things from the council members, things I hadn't really thought about before. It has definitely made my job more satisfying. These changes did not occur overnight and I have a long journey ahead, but I now have other travelers who are headed the same way and they are there to lend a helping hand.

2. Marti Rheault, RN, MSN, (Clinical Nurse Specialist)

My transformational story is in a way only an introduction, as it is not complete. My day-to-day professional and personal experiences continue to add to this story. I am not the same person today, that I was yesterday, nor will I be the same tomorrow. I truly believe that my transformation began with my arrival to a Michigan hospital in 1987 as an institutional nurse (although I did not know it at the time).

One day, as I was helping a nursing peer with patient care, she shared with me many highlights of the patient's life. When we stepped into the hall afterward, I thanked her for sharing that with me, and commended her for her interaction and caring for her patients, really knowing their story and incorporating it into their care. She informed me that she sees her patients as someone's child, someone's sibling, someone's parent, some-one's friend. I was so touched by this, that my eyes filled with tears. I began to wonder if this was how I treated the patients for whom I was priv-ileged to care. I hoped it was. This was an important experience in my transformation.

Around this same time, I was invited to become part of our Unit-Based Council or Partnership Council. I really did not know what this council was all about, but I wanted to get involved with unit activities. In fact, the council itself was struggling with its identity and purpose. Initially, it felt like a decision making body to both its members and the remaining staff. This lack of clarity continued as I remained on the council after transition-ing into the Staff Educator role. As the Education Resource, I felt that I was supposed to be the information disseminator. I was used to being the one who presented to a group of learners. I wondered if that was what I was supposed to do here. I felt that all I needed to do was anticipate and offset crises. I felt that I was doing a good job if staff were educated prior to change and any type of chaos was avoided. I realized our partnerships with each other and our peers were not strong.

Over time however, with the support of council members, clarity was gained. I do feel more comfortable with my role as resource. As our partnerships strengthened, so did our Partnership Council. This did not happen overnight, nor without the help and support of each other being willing to learn and grow together. We have created stronger partnerships by getting to know each other as people, which has allowed us to trust, be vulnerable, and be open to learning. We are all represented equally as peers, and although we may wear different hats, each role is important in delivering professional patient care services.

I have learned that I do not have to be the one to build the bridges, but am the resource for the staff to build their own unique bridges. I have also learned that trying to anticipate all needs in order to avoid conflict and chaos prevents us from reaching new levels together. Often crisis creates the need to learn and stimulates us to think of things we may not have thought of before. I truly believe in the words of Leland Kaiser, (1994) "We are the problem. We are the solution. We are the resource." True partners are able to see themselves as part of a problem, but also recognize that the solutions and resources to the solutions lie within each of us as "we." It is my feeling that with true partnerships there is no "we/they" thinking only "us" thinking.

3. Margie Bosscher, RN (Staff Nurse)

First of all, I wish I had kept a journal all these years. I don't know where to begin. This is a hard story to write because it is intensely personal. Until now, I have not shared it in writing and really prefer to share it in person. The written word is much more difficult, and besides, I continue to marvel that anyone would ever want to read anything I might put in writing. I think it is a symptom with many nurses. We couldn't possibly have anything interesting or important to say. The result of this self esteem problem (in my opinion) is the lack of articulate clinical nurses who are able and willing to share their practice and wisdom. I am sharing with you my perceptions of a time when I was growing and changing. Someone else may have seen it very differently, but this was how I perceived it.

My practice setting and changing professional mindset.

In order for you to grasp my transformation, you need to understand a little about me and the practice arena I found myself in. The time I want to speak to you about is in the late 1980's. At that time I was a "float" nurse in the medical-surgical float pool at a large metropolitan hospital. I had three school aged children and was working part-time. I worked the float pool only two weekends a month, and the unit of my preference was the oncology unit. I felt I could give good care to extremely sick patients and keep my skills very current with my sporadic work schedule. Although I consider this to be some of the most rewarding work of my career, I did not realize it at the time.

I was becoming increasingly aware of how nurses were being betrayed (OOPS, Freudian slip) portrayed in the media and I was extremely sensitive to what people said about nurses in general. I was so proud to be a nurse. I remember being so proud when I graduated from a well respected diploma program in the late 70's. I remember being proud to wear my cap. I remember how proud my parents and husband were when I graduated. When I started to hear these snipes about nurses and nursing in general, I took it very personally. I was distraught about how nurses were portrayed on TV shows, on get well cards and novels. I was saddened by accomplished and expert colleagues who were "burned out" and leaving the profession, and in their wake leaving a void for nurses and patients.

I was at a low point and hesitated to tell people I was a nurse, and started looking for a new profession/career to pursue. Then a colleague and friend told me about an opening in her unit. She thought it was the kind of nursing I might enjoy--since she herself had found it to be immensely satisfying. I don't think I ever told her I was thinking about quitting the profession all together. I applied for the part-time position in Same Day Stay (SDS) not even knowing what they did there, but knowing I needed a change.

The change in practice and culture saved me and really is the beginning of my transformation. The change from what I was doing was so profound,

I really experienced a honeymoon period of sorts. I loved this new practice. Same Day Stay patients were patients who were admitted and discharged the same day. (Catchy name, huh?) The unit was open from 7:00 a.m. to 7:00 p.m. and the nurses there worked a combination of 12 and 8 hour shifts. The patient population was adult and pediatric medical and surgical patients. This unit was separate from the Outpatient Surgery Department (OPS); those patients were discharged from the recovery room. The patients who came through Same Day Stay were a little more acute, often having an underlying chronic condition or requiring a longer recovery phase. I loved admitting and discharging my own patients. I loved the partnership and mutuality required. I loved the teaching and the direct feedback from follow up calls made the next day. Most of the time my patients wouldn't even see another nurse unless I was being relieved for break or a meeting. I loved the autonomy. What my job was, and what I was supposed to do, seemed so clear.

About this time the hospital I worked in was making some changes in the nursing division toward a more professional practice for nurses. The change evolved around supporting nurses to move from institutional practice toward a more professional practice. This move was being supported through the implementation of the Clinical Practice Model (CPM). This model had already been implemented in the Critical Care and Medical-Surgical areas and now the Special Services (which included SDS, OPS and the OR and PACU) would be implementing this model as well.

What I haven't told you about SDS is that it was a 17 bed unit that really had very little to do with the rest of the hospital. It was an island. Remember I said I applied for a position there without really knowing what they did? This was part of the culture. We liked being an island. We did not really know (or care) what other units did and we did not really care if they knew what we did. We considered ourselves separate and different. "We're different!" We loved to say it in our uniquely arrogant way. It was fun being an island, we didn't have to pay attention to anyone else. Our patients originated in our unit and then went to the other areas, and then they came back to us. We never really paid much attention to the fact that the patient flowed through the system, or how they flowed through the system. We began to hear our patients for the first time say things like "don't you people ever talk to each other?" Every area they went to asked them the same questions over and over. Every area had its own documentation page or tool, and we just all did our own thing.

What was required in this CPM implementation was a representative from SDS at the Professional Practice Council (PPC), the nursing practice council. Being the new kid on the block, and not involved in any unit activities, I volunteered for this position. Now, lest you think this a noble thing that I did, let me inform you, the reason I volunteered for this position was because it fulfilled a committee requirement for my yearly performance appraisal. Yes sir! Committee work looked really good at performance appraisal time, so I wanted to be on one.

I really didn't understand what the Clinical Practice Model was. I thought it was forms, papers, tools, and things you had to write on and fill out. I didn't know what it was, nor how it was going to support professional nursing. I didn't know what professional nursing was. We thought we were professional. We didn't understand nor think this was anything we wanted or needed. Hence my quest as representative from SDS: find out what this CPM thing is and why it won't work in SDS (we're different, you know) and then be done with it once and for all.

You might be getting the feeling that I was a little negative about this CPM thing. Well, you would be right. I spent considerable energy being negative about it and making sure others stayed negative about it as well. I thought and said, "These are inpatient concerns, we are an outpatient department. We're different. We don't have time for this."

Learning my role as leader and follower.

The next couple of years I began to learn my role. I started to research the CPM to find out why it wouldn't work in SDS. I started reading the guidelines and the Core Beliefs and the philosophy. I started spending time with a CPM partner discovering and learning about professional practice. I attended monthly Professional Practice Council meetings for a very long time without really being able to contribute. I spent time with a recently hired colleague whose practice I admired, she came from ICU and was using the model and she loved the support of CPM. She spent time with me explaining why this was valuable to patients and nurses. I owe her a great debt. What I learned and found out astounded me. I had been so arrogant and so wrong. This was the very practice I had longed for and hoped for and had been too blind to see. This is what I was taught in nursing school, yet every time I tried to be this kind of nurse someone would call me an idealist and remind me I was in the real world. The philosophy of the CPM paralleled my own. I couldn't believe it.

The Core Beliefs paralleled my personal belief system about the patients I cared for and the people I worked with. What I heard in the Professional Practice Council were nurses sharing professional wisdom and solving problems. The respect for their differences and the clear reason and purpose for us all to practice here was so refreshing. The focus and center of their speaking and listening and learning was 'what would be best for patients?' There were experts there from every specialty area. They could build on each others' expertise and work to solve differences for the benefit of patients. It was amazing. I started visioning on my own and seeing the possibilities of what this meant and what truly could be. This was a pivotal time for me and a time for some deep reflection and soul searching.

The soul work I needed to do was deeper than any work I had ever done before, and it was intensely personal. But now in reflection, I don't think they are so different from others. Many things were troubling to me, in my personal and professional life. I started doing a great deal of reading. I read the kind of books people either seem to love or hate: books on interpersonal relationships and communication. You know the kind, self help books. I devoured book after book, and guess what? As I read these books I started recognizing people. And guess who I recognized? PEOPLE I

WORKED WITH!! Oh boy this was great. So the problem was EVERY-ONE ELSE! Then one day, I realized after reading a quote from the sixties: **"if <u>you</u> are not part of the solution, then <u>you</u> are part of the problem."** I don't even remember where I saw it or what I was reading, but it made a huge impact on me. Now was the time for some truth.

I went to a place in my own heart to see what was really there and started asking myself questions that really mattered. I started to gain insight and clarity on a couple of things that profoundly changed who I was. As I read, I recognized some behaviors of people I worked with, but I didn't recognize the behavior of the most important person I worked with day in and day out--ME--the only person whose behavior I could change or do anything about in the first place. No, I hadn't recognized ME in those books. And believe me, I was in there big and bold. This brought me to one of the most profound realizations of my personal and professional life. **I can't change anyone but me. I am the only person in the whole world that I have any real control or power to change.**

At first this was a scary realization. Old habits die hard, and this was a habit. A habit of thinking that everything wrong around here was because of everyone else. You've heard it all before. "They won't let us." "Guess what they've done now?" "They did this or are going to do that...they, they, they." It occurred to me I didn't know who "they" were (and worse yet, no one could tell me). I began to suspect that I was the "they." In realizing I couldn't change anyone but me, the "they's" in my world started to disappear. I started thinking about what it was that I could be doing differently. Were there things about my behavior that if I change it would improve my work environment?

I had a second profound realization. This came from my big sister, where I get lots of profound stuff as well as love and support. The people we are surrounded by are like a mobile that hangs from the ceiling, subject to the air currents and environment. Every individual character that is suspended on the string is affected by every other individual character, and together, they make up the whole of the mobile. If one character in the mobile makes a change, no matter how subtle, the rest of them have to adjust to accommodate the change somehow. I thought this was amazing, and yet we see this in families all the time in the hospital. If a family member is sick or injured, the whole family is affected. This is pretty basic to systems thinking, but it gave me much to think about in my immediate environment.

I decided there were some things I could change about myself that would make my environment a more pleasant place for patients and my co-workers, so I set about to make some conscious decisions about how I practice, and how I communicate and interact with people. I made conscious decisions about being a good role model for my peers and students through the practice I performed and the documentation of that practice. I truly decided to live in the moment, for it is all any of us really have. Yesterday is gone and tomorrow isn't here yet.

I began to recognize that once a patient and family had received my care and services, that care and service was a part of their experience, and I was obliged to make it as positive as possible. I recognized the impact of participating in gossip and indirect communication as a very negative thing, and wished to separate myself from it. I began to value relationships outside of nursing and become involved in committees and task forces where I may be the only nurse or would meet and work on projects with nurses I did not know. I have great value for those relationships and have made wonderful friends and acquaintances across a practice boundary that before I would never have had the confidence to pursue. I began to realize, it is easy to find people who will beat you up and beat you down. There is pure joy in finding and connecting with people who share a vision and want to participate in creating a culture of respect and mutuality, for those we are privileged to serve and with those we are privileged to serve with.

As this process continued to develop, my manager began to invest in my leadership. This particular unit had tried a CPM implementation before that had failed. Looking back, it appeared that the failure had to do with the fact that what we were trying to implement had everything to do with what we did at the bedside day in and day out, but the decisions about what needed to be done were being made away from the bedside by managers and directors. We liked that because it protected us from being involved and from having to take any responsibility. Besides, that was how things were done then.

About this time, a curious thing happened to me. My manager started giving me books and articles to read about leadership. She sent me to seminars and encouraged me to get involved in leadership activities. I was very reluctant. I thought this was management stuff and way out of my league, I was a staff nurse after all, and this leadership stuff was for managers. But, she continued to encourage me, telling me that the most important managing to be done was the management happening at the bedside. That is where the patient satisfaction and outcomes really sit. These leadership principles can be applied at the bedside as well as anywhere else. These skills would also help in the development of our council.

As my manager and I continued to work on these things, our relationship began to change. Rather than the hierarchy we were used to, we began to see each other in a different light. She recognized my expertise at the bedside, and I was beginning to see her expertise as a manager and an operations resource. We realized we both had a different contribution to make, and neither of us was less. It turned into a much more collegial relationship that was very productive. We had different wisdom, and both were valuable. We developed a strong partnership.

Another part of the process of moving toward professional practice was connecting with the nurses from the other departments. Remember I told you we were an island? Well, I had no connection really with the nurses from the units through which our patients flowed--the operating room and the recovery room. Somehow, we decided it would be a good thing to spend time in these other units to help move along our process. I worked side by side with a nurse in the operating room and I couldn't believe what you have to know and be able to do to work there. Then, I went to the recovery room and worked with a colleague there. I couldn't believe what you have to know and be able to do to work in the recovery room. Those nurses came to my unit, worked beside me, and they couldn't believe what you have to do to get people ready for surgery. This included all you have to know and do to discharge patients in the same day. This was a profound learning experience. I developed great empathy for my colleagues that day and established relationships that are strong to this day.

The Partnership Council changed me.

I want to tell you about the development of my Partnership Council, because it is another part of me. Our council really developed as we worked together in changing our documentation system. The system we were using was archaic, and needed to be changed to reflect our practice and to protect us as professionals. Another problem was that every unit in Special Services had their own documentation tool, they weren't connected. We decided to pilot a tool called the Day Of Event Summary. Every nurse who cared for the patient would document on the tool; therefore, we would all be connected by our documentation, as well as being able to communicate to each other with this tool. We had, prior to this time, been using a narrative documentation tool with a graphic sheet and a checklist. We did abundant physical assessment and education, but had nowhere to document it. The implementation of this Day Of Event Summary (DOES) and an Education Record allowed us to document using nursing process in a flowsheet style and take credit for patient education. This was practically unheard of in the outpatient arena at the time.

Prior to implementing these tools we educated ourselves and our colleagues. We had side by side charting tools that showed the old tools and the new ones; we spent time going over guidelines and learning about flowsheet documentation. When we implemented the tools our practice was staring us in the face. The accountability was frightening. The tools centered us on patients. We needed to discuss things like assessing breath sounds and how patients were assessed, educated, and given individualized care. We realized that everybody did something different. We recognized that we were very good at being together as friends and women. It was one thing to talk about kids and recipes, it was quite another to talk about patients and why as a nurse we did, or did not do, something for patients. We were good at the tasks we did, but we weren't consistent with our scope of practice. The tools brought more consistency and the beginnings of our council. It is the place where discussions about what and why you do or don't do things for patients happens.

We experienced a successful tool implementation, and the development of a stronger council on the day of our tool implementation, when everything was incredibly busy and chaotic, a patient coded and died on our outpatient unit. A very unexpected event indeed. This experience changed my professional life. We didn't have the necessary papers when something like this happens so we had to call an inpatient unit to get a death certificate. I will never forget the note that came attached to it in the pneumatic tube system. It said something to the effect of, "This must be so hard for you, our thoughts are with you, please call if you need anything else." I will never forget the compassion and caring that note represented to me at that moment. You see, we are pretty good at showing compassion and caring for our patients and their families. It never occurred to me that those same skills could profoundly affect our culture at work as well. I learned a great deal about being a compassionate colleague that day, and I thank the colleagues on the other end of that note. I am so grateful.

This is the end of my story, but not my journey.

I've learned so much along the way and developed relationships with new friends and colleagues as well. My transformation started with me, my attitude, and my beliefs. It wasn't until I looked at myself from a different place that I was able to see that the environment I worked in had everything to do with me. I work in a different environment now. But the important learning and lessons have gone with me to be applied and built upon and expanded. You see, I am still growing and learning, and I suspect you are too.

4. Deb Chapman (Patient Care Associate)

My name is Deb Chapman. I am a Patient Care Associate. Before I tell you about my job, I will tell you a little about myself. Before coming to work at this hospital, I was a stay at home mom with four children. When the last one began pro-school I decided it would be a good time for me to go back to school. I went to the Grand Rapids Educational Center. They have a program that teaches you how to become a Medical Assistant. After I graduated from the program I worked in an office of four doctors doing billing, insurance, phone work, etc. Then I had an opportunity to go to another office where I worked seven years. I worked the front desk, put patients in rooms, worked with insurance companies, etc. I was only working part-time at this office and another part-time job opened up at a resident home, so I also took this job. At this resident home I had an opportunity to work with alert residents, and also with residents who had Alzheimer's disease. I learned so much, especially from the Alzheimer's residents. While working at this resident home I realized how much I enjoyed taking care of patients and their individual needs.

I heard there were job openings at the hospital and decided to apply and was fortunate to get a job in a Urology unit. I was a little nervous about coming because it was such a big place. After working in an office of five people it seemed huge, but I was also excited about being able to work in a hospital setting. I have been here for two years. It didn't take me long to get to know the nurses and staff on 7-North and find them to be very caring. I am part of the support staff on 7-North. In my introduction I mentioned I was a Patient Care Associate. As a Patient Care Associate (or a PCA) I work directly with nurses.

My job has much variety to it. I have an opportunity to do many different things such as weights, vitals, blood sugars, running to the lab, baths, and postmortem care. We also have other support staff on our floor called Environmental Care Associates (or titled ECAs). They take care of our patients' rooms, transfer patients from one room to another if necessary, and keep our floor disinfected and looking nice. We also have other support staff; they are our secretaries. They answer phones, call lights, and questions from doctors, nurses, patients, and patients' families.

Sometimes in my job we have opportunities to work long periods of time with the same patient and their family. I can remember one particular family was not completely satisfied with the care their loved one was receiving and our staff became aware of this situation. Our staff did not want this situation to continue and decided that it was important to sit down with the family and find out their concerns and how we could better meet their needs.

Some staff and family met together and decided it would be good for this patient to have primary nurses assigned to her on each shift. They decided to assign Carol Glass, a wonderful and caring nurse, on the day shift. This particular patient was in the area I worked in so I also had the opportunity to work with the family each day. Knowing they were concerned about the care she was receiving made it especially challenging because we wanted this patient and her family to know we give great care and each patient is important.

Carol and I formed a partnership and each day we worked together we would talk and go over our plans for this patient's care. Together we tried to find out what concerns the patient and family had. One thing we found to be very important to this patient and family was to have her hair washed often. Knowing this ahead of time, I could try and plan my day so I would have time during her bath to wash her hair. Her daughter was a Certified Nurses Aid and would often be in the room to help with her mom's bath and hair. We began to develop a real rapport. Soon we were able to talk about everyday things including concerns about other family members. It was really neat to watch the changes in this family and how they felt about the care they were receiving.

As time went on this patient was at a point where she could be transferred to another facility. I was sad to see her go, yet was happy she was able to go to her new place. Shortly after she left, her daughter contacted Carol Glass to tell her that her Mom had passed away. I was saddened and surprised of her death. Carol and I talked and decided to go to the funeral home to see the family. It was sad to see their hurt, but a wonderful feeling to know they knew we cared about them. When the daughter saw us, she came up to us, hugged us both, and introduced us around. It was a great experience knowing that she knew we really did care about her and her family.

Something else happened that evening when Carol and I went to the funeral home. Carol began talking to me about Partnership Councils and what an important role it plays on our unit. Carol is one of the Coordinators of the council. Carol expressed a desire to have me become part of our Unit-Based Council because she said it is real important that we have all the roles represented on our council. After she talked with me I became interested and decided to go to a meeting.

I was a little nervous about my first meeting. I wasn't sure what I was getting myself in to, but I am glad I took that first step and became part of the council. I liked finding out first hand what decisions had to be made. It was important to find our Unit Director, Clinical Coordinators, and Staff Educator supportive of our needs. Our number one goal was to meet the needs of our patients. In order to do this we had to be a team, that included each worker on our floor. One person could not possibly meet all the needs so we had to come together and decide the best for us as a team to meet the needs of our patients.

Let me give you an example. Our council decided we needed to concentrate on making the patient's family feel they were welcomed and also invite them to be a part of the patient's care. So we formed a shared work team from the council focusing on the family. Some of the things the work team wanted to change were making our pantry into a family kitchenette with coffee available at all times. The work team also decided we should have less clutter at the front desk and floor in general. One other idea was to have plastic holders on each bedside table with information readily available to patient and family regarding things like their telephone number, room number, and meal information, etc.

The shared work team gathered all this information and brought it back to our council. We were happy with the ideas and asked the members to go out to their peers One-on-One and ask for their opinions regarding the ideas. For the most part we got positive feedback on our ideas. We did get one concern back from one of our Environmental Care Assistants (ECA). She was concerned about the plastic holder on the bedside table because she was the one that cleaned that area and did not want anymore clutter. Whether I agreed or disagreed with her I needed to share her concerns because she is part of our team and her opinion does count. After listening to her and the others I was able to give back to our council both the positive feedback and concerns. Whether we agree or disagree with our peers, we need to let them know they are important and their opinion does count.

Our council represents our floor. They represent our team. I feel like Partnership Council has been a very important part of making our unit run smoothly and help create team work and spirit. It is a privilege to be a member and to watch how easy things come together when we value each other. We are here with the same goal in mind, to give our patient the best care possible and really show the community that we care about our patients and one another.

5. Barren VandeZande, RN, BSN (Clinical Coordinator)

Looking back, I am unable to recall the exact moment or what really motivated me to enter the field of nursing nine years ago. Perhaps it was the pressure of the clock ticking and still being undecided about my major in college or even more strongly, the people oriented, caring aspects of nursing which drew my attention. In retrospect, I can't say that it truly was a conscious decision; however, I can say that it is a decision that I am glad to have made.

Upon graduation from nursing school in May, 1991, I found myself in a situation which was unique in many ways. I was one of two males in a class of sixty five, at a time when it was still considered relatively unusual for a male to be entering a predominantly female profession. I was a

Canadian attending an American school--and with graduation came the reality of large school loans, the necessity of writing two board exams to obtain licensure in both Michigan and Canada, and an uncertain future as jobs were difficult to find in Canada. Here, at what was supposed to be the high point of my life, full of promise and potential, I found myself without a job, money, experience, and really wondering if I had made the correct decision.

With few other options, I began to work in a factory in Canada working full-time doing assembly. After receiving my Canadian licensure, I once again attempted to find a nursing job in Canada without success. At this point I needed to make a decision--a decision to leave Canada and my family and pursue other potential jobs in the U.S. My search brought me to this hospital where there was a nursing position posted for an RN on the Orthopedic unit, full-time evening shift. At the time, this was the only position available of all of the hospitals in the area. I submitted my application without much confidence as I was one among numerous applicants.

I believe this is where my first true lesson was learned. I really believed that I did not have much to offer at all. I did not have any hospital related experience other than my experiences as a student. Many of my peers had worked as externs in various hospitals during the summer months, whereas I could only offer such experiences as construction and landscaping. I realized that it was not my experience which really mattered, but my being a person with unique qualities and characteristics. This had a significant impact on me at the time and continues to influence me today.

I accepted the position immediately and worked in the staff nurse role for approximately two years before I became a Clinical Coordinator. The Clinical Coordinator role is similar to that of a first line manager on a hospital unit including responsibilities such as staffing, scheduling, staff evaluations, management of patient admissions/discharges/transfers, and addressing patient relation/risk management situations.

The transition from being a staff nurse to becoming a Clinical

Coordinator in many ways was a difficult one for myself. There was much to learn in relation to my new responsibilities. The majority of my learning has resulted from my interactions with staff. Since my childhood I have been continually encouraged to be responsible, make good decisions, explore all the options, be efficient, independent, and reliable. These qualities are considered essential and good, however, some manner of balance is necessary.

Some of the key contributions I feel that I am able to make in the Clinical Coordinator role, to not only my unit but the hospital as a whole, are as follows:

- Integrating and role modeling the Core Beliefs in my own practice and encouraging others in this direction. I continually make an effort to integrate the Core Beliefs into everything that I do and attempt to make it the center of my focus. The Core Beliefs not only help in providing clarity in terms of vision but also to provide direction in the decisions that I make independently or in partnership with others. I realize that any decision that I make will in some way have an effect on another. The Core Beliefs assist me in making the best possible decision and ensures that I explore all the options carefully.

  Being a role model to others in this manner is essential. I am an individual who strongly believes that your walk is stronger than your talk. Many of the Core Beliefs are similar to principles I have valued whole life. Therefore, living the Core Beliefs is natural for me and is almost automatic. I truly try, however, to exemplify these, not only in the decisions that I make, but also in my interactions with fellow staff, physicians, patients, and their significant others.

- Sharing expertise and acting as a resource to enhance practice. As a Clinical Coordinator, I find myself in a position in which my expertise is frequently sought and valued. I constantly make myself available as a resource to staff to enhance the decisions that they make related to their practice. I readily admit that although I may possess some expertise in an area, I am not by the same nature an expert. I can, however, facilitate the sharing of information and meeting needs which have been identified to enhance the practice of my peers overall.

- Recognizing each peer as a potential resource. Each individual on our team possesses unique strengths and is a leader in their own way. I have discovered that I not only have learned much from those with whom I have interacted, but also that with each interaction I have the potential to learn more.

- Promoting and facilitating development of leadership skills. As a Clinical Coordinator I feel it is also my responsibility to help promote and facilitate the development of each individual's leadership potential. Most of us think of leaders as those who occupy some formal position of leadership. The majority of individuals, however, are informal leaders with the potential to be highly effective in their unique individual way. It is only through partnering with these individuals that one is able to achieve a glimpse and perhaps a realization of this potential.

6. Kristin Root, BSW (Social Worker)

I am happy to share my journey with you as a Medical Social Worker. I work mainly on the Orthopedic floor and in the Outpatient Center. A real turning point for me in my journey was when I was asked to participate on a team in developing a Clinical Pathway for Total Hip/Total Knee patients. I can clearly remember all of the disciplines that were involved with these particular patients around one table discussing the care we provided. It was amazing to me how many people/disciplines touched this one person's life in a matter of days, hours, minutes. I was totally unaware of the importance of each discipline and their role with regard to the patient until this connection--it didn't take long to realize how much better we could be. One particular example was how much duplication there was between disciplines. Physical therapy, outpatient therapy, nursing, social work, residents/physicians were all asking the same questions. One patient would get asked five-six times if they had any stairs in their home, was there anyone to help them when they went home, did they have any equipment--it was awful! We frequently got asked by the patient, "Don't you guys talk to each other? I just answered the same question for the last five people that were in here!" It was a very frustrating and unpleasant experience for them.

After realizing this, we decided this was an area we needed to work on and make some changes. We started talking about all using the same documentation tools like the Patient Profile and Education Record. Each of us would refer to these tools, which were part of the CPM framework, before going into see a patient and each of us would chart on these tools. This way if the information was already there, we would not ask the patient again and we would chart any new information that was gathered for the next person. Well, as simple as this seems now, it was a huge change at that time. I can remember feeling very threatened and defensive. I had always asked the patient those questions and I wondered if someone else had already gathered that information, what was I going to do?

I was scared that there wouldn't be a need for social work anymore and I had just worked myself out of a job. Our group was definitely committed to the patient and so we went forward with our changes. It didn't take long to realize how much better this was for the patient and they noticed the difference. I often hear, "How did you know that about me?", and "Wow, you guys really do talk to each other!" I also learned that these changes and the other disciplines made me a better social worker. I am able to discuss more pertinent issues with the patient now and learn more about their story because I already know the basic information and am able to go from there. We have been able to save time, decrease length of stay, and increase patient satisfaction. I am no longer caught up in tasks, but living the partnerships with other disciplines and the patient.

I am also involved with the Partnership Council on the Orthopedic floor. We have recently rebuilt our council and this has been a huge learning experience. The collaboration, expertise, and wisdom in these meetings is incredible. I sometimes wonder what I have to bring to this group, but am quickly reminded of our reason for being there--our common goals, values, the patient, and strengthening our partnerships. I could not do my job as a social worker effectively without partnerships.

Finally, my current challenge is bringing the Core Beliefs and Principles of Partnership to the Social Work Department. I have shared my journey and the ideas with some of my colleagues and their response is, 'This is Social Work. We already do this." They think they are there, like it is an ending and everyone else is finally coming around. This is a journey--it never ends--it is always learning and connecting with each other and the patients in a deeper sense--it is life. Fortunately, my department is open to the ideas and beliefs based on CPM and Partnership Councils. My hope is that by planting seeds, we will grow as a department, as a health care system, as a consortium.

I am excited to be on this journey with all of you.

7. Tracy Christopherson, RRT (Respiratory Therapist)

I was introduced to the Clinical Practice Model about four years ago. At that time I was the Adult Critical Care Clinical Specialist for the Respiratory Care Department. I was working on an interdisciplinary project with a nurse colleague of mine who was the Clinical Nurse Specialist for the Surgical Critical Care Unit. We were designing a process to be used by the nurses and respiratory care practitioners regarding drawing and analyzing glucose samples. This would be the first time the staff members from both disciplines would have shared accountability related to this procedure. At one point in our discussion of how to design this practice change my colleague stated this would be important to bring to the Partnership Council. My first response was "What is a Partnership Council and why would we need to talk to them? Aren't we the clinical experts?" She proceeded to explain the purpose of the council and that there are many members on the council each representing a different area of expertise. This would bring a perspective to our work we would not have obtained on our own. Once I understood the purpose of a council, it made sense to me that this would be our next step. Of course our department didn't have a council at that time so we took the issue to our staff as a whole; however, a seed had been planted.

I was aware there was a growing concern within our department that they were not involved in the decision making processes that were taking place. In the past, we had what was called a Quality of Work Life Task Force. It was made up of staff members and the management team. It mostly was a place for the staff to voice their concerns. It was not focused on practice issues and the solving of the issues rested solely on the management's shoulders. For various reasons the task force dissolved after a period of time. I saw the implementation of a Unit-Based Council (UBC) within our department as a way to give the staff a voice and get them involved in the decisions that were being made related to their practice. The biggest challenge I saw was in helping the staff to understand that the UBC or Partnership Council would be different from the Quality of Work Life Task Force.

By the time we began to establish our UBC I had taken on a new role as the Research, Education and Project Coordinator for the department. This role moved me farther away from the clinical setting. Initially I did not see this as a problem but as time went on I began to understand the impact it would have on me and my ability to partner with the staff in our department. Because I was the one person in our department most familiar with the Clinical Practice Model and Partnership Councils I also acted as a co-chair in an effort to help get the council off the ground.

It was my feeling that as a discipline we were good at building partnerships with other disciplines but when it came to partnering with our peers we were challenged. There were many times when I would leave our council meetings frustrated because it was so clear to me that this was exactly what we needed to have and I just wanted so badly for it to be as clear to everyone else. I felt like I had climbed a mountain and saw "what could be" on the other side and I was constantly trying to get the others to cross over. On the other hand there were days when I was astounded by the wisdom of my colleagues. It is through these frustrating and rewarding times that I realized that the only person I can change is me. Although we had all embarked on this journey together we would not all arrive at the same place at the same time. I needed to be patient and concentrate on what I could do personally to change my own patterns of behavior.

I began to learn more about the Clinical Practice Model. The more I learned the more I felt this model had exactly what the respiratory care profession needed. As a profession we were not taught how important it is to look at the patient as a whole, we were taught how to complete the task. As respiratory care practitioners we were in the process of transforming our practice from institutional to professional and I could see how the tools developed under the Clinical Practice Model would help us with that transformation at the bedside. I got involved in writing three different practice guidelines from an interdisciplinary perspective and invited a few of the staff members to join me.

We all learned a great deal from that experience. We became clearer on our own scope of practice as well as the nursing scope of practice. Before this experience, I thought I knew what it was a nurse did but I came to the realization that I had only looked at what was on the surface, what I could see with my eyes. There was much more to a nurse's practice than what met the eye. This also made me realize, since that was how I saw them, maybe that was how they saw us. That is why I got even more involved in implementing the Partnership Council and Clinical Practice Model in our department and began sharing the work with my colleagues across the country. It was a way to establish our scope of practice and integrate that practice at the bedside. It became a part of my mission not only for the benefit of my profession, my department, and the hospital, but also for the benefit of the patient.

When I began my journey I was in a management/support role and now I've come full circle to once again practice at the bedside. This transition has probably brought me one of the greatest learnings of my journey. As a member of the support staff I was continually frustrated by the inability to build the necessary partnerships. I was perplexed at the continuation of the we/they mentality throughout the department. I thought I was doing everything I could to be a good partner, but it wasn't until I made the transition back to a staff role that I finally understood what was missing: relationships.

Two things brought me to this realization; one was that I didn't really "know" the people I was working with and; two, I hardly ever conversed with or saw people from the management/support staff. It is difficult to have a relationship with someone you do not spend time with. I finally understood I had not done the work necessary to build and maintain relationships with my peers. It was not enough that we worked in the same department, that we sat at the same table together and talked about the same issues, that we cared about the same things. We did not know each other's story. The farther I had gotten away from the clinical setting and the staff that worked in that setting, the fewer my relationships. After all, I did not spend the majority of my day with these people anymore. I was away from the clinical setting working at my desk or attending meetings. I am now working very hard to re-establish those relationships because I finally understand the importance.

When I returned to clinical practice I was excited because my practice looked much different than it did five years ago when I last practiced at the bedside. It looks different partly because of the advances in technology and the utilization of protocols but mostly because I am different. I am much more centered on the patient and where they are in the moment. I am not proud to say there was a time when I would have what might be called a "demanding patient" and I would be frustrated in trying to care for them. I would think, "Where do they think they are, a hotel? Don't they realize I have other patients to see?" Today I do my best to establish mutuality with my patients. I always try to understand where they are in the moment and then in partnership with them determine what would best meet their needs at that time.

I never really considered the patient's family as part of my responsibility. Most of the time they were just there. We would have a little conversation or not and that was that. Many times as a respiratory care practitioner I would be left alone at the bedside of a dying patient to provide ventilatory assistance while the family gathered to say good-bye. This has always been the most uncomfortable part of my job. I would close myself off to the moment, to what the family members were experiencing, to the grief, the love, the pain. I would stand there like a stone wall not speaking or showing any emotion. I felt if I let down that wall, if I for one moment would allow myself to feel what they were feeling, I would crumble.

What I have learned is that to be with someone at that time in their life is a privilege and it is a moment to be shared. It is my accountability to care for that family as much as I have for that patient, for they in fact, are one. A short time ago a patient was brought into the Emergency Department, intubated and being mechanically ventilated. He had suffered a massive CVA. The neurologist who came to examine him was new to our hospital and was not familiar with our processes. After examining the patient he announced there was nothing that could be done for this gentleman surgically or medically and asked me what was the next step he should take. At this point he had not talked with the family and I knew the next step would hinge on their decision.

To me the most important thing for him to do was to meet them where they were at, and, to do that, he needed to know their story. I told him that this patient was a 79 year old who had been preparing to celebrate his 80th birthday three days from now with over 100 friends and family members, one of which was a son he had not seen in three years. It was my feeling they would want that one son to see his dad before they withdrew life support. The physician went out to talk with the family and when he returned he thanked me for giving him the information. Knowing where they were in the moment had made it much easier for him to establish mutuality with the family. My feeling had been correct and they would wait for the one son to arrive to say good-bye before withdrawing life support. Later when I found myself alone with the patient and his family I realized as the tears rolled down my cheeks how far I had come, what a privilege it was to be there and as much as I had contributed to their journey they were contributing to mine.

8. Jeanne Roode, RN, MSN (Director)

Over the past 15 years I have been a nurse manager for several inpatient care units at a 529 bed acute care teaching hospital. Most recently I am responsible for two 41 bed medical-surgical units focusing in neuroscience and urology. I have experienced many changes over the years, but none quite as significant as my personal journey from an institutional manager to a transformational leader.

Institutional Manager

Fifteen years ago I was an institutional manager. I was highly respected by my superiors and colleagues as a strong leader. My budget performance looked good, policies were in place, and my unit received positive marks from inspecting agencies. The positive inspections were due in large part to the fact that the night before being reviewed, I personally wrote care plans for each patient and completed missing documentation. No one ever read them but they looked good. Back in those days care plans were disposable and rarely written. Admission assessments were seldom completed and after admission, were placed in the chart and never referred to again.

I believed in professional nursing practice and the use of the nursing process but didn't know how to get there. I believed that my staff were not at a professional level and it was my job to get them there single handedly by "cracking the whip" and forcing professional practice. It was around this time that I became aware of unusual activities occurring within a division-wide documentation committee and decided to become a member of this committee to control the process. A visionary leader, Bonnie Wesorick, had joined the committee to introduce philosophies for a new way of documentation. Because the documentation she was recommending looked long and arduous, I saw it as my role to protect my staff by fighting against the recommendations. After all, I was the defender and guardian of my staff. They were already busy enough, I didn't want to take more of their time. As an informal leader, I busied myself as the champion of the opposition, fighting the implementation of our Clinical Practice Model.

I viewed myself as supportive of my staff but in essence I was suffocating them. I thought it was my role to order things to happen, to be in control, and I thought I knew what was best for the practitioners. In addition, my understanding of the scope of nursing practice was limited. I did not value knowing the patient's story. The tools and resources to support it were weak. No one ever read the documentation unless there was a problem. I saw the documentation as a task rather than as a support for the core values of the Clinical Practice Model. I didn't understand the core values.

Personal Transition

I began a major personal transition when I, as the leader of the opposition, began a series of difficult and painful discussions with Bonnie Wesorick who had an ideological vision which far exceeded my readiness as a realist to comprehend. I also began to dialogue with my colleagues about practice issues and about changing our leadership paradigm from one of control to one of shared decision-making and shared accountability. This was very difficult. Letting go was such hard work. I had to take risks with my colleagues and began to feel alone. This was a time of great chaos. I began my own inward journey to obtain clarity on my personal mission and core values and how they aligned with an environment that was changing and calling for new leadership. I began to realize that I was fighting to keep things the same even though I was not satisfied with our current state. I was attempting to control something I could not understand. It was in the letting go and being willing to be influenced that I was finally able to move forward. I could begin to visualize a brighter future with excellent quality, individualized patient care provided by expert practitioners who cared about outcomes and partnership. In my dream, I was no longer alone.

I began to share this dream with key staff on my unit. Through dialogue I discovered that we shared a common dream. As we talked about where we were and where we needed to head, we became clearer on what mattered most. We could see that we had been spending much time on things that didn't matter at all. Those staff began to dialogue with other staff and I began to realize the importance of creating a structure that supports each provider in their practice. I believe that it is difficult to remain empowered as an individual for any length of time and that Partnership Councils are necessary to connect us, continue growth and build momentum. I could not do it alone. With that realization and the formation of our first Partnership Council, I was no longer alone.

The transition period was ripe with lessons. I tried some institutional tactics when things felt out of control. On one occasion, I noticed that documentation on the patient assessment tool was lacking. I compared my staff with those from other departments and decided to correct the situation at once. I put out a memo to my staff stating that the assessment tool reflected their professional practice and they were accountable to complete it. Failure to do so would result in corrective action counseling for lack of compliance with departmental policy and procedure.

Over night there was immediate compliance with the completion of the tool but for the wrong reason. They were driven by fear. Needless to say, I did not use corrective action and over time completion began to taper down. Instead, I and the Partnership Council members learned to accept each person where they were at and encouraged them to grow through the use of One-on-One positive reinforcement. The end result was a clarity and valuing of the professional services they provided and an appreciation for knowing the patient's story using the assessment tool. I learned that you cannot force professional practice. No matter how hard you try, you cannot force others to value something. It is only through building relationships and positive reinforcement that growth occurs. This takes a tremendous amount of time, but when all members of the Partnership Council are providing One-on-One reinforcement with their colleagues, the momentum builds so much faster than I could ever have done by myself.

Transformational Leader

Leadership is not position related. I had been a manager, but I had not been a leader. Similarly, I saw that many of my staff were leaders even though they did not occupy line positions in the hierarchy of the organization. I am now a learner. I am no longer a controller. I am now a facilitator. I realize that I have not arrived and that I am on a continuous journey. What I am today will be different from what I become tomorrow. I must change as the needs for leadership change. What will not change however, are my guiding principles. I no longer view my staff as subordinates and myself as the boss. They are my valued colleagues who have an expertise which is uniquely different from mine. I believe that anything is possible and that I must help colleagues to see that they do not have to adapt to reality but can change it.

There are still times however, when the stress builds, when something doesn't go as planned, that I need to consciously remind myself not to slip back into my old controlling habits. It's so easy to develop a quick fix corrective action plan when a quality issue arises or when financial indicators are off. Bonnie Wesorick aptly calls this phenomenon "institutional retreat." Sometimes when I feel a loss of control, I may try to order things back into place. Instead I need to remind myself that I am not alone, that my practitioner colleagues share in the accountability and that together with our collective wisdom, we can move mountains.

I have the privilege of being part of two very active Partnership Councils. We take time each year at our annual goal setting retreats to reflect on where we have been, how far we have come and where we want to head in the coming year. I no longer have separate goals for my units. Instead, I share with my partner colleagues the same goals and together we work to accomplish them. We have committed ourselves to being continuous learning councils through the use of dialogue. We have had special educational offerings to learn the tools of dialogue such as the use of advocacy, inquiry, and own thinking. We are learning to uncover our assumptions and listen to our own thinking. We are gaining a new awareness of ourselves and each other which is making us better partners.

Often, the goals of our councils lead to shared work teams where anyone, not council members have an opportunity to be actively involved in an initiative. Examples of this have included a team to improve our anticipation of patient needs thus decreasing the need for patients to ring their call lights, a team to improve the care we are providing to our patients' famil members, and a team to eliminate things that slow us down in our work environment and keep us away from our patients. So much has been accomplished through these teams, it is a great source of pride to the unit.

Advice I would give to others who are implementing Partnership Councils is to keep the focus on what is best for the patient. It is unbelievably easy to become sidetracked by what is best for us as the providers. Certainly that is important, but we must always be mindful that we exist to provide care to our patients and their families. With this in mind, decisions we make must always be with their best interests in mind. Staying principle centered helps to facilitate decision-making through the use of consensus.

Being a partner on the council has led me to develop trust that decisions we make through consensus are of quality. They are better decisions than I would have made independently because they include the collective wisdom and support of all roles.

The process of letting go takes courage. But it is through our vulnerability that we become strong. Implementing Partnership Councils strengthens our patience and demands that we listen. It is not an easy journey but the rewards are great. It has changed my life, it has brought joy and love to my work.

After reading the above transformational stories, a question emerges.

"What will our leadership legacy be?" How can we continually transform our leadership? The transformational stories show us that developing leadership within ourselves may not be easy but it is necessary. It is expected that we will experience cycles of clarity and confusion in our lives. Whenever we lose sight of our own path as leader we must remember what we are evolving. Fear will stop us if we let it. Confidence in the truth and doing what is right will sustain us on our journeys. Mission, relationships, core beliefs, and Partnership Councils connect us in shared leadership.

The following Parker Palmer quote (1990, p. 5) quote articulates the implications of a leadership legacy. "A leader is a person who has an unusual degree of power to project on other people his or her shadow, or his or her light. A leader is a person who has an unusual degree of power to create the conditions under which other people must live and move and have their being--conditions that can either be as illuminating as heaven or as shadowy as hell. A leader is a person who must take special responsibility for what is going on inside him or her self, inside his or her consciousness, lest the act of leadership create more harm than good."

We can connect with each other in ways that energize all of us. We can transform ourselves into the leaders needed now and for the next millennium. We cannot go back to pretending that life is about having power over others. With these understandings about leadership we can continue the journey of co-creating healthy work places.

Chapter Three

Partnership Council Framework; What is the infrastructure that supports a healthy work culture?

"We need to be able to count on the other person's special competence. When we think about the people with whom we work, people on whom we depend, we can see that without each individual, we are not going to go very far as a group. By ourselves we suffer serious limitations. Together we can be something wonderful."
- Max DePree

Individual and collective work must be done to transform work cultures into a safe place for the individual soul to live, thrive and fly. The nature and importance of the work is captured in a story from the book *Character Sketches* (1986). The story begins by explaining how the silkworm was the center of wealth for the Chinese people as early as 2600 B.C. Despite the death penalty for anyone who took the silkworms out of the country, the eggs were taken to other parts of the world. In North America the silk-worm is called the cecropia moth. Many children take the cocoons from the trees into their homes to watch the miracle of transformation. The story of one small boy brings an important lesson to all. As he watched the moth struggle to emerge, he thought he could help by opening the cocoon making it easier for the moth to be released. He did not know that the struggle to get out of the cocoon was essential to develop muscle and push blood into the wings. What he thought would help, led to the crippling of the moth. As the story states, "He realized at the expense of the cecropia moth that present struggles are essential for future achievement." This book is about the same realization.

As with the cecropia moth, it takes work to transform our cultures. The desire to create a healthy work culture is not enough--just as the desire of the boy to help the moth was not enough. There are three clear lessons from the cecropia moth story. Lesson one is that each person is accountable for his/her own work to express his/her soul. To create a healthy work culture, each person will have to experience personal transformation. The second lesson is that what you think might help another with personal transition may in fact be detrimental. No one can do another's work or bring another's soul into the work place. There are some basic principles, awarenesses, and knowledge that can help others with transformation, and these must be respected. The third significant lesson from the moth story is: *you begin by being with others where they are, not where you think they should be.* In our work of creating a healthy work culture, we have killed some moths along the way. That is the bad news. The good news is that we have uncovered some learnings about transforming work cultures that we believe will prevent you from killing off some of your own moths.

We have learned that we need to create a safe place to do the work necessary to transform from bureaucratic, hierarchical cultures to ones of partnerships. We need a human infrastructure very different from the typical systems infrastructure that evolved solely around getting things done or getting ahead. An infrastructure that focuses on shared purpose, relationships and interpersonal communications is necessary, yet difficult.

What is the nature of an infrastructure that brings the soul back into the work place?

One major component of any infrastructure is how the people are brought together in their work. What is the role and nature of these gatherings? If we use the word "meeting" to describe the gathering, what images surface for you? Are you thinking, "This is all we need, another meeting. We are meeting-ed to death. Who does the work around here? It seems everyone is always at a meeting!" The old culture is rooted in meetings. One of the most important contributions of the hierarchical meeting infrastructure is that it brings people together. The downfall is in the way in which it is done. The infrastructure is often laid out on an organizational chart and then meetings related to the work, the tasks at hand, are held by those in charge. People are picked or assigned to certain meetings. It is a familiar structure that no longer works.

For more than a decade we have been creating an infrastructure that helps us come together in a different way, one that helps us create shared purpose, meaning and vision, healthy relationships and meaningful conversations throughout the organization. At the onset of this work, a major realization emerged. There was no norm, no usual process to bring the staff together or to even link them with the work at hand. One thing was for sure, there would be no success unless we brought the people together. The manner in which the people in the setting gather is the heartbeat of a healthy systems design. We began to question what infrastructures would help us do the work of soul relationships. What infrastructure would help us tap into the collective wisdom of our peers? What infrastructure would give ownership, not just to the mission, but to each person's personal work life and destiny?

We have experimented and tried many different approaches over the years. There are some patterns and basic principles that have emerged from our work. These principles became clear both from our mistakes and from our successes. We have chosen to call this evolving infrastructure **Partnership Councils.** In the earlier years the councils were called *Unit-Based Councils (UBC's)* because the councils began and were solely reflective of a particular hospital "unit." As the work has evolved, the name Partnership Councils better reflects the system infrastructure that is needed today to create a healthy work culture throughout a health care system. The purpose of this chapter is to give an overview of the fundamental tenet and structural components of Partnership Councils. Having established a common ground based on the fundamental tenets of a Partnership Council, we can then explore the processes of development, the lessons learned, the questions that surface, and the clinical outcomes. Our goal is to build on this information throughout the remaining chapters.

What is a Partnership Council?

The Partnership Council is part of an infrastructure that creates a place to develop and enhance relationships and have meaningful conversations in order to tap into the collective wisdom necessary to achieve the shared mission and vision. It is the space to do the ongoing work to create and maintain a healthy work place. A healthy work place is one that is good for the provider and recipient of care. The Partnership Council provides an infrastructure designed to make sure the fundamental work to create a healthy work culture is carried out at all levels of the organization.

In what way does a Partnership Council differ from a typical meeting?

The Partnership Council is not just another meeting. The difference between the typical meeting and a council are clearly delineated in the following Wisdom From The Field. The comments were spontaneously given by colleagues who have lived and know well the usual nature of meetings, but are now members of a Partnership Council. Each perspective gives clear insights to the essence of a Partnership Council.

Wisdom From The Field

The following words are the responses of colleagues who answered the following question: **In what way would you explain the difference between a meeting and the Partnership Council?**

<ins>Meeting</ins>	<ins>Partnership Council</ins>
<ins>Pharmacist:</ins> "In a regular meeting you have a leader. They have an agenda. They have a decision that they want to make. It is usually one-sided. They are either providing you information or want a certain amount of information from you."	"There is no one leader. The leadership flows from one person to another depending on the subject. If you have more expertise you naturally come to the forefront and provide the information that is needed. Decisions are being made right there, right then. It is not that we are going to take this back, digest it and we're going to make the final decision and will tell you what we decided.

Things are discussed at the table, everyone gets a chance to voice their opinion. Everyone agrees that this is the best thing that they think and the decision is made there. We have consensus. Everyone agrees that this is the best-but not just looking at financials but looking at patient care which I think sometimes is lacking in a lot of regular meetings."

Patient Care Associate:
"I've been at meetings before where all of a sudden a problem arises and everybody is giving their opinion and it gets heated. Its not a fun meeting and you go away feeling worse than you had when you walked into the meeting."

"We meet every month. We are concerned together as a group about what's going on. We're out there finding out what's going on. We'll know if morale is down or there is a problem. We've got all those things--we can bring back and we know we are going to meet and we are going to be able to talk about it at the council meeting...instead of a real quick meeting. We can go to the council and tell them our concerns and something is going to happen. We know we are going to work it out as a team, as partners. It might take a little effort and a little listening but we're going to work it out with good feelings about each other, not negative feelings. At council you feel good knowing you have your support group, knowing people really do care and you walk out feeling better than you did going in."

Staff Nurse:

"Meetings are an opportunity to exchange information. Somebody else tells everybody there what is going on in the world, or the way things have to be or this is how we are going to do it. Then they may ask you. 'What do you think'?"

"A council is where a group of people get together and do the work of relationships and partnerships in a given unit or environment. There is a different sense at a council because you have the idea that everybody is spoken for there. It is not just a group of people meeting behind a closed door to discuss some future catastrophe or something. I know that although I'm not present at the meeting, the person who is there will bring my perspective and every body's idea is represented there. Also it's the quality of the work that is done there. It's not an exchange of information or plotting or strategizing. It's the quality of the work. the work we think matters most to the people who are doing it. It's not an agenda that we carry out in such and such a time. It's about what needs to be done to make our world what it needs to be. The relationships, the practice, all of that is there and the work evolves."

Staff Nurse:

"Through all the many meetings I used to go to we kind of all sat and listened to the manager telling us what was going on. Initially we didn't have any say and you didn't feel like you had any empowerment at all to change things. You just sat there, soaked it in and then went out afterwards and complained about your manager. You never had

"All of a sudden I felt more responsibility. It wasn't just someone telling us what was going to happen. It was us coming together to decide what was best for patients, for our units. You had to think and you couldn't go out and complain about what the manager had decided. You were a part of it. It made me more accountable and I became much more interested in changing some

ownership for what was happening."

things that I saw and wanted to change. You could have a say and you could change things. Sitting with co-workers and talking about those problems, usually we came up with some solutions. It was a nice time to share different problems and finding out you were not the only one with the problem."

Staff Nurse:
"What would happen at a typical meeting is that everyone would come, also people would come in at different times. Everybody wasn't always clear on the agenda of the meeting or the goals. People usually came in doing five other things while they were at the meeting. So many were not focused. So you take an hour of your day: yes people are in attendance but only half are really there and you don't get anything from the meeting. People lost eye contact, didn't have trust to say what you felt needed to be said. It is not a space to do that."

"You have a partnership and everyone is clear why they are there. You can be vulnerable there with everyone on the council. In the council you create a space right up front at the very beginning, a safe place. With it being an open council even if it is somebody who doesn't always attend, you can establish that partnership within a few minutes and make them a part of it.

I no longer go to any meeting without seeing it as a partnership. I would never want to take the time away from the care of the patient at the bedside if I couldn't see that the participation was going to help improve the care I give to each patient."

Educator:
"In a meeting there is usually a task. Those every two week meetings...you go, cover the agenda items, delegate tasks and then you leave. Also, input is sought from

"The work is ongoing. There are different components and certainly there are things you need to come to closure on but the work is ongoing. Unique is the nonverbals that happen at the council, the power of the

only those at the table."

partnership/relationships, the different disciplines and roles coming together and working together as equals. There is a powerful feeling that all peers are represented even though they are not sitting at the table. When I leave the council I'm not the same person that I was when I came in. It is the strength of really opening our ears, putting aside assumptions and the honesty, trust, respect, and knowledge at the table goes beyond words to describe. Some of it you just can't articulate but can invite others to come to see and feel what happens."

Manager:
"I do not think in standard meetings that all voices are heard; I do not think we focus on the use of dialogue. We are more into discussion and debate. We are pretty task focused. Sometimes the meeting is for information purposes, sometimes it is to make a quick decision. Typically the meeting does not involve getting input from others outside of the room. You have people meeting unwillingly."

"It is the only thing I look forward to every month. I really look forward to it. Partly because the leadership is shared and so I don't have to be there leading this meeting, I can be an active participant. I enjoy this. It is a place to be reminded that I'm not alone. It is a place where every thing that we talk about really centers around the purpose of our mission. It is so very clear. There is wisdom from all the types of roles and tracks. There is equal participation from all. Being able to hear all the voices is so important."

Physician:
"Many meetings, not necessarily all meetings are called by people who are brought together over a very

"I think there is truly no set resolution to a particular problem but the issue is how can we as a group who again share interest, who have a specific issue. Oftentimes, the shape of the resolution of that issue already exists, perhaps in the mind of the person who has brought them together. The idea of the meeting is simply to develop consensus for that particular idea. It is probably a waste of a fair amount of people's time to do that."

First Line Manager:
"Staff meetings, I feel, often are perceived as the sharing of information. We are being told about this whether it be information about change in procedure or policies, or information based on different strategies or happenings. The role here is to listen. Things are just being communicated to us. It is not a place where staff can illicit feedback or provide input. It is more that this is to inform you. They just want to make sure you know about this or this is what is going to happen. There is a preconceived notion that there is already a plan in place and we are just getting your input but we've already decided what the action plan will be. This is a very hard thing to break. The meeting seems to occur at the worst possible time. This is very inconvenient in terms of interfering with care. It is hard to remain focused. There is a whole different aspect of participation and that lack of active partici-

common purpose generate a solution to a particular problem that is going to help us achieve our outcomes. That is a far different thing because that involves people first owning that there is a problem, then being participants in the resolution to that problem. It is true participation, not like the participation you might find in other meetings."

"It is a balance of individuals from various shifts, roles and positions. It is a different culture in terms of a meeting itself. It is not a session where they are being told this is what's happening. They are not just listening but active participants. They take a very active role and engage in dialogue. Value is placed on feedback. There is a perception that I can say what I want and nothing is going to happen to me for saying it. You get a stronger sense that boy there is more than just me out there. There is more than just my responsibility. What I do impacts others so much and we are all a critical piece in anything that occurs on the unit. The agenda is not generated by someone else, but by individual and peers."

pation where they really feel they are a part. The time issue creates a different perception. I need to cover this and we need to go on to the next issue."

Staff Nurse:
"A meeting is lead by one person with a tight agenda."

"We are all on a level playing field. There is no person that is more important than the other. We all have knowledge and experience to help us work together. It helps us work together on things I could never accomplish on my own. We listen carefully to what each other has to say. Only if we have all those slants will we be able to best care for patients. It is much better than any meeting I can attend because I can share my wisdom and receive and understand someone else's wisdom."

Respiratory Therapist:
"I think in regular meetings even though there is an agenda, a lot of people come with their own agenda. There are some things on the agenda that need to be accomplished. I don't think, depending on the kind of meeting, everybody has accountability to the results. Often it is not focused on what is best for the patient. The patient isn't even at the center of the discussion."

"We come together to find or discover or define a better answer together rather than coming and having somebody say they pretty much know what the answer is. Here we try to explore what is the best way to do something. The decision is centered around what is best for the patient. We really have to question whether we made the decision based on what is best for us, because it has worked right in the past or it is easier for us to do it this way or it is best for the patient. I think when you focus on the

Meeting, continued	**Partnership Council, continued**
	patient, it changes the outcomes of the answers that you come to...and we come to. We come there to share the knowledge and expertise we have. There is a great deal of respect at the table for that expertise. It is almost like putting a puzzle together and each person brings their piece and it all fits together and you come up with the picture instead of knowing what the picture is going to be. We focus on what is happening at the bedside and impacting the patient every day. We synergize with each other and you can really tell when people are together in a different way. They are fully present with what needs to be talked about."

In addition to the very descriptive comparison of the familiar meeting and a Partnership Council, the following verse is another way to capture the essence of our knowings related to the typical meetings. It also clearly supports the need for us to be together differently as we carry out our work.

Full And Empty

Our meetings are full
of schedules
timed talk and
quick decisions.

They are full
of words that swirl
at the surface
of deeper issues.

They are full
of giving information,
fixing problems,
and staying on track.

They are full
of ego building,
defending, blaming
and judgment of others.

They are full
of quieting the voices,
that bring questions and
unwanted truths.

Our meetings are full
and I am left empty.

Give me one clear moment
of silence
and the courage
to show my vulnerable self.

Let me be an invitation
for us to be together
in a meaningful,
genuine way.
- Laurie Shiparski

Used with permission: ©Shiparski, L. (1997).
Change Is Life. Poems Of Personal Transformation In The Work Place. Michigan: Practice Field Publishing

What is the purpose of the Partnership Council?

Every person within the organization must change in order to shift from old to new ways of thinking, practicing, and relating. We have found that without an effective infrastructure to support the transformational shift, it will be very slow or not happen. Without a foundation in place to support the work, we will in our humanness fall back into the old, familiar ways. As Fox (1941, p. 82) said, "Thought is so swift and habit so strong that unless you are very careful you will constantly transgress."

Healthy cultures are changing all the time. The purpose and the importance of the council becomes obvious during any change. Much of the change today is driven by cost or bottom line issues. There is great emphasis on becoming more efficient in carrying out our work. During these times, the cultures are at risk for dehumanization. The purpose, the meaning, and the human connections needed to do the work can be lost in the face of getting things done. The Partnership Council's purpose is to focus on the relationships needed to achieve the mission. The council keeps what is important in front of them at all times. It focuses on learning and improvement but never at the expense of relationships.

Many conversations about the purpose of the Partnership Councils have taken place over the last 14 years. Table Eight lists some of the key learnings that council members have shared about the purpose of their councils. There is no order of importance but each relates to the work at hand.

TABLE EIGHT

Key Learning About The Purpose Of Partnership Councils

The Partnership Council provides a continuous place to:
- Learn partnership.
- Create shared mission/vision.
- Continuously improve the process of care/mission.
- Explore things that matter most.
- Shift learning from theory into action.
- Link local team with each other and the whole.
- Coordinate and integrate the work of the unit.
- Move from individual wisdom to collective wisdom mind set.

- Eliminate incongruency by bridging the gap between what is and what matters most.
- Learn to trust self, self organize.
- Build trust with colleagues.
- Learn how to learn together - create a learning culture.
- Demonstrate that learning is lasting productivity.
- Begin and develop systems thinking.
- Address fiscal accountability.
- Address the process of change.
- Identify interrelationships that influence behavior over time.
- Experience leadership of wisdom, not position.
- Challenge, uncover, and explore decisions.
- Raise difficult questions.
- Dialogue on the whole of the profession, not just events.
- Tap each person's capacity to grow.
- Practice continuous learning.
- Move from event focus to global process/outcome focus.
- Teach and learn.
- Enhance people's capacity to learn.
- Synchronize expertise.
- Safely create, not just problem solve.
- Create a learning culture.
- Create a mechanism to uncover how decisions may influence others.
- Fight mediocrity.
- Learn to compliment one another.
- Understand and learn from experience.
- Move from blame to ownership mentality.
- Stimulate imagination.
- Dialogue on important issues.
- Connect work distribution.
- Define, change, and evaluate reality.
- Understand at a personal level what it is to be a part of a larger whole.
- Reflect with peers.
- Celebrate successes.
- Think about how to do things differently.
- Nourish each other.
- Humanize culture.
- Create a safe environment for exploring and learning.
- Learn from long term effects of decisions.

Before getting into specific operational and structural details, it is important to reveal some underlying assumptions about Partnership Councils noted in Table Nine.

TABLE NINE
Underlying Assumptions About Partnership Councils

Purpose: The Partnership Council is part of an infrastructure that creates a place to develop and enhance relationships and have meaningful conversation in order to tap into the collective wisdom necessary to achieve shared mission and vision.

- Collective work is necessary to create a culture that is the best place for anyone to practice and the best place for any person to get care.
- Positive outcomes are not sustained by one individual, one position, one role, one committee, or one discipline.
- All are accountable for the mission and the relationships necessary to achieve the mission.
- Each have different responsibilities.
- All have responsibility to one another.
- Every person must do their own changing.
- It is a practice field--a safe place to practice new learnings.
- We can learn from all situations.
- One person's voice is not more valuable than another's.
- We are never alone.
- Everything we do impacts others.

The assumptions in Table Nine clarify why Partnership Councils are different from the "typical meetings" described previously in the Wisdom From The Field. We are often asked, "What is the difference between the Partnership Council and our monthly staff meetings?" "What is the difference between the Partnership Council and a CQI team?" Table Ten compares Partnership Councils to other common organizational meetings. Looking closely at specific operational and structural details about Partnership Councils also help one see other fundamental differences.

TABLE TEN

Partnership Councils Compared To

	Partnership Council	Staff Meeting
Purpose	Creates a place to develop and enhance relationships and have meaningful conversation in order to achieve shared mission and vision.	To provide a forum for information sharing. Global update.
Format	• Agenda collectively set by members. • Format includes check-in; updates from shared work teams, one-on-one learnings; key learning/check-out. • Dialogue principles practiced at each session. • All sessions are "open" attendance. • Focus in continuous learning tapping collective wisdom.	Informal, more than one session to cover multiple shifts. Presentation of information with some discussion.
Members	• All tracks represented: provider (licensed & non-licensed), operations resource, practice/learning resource, and research resource. • Membership "mirrors" the workplace. • Provide shared leadership. • Focus is on building strong partnerships. • Preparation time is provided to understand leadership role (formal leadership training/mentorship).	• Members are unit/dept. staff members. • Attendance dependent upon multiple variables--inconsistent.
Frequency of Meeting Time/Duration	• Monthly gatherings. • Scheduled basis. • More often if necessary.	Usually monthly.
Decision Making	• Shared decision-making. • All members carry equal weight in consensus decision making process.	• Not usually a decision making group--input gathering and giving. • Discussion cannot be channeled into consensus decision making since all staff are not represented.
Linkages	• One-on-One - links each person to council which coordinates work. • Shared work teams - may be long term/short term. Meet separately to learn/work on topic/issue at hand. Short-term teams may emerge from one-on-ones, goal setting sessions, etc. • Centralized Council - Coordinators from each Partnership Council connect monthly - share and streamline work. • System Linkages/Council - Connections to link/connect work across the system.	• Only staff who attend meeting. • Inconsistent communication is a risk. • Meeting minutes available to staff for information purposes.
Agenda Items	• Centered on mission/vision. • Outcome focused. • Goal planning. • Continuous learning. • Unit/department ownership.	• Generally information sharing and input gathering. • Manager/CNS produce agenda. Staff may submit agenda items for discussion.

Other Common Types Of Meetings

	CQI Meeting	ADHOC/Task Force Meeting
Purpose	Continuous Quality Improvement (CQI) is a short-term process to solve a problem improve a process around stakeholder information.	A process to research and study a problem/solution and bring back to a larger group usually episodic but may continue over long period of time.
Format	• Based on "CQI" meeting approaches. • Structured to find solution.	Varies--often depends on leadership style. Group process to address issue.
Members	Trained CQI Leader/Facilitator. • Membership determined by problem/process for improvement. • Might involve many units or departments.	Leader variable. Generally by volunteering or by being appointed to chair.
Frequency of Meeting Time/Duration	Meets as decided by group to achieve goal.	Meets as decided by chair and/or group to achieve goal.
Decision Making	Group determines how to best streamline process and makes recommendations via consensus process.	Makes decision and then communicates them or takes recommendations to specified person/group.
Linkages	Members of team. No specified linkages. Input is sought from individuals/groups.	May be local or global linkages depending on scale of problem/issue.
Agenda Items	• Narrow, focused on one objective. • Group ownership.	• Narrow, focused on one objective. • Group ownership.

What is the structure of a Partnership Council?

The basic structure and purpose of Partnership Councils are the same whether they are unit, service, department, or system-based. The council is a mirror of the work place and represents its diversity. Every person is linked to the council. Therefore the voices of all disciplines, shifts and roles are present. Although the titles may vary in different organizations, there are four basic roles or tracks within each professional discipline. One can choose to be a practitioner or hands-on provider (licensed and non-licensed) or support staff for providers, an operations expert/resource often called manager, a practice/learning resource often called specialist or educator, and a research resource which may be represented by a person(s) and/or the integration of research utilization and quality improvement into the work of the council. *All roles and tracks are part of the Partnership Council.* Figure 1 summarizes the roles/tracks on the Partnership Council.

The council evolves around the mission and the relationships necessary to carry out the mission. The diversity of the council members is determined by the specific needs of the people they serve. Therefore each council's make up varies. Figure 2 shows a typical structure. Note that all roles and diverse disciplines are present. The relationships as designated by stick people are centered around the mission.

What are the responsibilities of the council?

The work needed to create a healthy work culture belongs to everyone, not just to the council. The work of the council is to coordinate the effort because there is no time that everyone can come together. We have found this to be true whether in an area rendering 24-hour inpatient services, scheduled outpatient services, or home care visits. Those who choose to coordinate the effort of creating a healthy work culture, by sitting on the council, commit to responsibilities and expectations as listed in Table Eleven. These are the responsibilities and expectations of all Partnership Council members regardless of their role (provider, operations resource, practice/learning resource, or research resource). *The credibility that each member of the Partnership Council brings to the table is how they practice and relate from day-to-day.*

Figure 1
Roles/Tracks on the Partnership Council

Role of Provider

- Brings practitioner or hands-on providers expertise (RN, physical therapist, physician, pharmacist, etc.)
- Licensed and non-licensed
- Include other support staff roles (secretaries, clerks)
- Each links to certain number of peers (One-on-One)
- Links to global providers

Role of Operation Resource

- Brings operation, fiscal or budget expertise
- Often called manager, director, coordinator, etc.
- Links to global operation resources

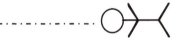

Role of Research Resource

- Usually not represented by a "researcher" role
- Integrates research and quality improvement into work of council
- Advanced practice roles key to integrate research
- Links to global research and quality work

Role of Practice/Learning Resource

- Act as a resource for the work of continuous learning in the areas of practice and/or standard of care and provide on-going educational support
- Often called educator, clinical nurse specialist, and case manager
- Links to global learning resources

Figure 2
Partnership Council

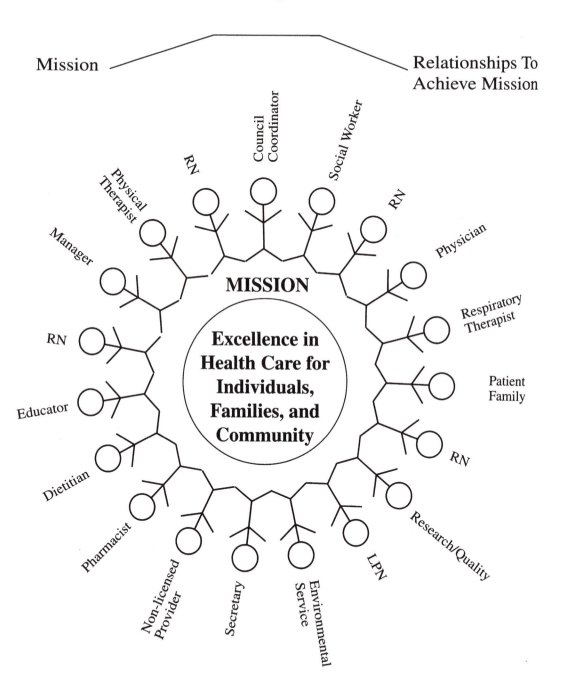

Mission ———————————— Relationships To
Achieve Mission

MISSION

Excellence in
Health Care for
Individuals,
Families, and
Community

Council Coordinator
RN
Social Worker
Physical Therapist
RN
Physician
Manager
Respiratory Therapist
RN
Patient Family
Educator
RN
Dietitian
Research/Quality
Pharmacist
LPN
Non-licensed Provider
Secretary
Environmental Service

TABLE ELEVEN

Role Of All Partnership Council Members

The members of the Partnership Councils are responsible, regardless of which track or expertise they bring to the table, to demonstrate principles of partnership and new ways of thinking about leadership. They are responsible to assure that their council is linked across units, settings and systems as appropriate.

Members' responsibilities and expectations:
- Know, live and role model Core Beliefs to colleagues, interdisciplinary team, patients, families, and community.
- Attend each session or be prepared to have another peer substitute if unusual circumstance prevent attendance.
- Work on becoming a good partner and develop partnerships with others.
- Center the decision-making process around what is best for patients and families.
- Be clear on the scope of practice of each member.
- Have open, direct, respectful, and timely communication.
- Mentor and be mentored, coach, facilitate, become teacher and learner.
- Attend and prepare for council sessions.
- Extend invitation to others to participate in council session.
- Connect shared work teams.
- Be receptive to feedback, constructive criticism and value diverse opinions.
- Strive to be good listeners.
- Discuss practice issues with peers.
- Assure that every colleague knows the purpose, structure and process of the Partnership Council.
- Demonstrate ownership of Partnership Council process.
- Communicate what is needed to best fulfill role.
- Value expertise of all tracks.
- Support each track and every peer in the process of continuous learning and transformation from institutional to professional practice.
- Know that each colleague is a unique, multi-dimensional person who has hopes, goals and dreams.
- Integrate dialogue skills and consensual processes during gatherings and in daily work.
- Celebrate successes.

Partnership Councils are rich with diversity and wisdom because people in different roles make up the council. Each person brings a different perspective because each fulfills a different role in his/her day-to-day reality or practice. Partnership Council role responsibilities have been identified by those in the roles of operation resource, practice/learning resource, and provider (see Tables Twelve, Thirteen, and Fourteen). Although people in administrative/executive roles do not sit on Partnership Councils, their roles in supporting the ongoing development of councils is critical. Table Fifteen identifies some responsibilities specific to those in administrative/executive roles (e.g., vice presidents, administrator, CEO, etc.).

TABLE TWELVE

Role Of Operation Resource

- Show how Core Beliefs relate to daily operations.
- Support staff to do what they need to do (e.g., attend council sessions, continuous learning opportunities, preparation).
- Help staff analyze and improve practice patterns and routines that impact service delivery.
- Integrate council coordinators into leadership team.
- Mentor council members on leadership skills and accept mentoring from them.
- Share information and broaden staff's perspective of professional practice beyond individual unit, hospital, state...
- Keep staff informed and help them understand financial and regulatory agency impacts.
- Help structure unit activities so each person can experience diversity.
- Seek others' personal thoughts, visions and opinions.
- Share personal thoughts, visions, and opinions.
- Strengthen staff in their ability to change and problem solve.
- Avoid rescuing or fostering dependence.
- See staff as colleagues and partners, not subordinates.
- Bring CPM values and beliefs to all other meetings you attend.
- Help unit leaders and council members grow in leadership and decision making.
- Assure Partnership Council has clerical support (typing, memo distribution, bulletin boards, etc.).
- Assure budget and Core Beliefs complement each other.
- Assure the Core Beliefs are an integrated piece of the interviewing process for new employees.
- Assure evaluation of performance is based on actualization of Core Beliefs.
- Help collaboration and build on the basic premise that all tracks must work together, for example, by promoting mutual respect for expertise.
- Assume accountability for operation resource role responsibilities as listed and share leadership with staff through empowerment process.
  - Strategic planning - unit based.
  - Creating and facilitating professional work environment.
  - Quality management.
  - Customer satisfaction.
  - Fiscal management.
  - Fostering interdisciplinary collaboration.
- Take risks by inviting new and different ways of being together.

TABLE THIRTEEN

Role Of Practice/Learning Resource

- Share information related to guidelines for care at council meetings as practice issues arise.
- Recognize importance of provider involvement with practice changes including standards, guidelines, protocols or procedures. Seek wisdom from providers via the council and One-on-One linkages.
- Invite other colleagues throughout the organization to attend the Partnership Council as appropriate (e.g., around change, to seek wisdom/input from all staff).
- Provide resources for shared work team.
- Facilitate care conferences and mentor providers in the same.
- Anticipate/coordinate resources to assist in meeting learning needs.
- Strengthen providers in their full scope of practice.
- Integrate Core Beliefs in orientation, preceptorship, and continuing education activities.
- Help staff members master and improve the tools/resources designed to enhance their practice.
- Mentor others, and allow self to be mentored. Know and tap each persons expertise.
- Celebrate success, recognize/role-model growth from "lessons learned."
- Facilitate and encourage acceptance of challenge, risk taking, and learning.
- Connect colleagues with resources that enhance their practice and relationship development.
- Provide learning experiences that strengthen each provider's ability to:
  - Know patient story
  - Establish mutuality
  - Prioritize care based on person's needs
  - Teach patient/significant other and colleagues
  - Deliver full scope of services
  - Recognize the human responses

TABLE FOURTEEN

Role Of Provider

- Uncover ways to continuously integrate mission and relationships into day-to-day practice.
- Develop One-on-One skills and bring learning back to council.
- Help peers value the time members spend at Partnership Council meetings.
- Provide leadership for the change and problem solving processes regarding professional practice issues (e.g., quality patient outcomes, professional practice environment).
- Consciously and consistently articulate and role model actualization of the Core Beliefs in day-to-day practice, especially during stressful times.
- Assist peers in understanding their accountability to the scope of practice and Core Beliefs.
- Consciously provide positive feedback to peers for professional behaviors (e.g., wholistic assessment, patient-centered decision making, individualized plan of care, professional exchange, and documentation of professional services).
- Facilitate and encourage an environment that supports risk taking and continuous learning.
- Enhance communication and problem-solving regarding professional issues by helping peer problem solving, role modeling decision making and using open direct communication.
- Problem solve areas that inhibit progress toward professional practice goals.
- Share positive approaches, techniques, and methods that support professional practice.
- Understand the role of all tracks: operations, provider, practice/learning resource, and research.
- Collaborate with all tracks and ask for what is needed, without expecting rescuing.
- Bring perspectives of other tracks and disciplines to colleagues.
- Articulate and role model scope of practice to colleagues, physicians, interdisciplinary team members, patients, family and community.
- Recognize that peers will learn and develop at different paces.
- Help colleagues see each other as resources.
- Demonstrate receptiveness to feedback, constructive criticism, and diverse opinions.

TABLE FIFTEEN

Role Of Administrators/Executives

- Know the mission and vision of each department/area.

- Integrate how Partnership Councils support the current initiatives and strategic direction of the organization.

- Be open and willing to work on your own personal transformation as Partnership Councils expand shared leadership. Tell others of this intention in an honest, vulnerable way.

- Articulate to the Board of Trustees, physicians, and administrative colleagues the purpose and the cost benefits of Partnership Councils.

- Allocate and deploy human and fiscal resources to support Partnership Councils.

- Support and participate in the implementation and on-going development of Partnership Councils and members.

- Utilize the Centralized Partnership Council and/or individual councils as vehicles to interact with staff for achieving mission and vision and to keep staff informed of strategic operation issues.

- Discuss with all directors and managers their personal progress and the progress of their units during each phase of implementation and development of Partnership Councils. Support them in continuous learning and evolving.

- Continuously invite and support interdisciplinary Partnership Council development to support integration at the point of care.

- Develop a strong partnership and meet frequently with the system wide person who is coordinating and supporting the ongoing development of Partnership Councils (sometimes called the CPM Coordinator).

- Share expertise to help balance staff and patient needs with realities of business in health care.

What approach assures that all are involved in the work of creating a healthy work culture?

Partnership Council members must first commit to meet together on a consistent basis to help coordinate the work of creating a healthy culture. Members in the provider role must also commit to developing a partnering relationship with a designated number of their peers. This partnering relationship between peers is called **One-on-One**. One-on-One partnering not only helps build relationships but assures every voice is connected to the council. At least once a month every council member interacts with each of the peers with whom they have a designated One-on-One linkage. Figure 3 on page 91 provides a visualization of how a council member links their peers to the Partnership Council via the One-on-One process.

We have found that the ideal number of peers for each provider on the council to link with is five to six. Any more than six has often proven too difficult because of the purpose and nature of the partnering relationship. The significance of the One-on-One relationships in creating a healthy work culture cannot be underestimated. For that reason, we have dedicated a significant part of Chapter Five to the One-on-One partnering relationship between council members and their peers. The necessity of having One-on-One connections also determines the size of each Partnership Council. For example, if a clinical area has 50 staff including RNs, LPNs, and secretaries, there would be 10 council members encompassing all roles. In addition, the manager, educator and key disciplines would also be in attendance. Patients can be included as needed. Figure 4 on page 92 shows examples of different Partnership Councils that mirror their unit or department. In these examples the Respiratory Department is much larger than the endoscopy unit as evidenced by the number who sit on the Respiratory Department Council.

There may be times when an urgent issue arises and an emergency council session and/or input from members and their peers is needed immediately. One method that has been beneficial in connecting all the Partnership Council members in a timely manner is the use of a phone tree.

When an urgent issue arises, the council coordinator(s), in collaboration with other leadership roles as appropriate, activates the phone tree to pass on information to each council member. Each Partnership Council member is responsible to phone and pass on the information to another member until each member is notified of the urgent communication. See Figure 5 on page 93 for an example of a Partnership Council phone tree template.

How do councils link to distribution of shared work with peers?

As councils come together and focus on what is necessary to achieve the mission and strengthen relationships, it is not surprising that further "work" will need to be done. All work on the unit is coordinated through the council but every peer is accountable to the area's work. Figure 6 on page 94 shows how shared work teams link to the councils. See Chapter Five for exploration of shared work and its importance in a healthy work culture.

How do Partnership Councils Link Throughout the Health Care System?

One of the greatest strengths of Partnership Councils as a system infrastructure is the powerful connection of all of their work to the centralized Partnership Council session. The centralized council session occurs once a month and membership consists of all the Partnership Council Coordinators throughout the organization/system (see Figure 7 on page 95 for a visualization of a Centralized Partnership Council). The purpose of the centralized Partnership Council is to continue and connect the work of individual Partnership Councils. The centralized Partnership Council also provides a way to communicate global learnings or changes back to each Partnership Council throughout the organization/system. Chapter Seven explores the significance of systems thinking linkages and further describes the purpose and outcomes of the centralized Partnership Council. See Figure 8 on page 96 for a general overview of the linkages.

Figure 3f
Partnership Councils And
The One-On-One Process

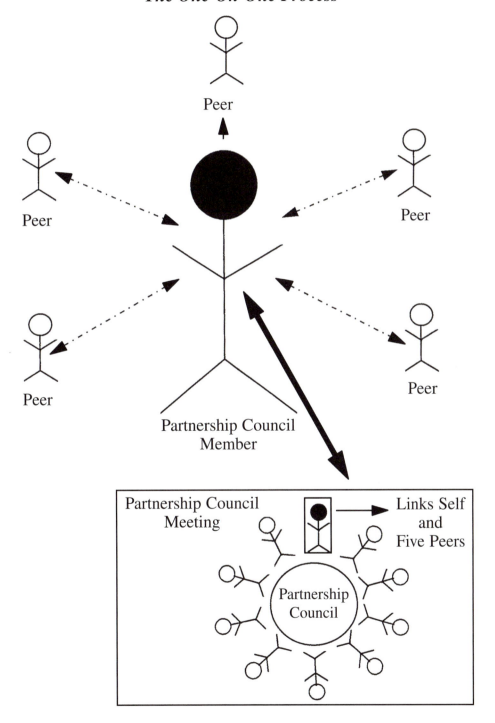

Peer

Peer

Peer

Peer

Peer

Partnership Council
Member

Partnership Council
Meeting

Links Self
and
Five Peers

Partnership
Council

Figure 4
Examples of Various Partnership Councils

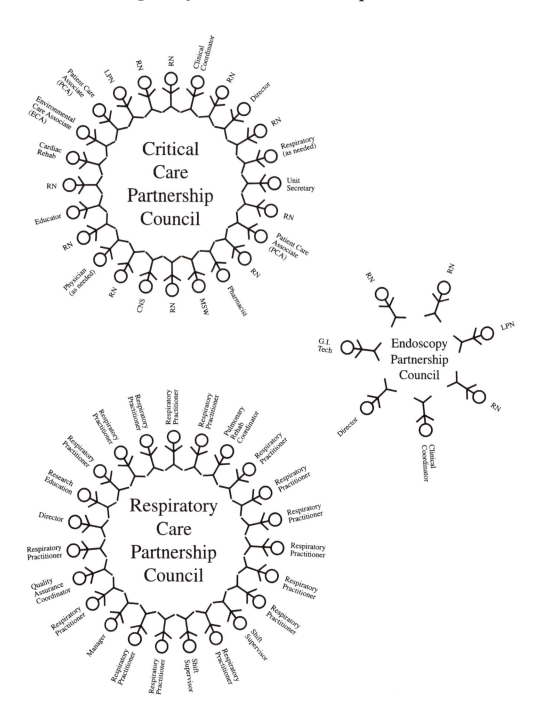

Figure 5
Partnership Council
Phone Tree

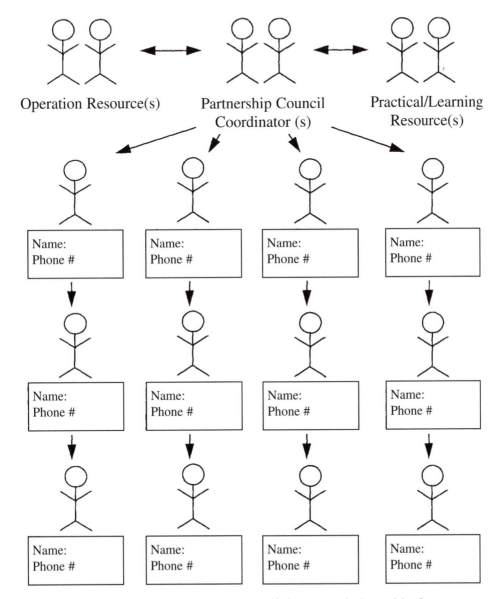

Operation Resource(s)   Partnership Council Coordinator (s)   Practical/Learning Resource(s)

If you do not get an answer when you call the person below, skip that person and go to the next. Please re-try the first person at a later time. Thank-you.

Figure 6
Shared Work Teams Link to Partnership Council

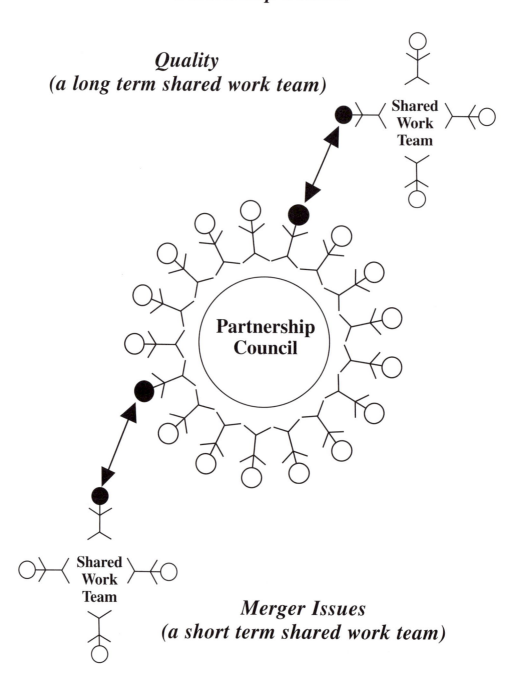

Quality
(a long term shared work team)

Shared
Work
Team

**Partnership
Council**

Shared
Work
Team

Merger Issues
(a short term shared work team)

Figure 7
Centralized Partnership Council

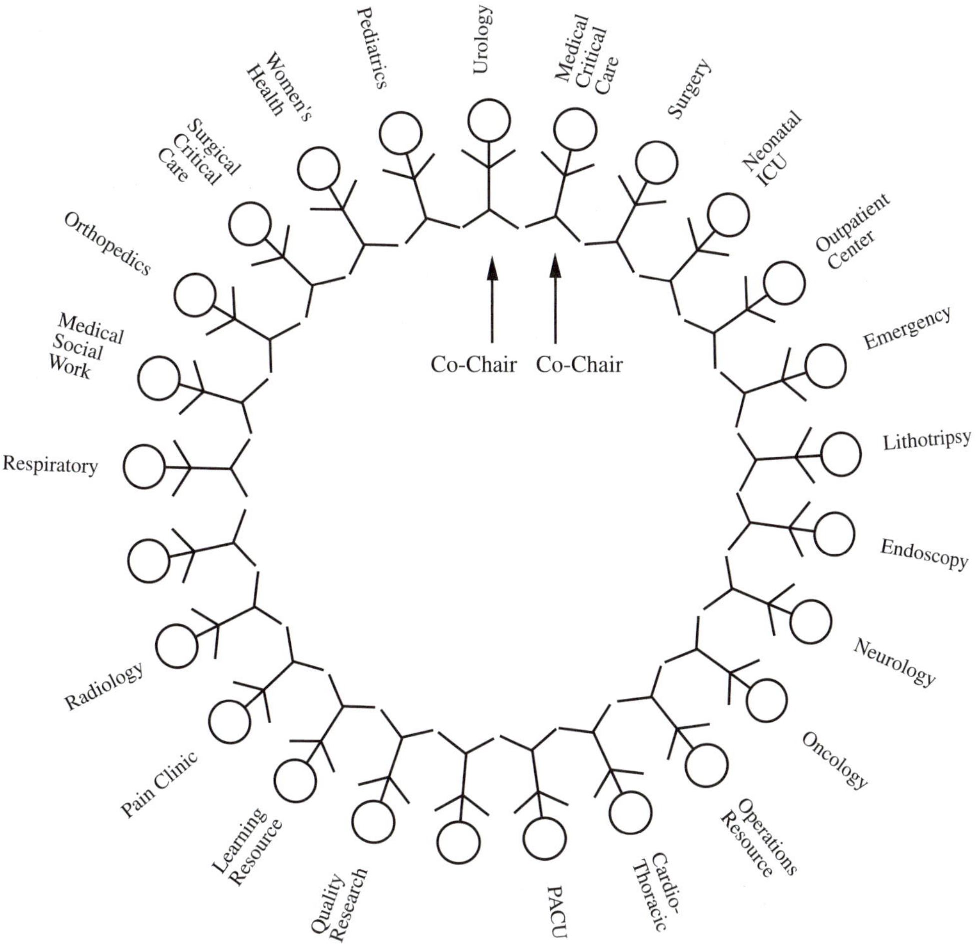

Women's Health · Pediatrics · Urology · Medical Critical Care · Surgery · Surgical Critical Care · Neonatal ICU · Orthopedics · Outpatient Center · Medical Social Work · Emergency · Respiratory · Lithotripsy · Endoscopy · Radiology · Neurology · Pain Clinic · Oncology · Learning Resource · Operations Resource · Quality Research · PACU · Cardio-Thoracic

Co-Chair   Co-Chair

Figure 8
Partnership Council
Core Linkages

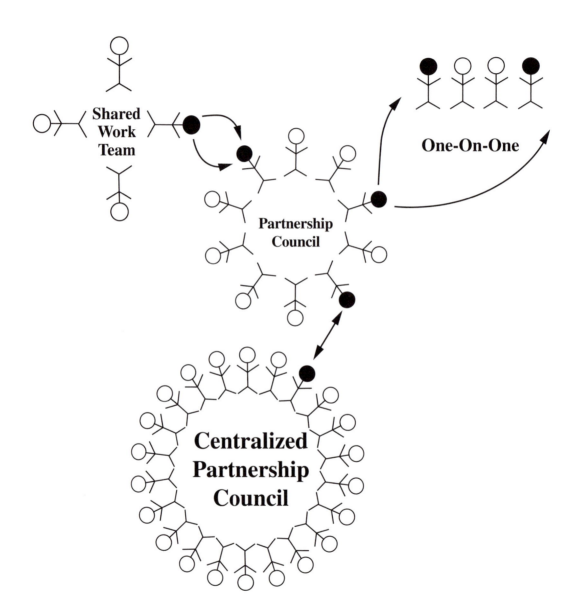

Shared Work Team

Partnership Council

One-On-One

Centralized Partnership Council

Who coordinates the Partnership Council?

The Partnership Council is coordinated by a practitioner (provider) who is selected by the members. This role is not a position of hierarchy. It is important for two reasons: one, this role supports the coordination of the council's work; and two, it links the council to others within the organization. It is suggested that a provider lead the Partnership Council because the work evolves around the service rendered and providers are the experts. This also breaks the old mindset that managers are the leaders. Every member on the council is a leader.

Some Partnership Councils have two coordinators to best meet the needs of the council. Members can either nominate themselves as the Council Coordinator or another council member can nominate them. The nominees are encouraged to tell their partners at a council session why they desire the role and why they believe they can serve them in this vital leadership role. The following Wisdom From The Field is an actual excerpt of what a current Partnership Council Coordinator wrote and read to her colleagues on her council as she sought the role of council coordinator.

Wisdom From The Field

I hope to be chosen by you, my colleagues, to coordinate our Partnership Council. I will continue to strengthen the partnerships I have with each of you and work to develop new partnerships. I value the wisdom of every person that provides care on our unit and believe having a Partnership Council is the most important way to tap into that wisdom consistently. I know how much I have grown personally and professionally since I joined the council two years ago.

I would also love to be your representative on the Centralized Partnership Council of this hospital. I feel we have so much to share with others and know how valuable it is to bring others insights to our unit.

I am encouraged by your willingness and enthusiasm to continually learn. I trust that we will learn together--I will need your support if you select me for this new challenge!

Partnership Council Coordinators are selected either through a traditional voting ballot or via a consensual process. Most often the Council Coordinators serve in their role for a two year minimum. This approach has evolved from the observation that it sometimes takes one year of experience for a Council Coordinator to truly learn how to effectively be a Partnership Council Coordinator. Many councils that have two Coordinators rotate one of the Coordinators every other year to create a natural mentorship of the most recently selected coordinator. Experience has also shown that Council Coordinators who are provided support in their role development tend to coordinate a strong, effective Partnership Council. For that reason, a competency-based development plan has been developed for new Partnership Council Coordinators (see Chapter Eight for details and Appendix A for an example).

What is a Partnership Council session like?

Partnership Councils meet on a routine monthly schedule or more often if needed. The usual day and time for the monthly gathering is determine collectively by all council members. The length of the actual session may vary from council to council, but usually ranges from one to three hours. So far the process may sound rather familiar, and maybe you are wondering if this is a new name for the old ways--especially when we talk about selecting a meeting time, length of meetings, who will coordinate and agendas.

The following keep the Partnership Council from becoming another meeting: the purpose, its focus, who is present, the connection of the voices of all colleagues, and how the work is carried out. The council connects everyone to the mission and the work of relationships. Dialogue skills form the foundation for being together differently. For example, you will notice on the agenda the word check-in (Figure 9). A check-in provides a powerful new way to begin the time together. It provides a moment for each person to focus on the special time that has been set aside for this important work. It begins by honoring the presence and voice of each person.

Figure 9
Sample Partnership Council Agenda

PARTNERSHIP COUNCIL
Session Agenda

Time	Method	Content
		1. Clarify Objective: Partnership Council Session a. Welcome/Introductions b. Check-In 2. Review Roles Leader: <u>Margie</u> Recorder: <u>Carol</u> Timekeeper: <u>Marti</u> Facilitator/Advisor: <u>self (group)</u> 3. Review agenda
		4. Work Through Agenda Items: a. Shared Work Distribution 1. QI (Marti) 2. Education (Carol) 3. Fiscal (Jeanne) 4. Patient Satisfaction (Darren) 5. Central Partnership Council (Marcia) b. One-on-One's c. Interdisciplinary Practice - Explore
		5. Review Meeting Record
		6. Plan Next Steps and Next Meeting Agenda
		7. Evaluate Meeting a. Check-Out

a-cqi

Have you ever arrived at a meeting feeling a little frustrated or rushed or worried about something else that does not relate to the session? Check-in provides a time to be present to the moment for yourself. Check-in is a process that centers on relationships. It provides an opportunity for the group to focus on the presence of each colleague. It is an invitation to be together differently, slows the pace and acknowledges that everyone comes to the meeting within his/her own circumstances. The group is able to practice the skills of listening and the reflection of silence. The check-in is not a time to fix or do, but to listen and to be with each person where he/she is. It is in that recognition that the pace and the conscious intention of the meeting is brought forward. It frees each individual to get on with the work at hand.

In the initial phases of council development, it is natural for many to think of this as any other meeting. It is easy to see why some may think so--that is all they have known. Expectations of the Partnership Councils can be clouded by the past ways of working together. Historically, staff attended few meetings. Their understanding of meetings came more from perceptions than attendance. In a hierarchical culture, when a meeting occurred, the staff wondered what would happen to them next. If nothing happened, then they wondered what people do who go to meetings all day...certainly not the work at hand.

Often there is little valuing of meetings at the staff level. Therefore supporting another peer to go to a council session does not automatically happen. When staff leave the work setting and go to a meeting, someone must continue to "do" the work of providing patient care services. There is not a natural trust that what is happening away from the work setting is important. When the purpose and work of the council is unknown, it is even easier to have little respect for it. The work of each council member is to help peers understand the difference between the council sessions and the old meetings or other meetings. This is done during the One-on-One time between council members and their peers.

An important aspect of Partnership Council sessions is that they are always open sessions--everyone is invited all the time. One learns to appreciate the value of this when new wisdom speaks and trust is built by advocating "open sessions." This reinforces that this is our work, "there are no secrets," and maintains an openness to listen in order to achieve shared understanding and decision making. Council members sometimes struggle when doing their One-on-One with a peer who may be "hot" about an issue or who has a uniquely different perspective than their own. We often find ourselves comfortable discussing family vacations, hobbies, and our children, but discussing our actual practice may not always be comfortable. Our ability to discuss practice issues grows as the trust in the relationship deepens and an understanding of the Partnership Council grows. Inviting a peer to a council session who has strong opinions on an issue or topic can help build trust and understanding.

Over the years we have learned the value of having some structure to council sessions yet keeping an "openness" to invite dialogue, consensus, and continuous learning. Agendas, meeting minutes and peer feedback sheets all serve as valuable organizational and communication tools for an effective Partnership Council meeting. There have been, and no doubt will continue to be, many suggestions for improving the processes of Partnership Council meetings. While some suggestions are appropriate for councils, others can interfere with the work. Continuous quality improvement (CQI) started with enhancing group work and includes how to run successful meetings. Many Partnership Councils have adapted the Seven Step Meeting Process Agenda (Quorum, 1992) to help facilitate an effective council session (see Figure 9 on page 99 for a sample agenda). While having a format can be valuable, participants are cautioned to not get "stuck" in the agenda format and thus forgo the principles of consensus and dialogue that are central to the Partnership Council

Where do you begin?

This chapter has focused on the infrastructure of a Partnership Council. Often we are asked, "Where do we begin" Table Sixteen gives a few beginning tips. See Chapter Eight for further details.

Although understanding the basic structural components and linkages of a Partnership Council is important, clarity on the intention and purpose of councils is even more important. By focusing on the relationships needed to do our mission work we create the intangible aspects and awesome experiences of a Partnership Council. Meg Wheatley states, "Relationships are all there is" (1992). Now it is time to explore ways in which Partnership Councils can bring meaningful relationships and conversations into our work culture.

TABLE SIXTEEN

Partnership Councils: Where To Begin

- Provide information for all staff related to the organization's commitment to focus on creating a healthier work culture, a culture that is best for both providers and recipients of care.

- Discuss the connection between shared purpose, healthy relationships and meaningful conversations, and the health care culture.

- Examine the characteristics of the present culture, i.e., nature of leadership, participation, cultural patterns and show how they compare to a changing, expanding and healthy culture.

- Explain the goal of creating a flexible infrastructure that brings people together to concentrate on ways to continue learning and improve the work of the mission and relationships necessary to achieve the mission.

- Explain the nature of the infrastructure so each person can relate it to his/her role, such as:

  - What is a Partnership Council?

  - Explain the purpose and the way the council differs from usual meetings and other committees.

  - Explain the infrastructure and how it strengthens relationships and connections by including all tracks and diverse roles.

  - Review the responsibilities of council.

  - Explain the One-on-One concept.

  - Review the responsibility of each person on the unit to the work of healthy cultures.

  - Discuss who leads the council and how that role links with the other councils.

  - Talk about shared work teams.

- Put out a call for volunteers to be a part of this work. An invitation is extended to everyone.

Chapter Four

Relationship Dynamics:
In what way are meaningful relationships and conversation strengthened in Partnership Councils?

"When people see the respect and dignity we have for one another they will know this is a good place."

- Bonnie Wesorick

The quality of life parallels the quality of relationships. It takes work to initiate and sustain healthy relationships. When we avoid the work of relationships, the quality of relationships and the quality of life decline. The avoidance of relationship work is common in the work setting. We often fail to notice, because we disguise our actions. The nature of conversations give you a clue about avoidance.

A common expression by those who have found it unsafe to bring their soul into the work setting is, "Hey, I don't get involved in the politics around here. I come and do my work and get out" This statement is a common symptom of an unhealthy work culture, one in which it is safer to withdraw or disconnect from others, than to engage. Once the work setting is depersonalized, dehumanization becomes a norm, and after a while it is accepted, expected and even considered appropriate. It does not happen overnight. There are many stories and a history that explain why people decide to disconnect from those with whom they work daily.

How do we stop the dehumanization cycle and engage others in the work of healthy relationships?

The council provides the space and invitation for us to learn to be together differently. It is a place to stop "doing" and concentrate on our relationships that are necessary to achieve the mission. The council infrastructure stops the hamster wheel of activity and the cycle of dehumanization. It does this by providing the opportunity for meaningful conversation as well as the time necessary to develop relationships around what matters most in our work. Once the space is created, its boundaries become endless and stops dehumanization.

Dehumanization

You speak
but I feel nothing.
My ears hear
My eyes notice
My mouth responds
But I disconnected from my soul long ago.
It is easier this way
At least it seems so
Til I realize that
When I speak
I do not hear
I do not feel
I cannot find my soul.

- Bonnie Wesorick

There are three phases to council development as listed in Table Seventeen. The first phase is to learn partnerships within the council. That is the focus of this chapter. The second phase is reaching out and forming partnerships with others, both One-on-One (see Chapter Five) and also across the setting (see Chapter Seven). The third phase is the ongoing work through Partnership Councils to create a healthy work place. The third phase is discussed in Chapters Five, Six, Seven and Eight.

TABLE SEVENTEEN

Phases of Partnership Council

Phase One: Learn partnerships within the council.
Phase Two: Reach out and form partnerships with others.
Phase Three: Co-create a healthy work place via partnerships.

What are common situations that Partnership Councils face in the initial phase?

Once the members make a choice to be a part of the work to create a healthy work culture, they recognize the need for new skills. The interactions between people often mirror the realities of their work place. People will come to the Partnership Council armed with expectations and relationship skills molded by the insidious, yet deeply embedded, patterns of the past and present norms. Learning to come together and pay attention to relationships, as well as to getting "things" taken care of, is not typical. The natural inclination for the members is to begin with the work of finding solutions, getting answers and fixing the problems on their units. In a world focused on measurable outcomes and results, it is unusual to think that learning to be a partner is as important as how many items were addressed on the agenda.

The need for dialogue skills surfaces immediately when councils are initiated. The members come to the table with many assumptions and expectations of each other that are based on old boss/subordinate mindsets. They are accustomed to being together as staff/manager, discipline/discipline, teacher/learner, expert/novice and licensed/non-licensed, not as partners. They are used to "doing" together, not "being" together. The desire for it to be different is often buried in the old ways of being together as evidenced by the following Wisdom From The Field.

Wisdom From The Field

A group of leaders was gathered to talk about what could be done to create a healthy work culture. The group was made up of people who worked in this very bureaucratic and hierarchical culture. The conversation was filled with what one member called "the typical fight for power and control." Fear is often disguised in conversations by patterns of competition, judgment, blame and the fight for power. Fear was thick in the room. Although the group believed a change was needed, there was fear of who would "dictate" the change. Historically, whoever spoke the loudest, and had the most power would determine the way the work would be done. The group was responding in the only way they knew in this culture.

The facilitator consciously used the principles of dialogue. The facilitator's intention to respect and be present with the others was evident by demonstrating listening without judging, competing, blaming or defensiveness. Gradually the usual patterns of communication, so familiar to the group, began to change. As they were listened to, they began to listen. A peer acknowledged that the present culture was not one that welcomed questions or discovery but one that preferred answers. As questions were asked from a genuine need to uncover and deepen the understanding, the nature of the group's questions changed. There was a shift from questions of blame and manipulation to questions of wondering.

The conversation at the meeting was not only reflective of the nature of their culture but also a symptom of the need for a healthy culture. As the conversation changed, a safe place to share thinking and even feelings was created. The members of this group desired a healthy work culture, but no one was certain how to make it happen. There was agreement that the usual patterns were not successful or healthy. The following verse is another way to think about what happened.

Loosening The Jaws Of Fear

There was tension in the air.
The initial polite expressions
could not disguise the
troubled or empty eyes.
Questions swirled with suspicion
accusation and defensiveness.
Blaming stifled exploration.
A hint of the soul could be felt in the passion
But the words were too harsh to be heard.

An invitation was offered
to a safe place for all.
Words were not judged
assumptions were checked out.
Listening could be heard
and genuine inquiry unfolded.
Compassion seeped in
Fear was dispersed, and
respect was felt in the moment.

- Bonnie Wesorick

What is the first work of the councils?

The first work of the council members is to learn to live the Principles of Partnership and Dialogue amongst themselves. This is ongoing work. The council members become aware that the common old behaviors, as listed in Table Eighteen, are quite contrary to the common new behaviors of the partnership paradigm. Learning to live the new behaviors is a challenge for everyone.

The ability to first recognize and then shift from the familiar and almost unconscious old behaviors to the new behaviors in Table Eighteen requires living the principles of dialogue and partnership. The conscious intention to learn and listen deeply to another brings forth the compassion in the heart and offsets the tendency of the mind to judge or blame. Being heard by others gives rise to courage to bring the unspoken from within. The connection of purpose and mission silences the fear and erases the competition. It takes work to break the old patterns which are embedded into the daily patterns of thinking, relating, and practice.

What are the barriers that interfere with the work to create healthy relationships?
Fear

Fear is a common barrier to the work. Fear, as most threats, is a reflection of past relationships and is especially common in the old boss/subordinate or power/control culture. Fear generates the doubt that the council is a safe place to be together differently. One thing that offsets this fear is the ability to talk about it. Zigler, (1988) notes that f-e-a-r is really nothing more than "**f**abricated **e**vidence that **a**ppears **r**eal." Once the fear is recognized and spoken about, the chains are broken. It takes courage and vulnerability to verbalize the fear.

An example of such courage and vulnerability is found in the approach by a manager who said in the first council session: "I have been quiet most of this meeting because I do not know how to be with you as a partner. I know how to be with you as a boss. I haven't spoken because I was afraid of saying something that would make you think I don't want to have a partnership."

TABLE EIGHTEEN
Differences of Behaviors in Old and New Paradigms

OLD BEHAVIORS Bureaucratic, Hierarchical Relationships	NEW BEHAVIORS Empowered Partnering Relationships
FEAR: This approach is rooted in the belief that all power, all security sits outside of oneself and security is dependent on another. It leads to personal power over another and even over mission.	**VULNERABILITY:** The willingness to look at oneself, know oneself and connect with others as you are, not as you think others desire you to be or you are supposed to be.
COMPETITION: This approach is focused on being better than another, rather than striving to tap into the capacities of another. It is limiting to both oneself and whoever is in the race with you. Competition is rooted in power, control and comparison. It implies that for one to be great, another has to be less.	**COMPASSION:** The ability to see and care for others, as they are, with no desire to judge them, but instead a willingness to accept and learn with them. It gives one the ability to see potential in others beyond their present limitations. It helps us connect with the positive and allow the negative.
JUDGMENT: This approach is based on a hierarchical mind set, wherein another's action, potential and capacity is narrowed and determined by the mental perspective of another. It is a process that insidiously gives permission to perpetuate boss-subordinate behaviors.	**SYNCHRONY:** The ability to connect with a shared purpose and meaning through mission. Just as two eyes see one image, partners have one common mission.
BLAME: This approach is an escape from accountability by projecting the "cause" of an event to another. It is often rooted in fear and powerlessness. It decreases the opportunity to uncover the truth.	**FORGIVENESS:** The ability to let go of the past and discover the potential within an individual or present moment. It is a shift from a judging to a compassionate mind set.
ENTITLEMENT: This approach is based on the notion of separateness and exception to fundamental principles because of personal importance.	**MOTIVATION:** The ability to connect with others around their purpose and passion.
RESCUE: This approach is to fix things for others. The action is not to tap into the capacity of another but do it for them.	**DIVERSITY:** The ability to uncover different views, not to analyze or prove but to learn and connect the differences without dominance.
INDIFFERENCE: This approach is rooted in detachment and disinterest in the presence, the actions, and the words of another.	**TRUST:** The ability to accept and respect the worth of another without proof. There is a willingness to build a meaningful relationship.
	ACCEPTANCE: The ability to be with others as they are at that moment.

A staff nurse replied by saying, "Thanks for sharing that because I was sitting here thinking your silence meant you didn't support this and really didn't want to be a partner." This was the beginning of their learning to be together differently.

To show one's vulnerability and bring it to the surface takes great strength. It is also fundamental for healthy relationships. The humanness, the personhood becomes evident in vulnerabilities as well as in strengths. Block (1993) noted, "It is vulnerability, not strength that makes one's humanness more visible" (p. 43). Within hierarchical cultures, it was not safe to be vulnerable, and therefore fears were often not expressed. Partners bring their whole selves to the table and that includes their fears. Councils consciously attempt to create a safe place for that to happen. Once someone speaks at a council and the fear is dissipated, it gives courage for the members to do the same in other interactions. It begins a new cycle.

Competition

Another barrier to partnership work is competition. Competition is based on comparing one person's performance to another's and is expressed in diverse ways. Insidiously, comparison of abilities to "do" became equated with worth. If I am more important or can do more than you, then I have greater worth. The hierarchical model thrived on competition. To climb the ladder of success, individuals had to show they were better than others. This resulted in such thinking as, "I am more important than you, because I can do this and you can't." "I have more education than you, I have more experience than you, and therefore what I think is more important." "I can get more done, carry a heavier assignment, and am faster than you."

Competition violates the partnership principles of equal worth and potential. It is associated with such dysfunctional thinking as, "I deserve more respect because I can do things you can't do...or I do them better than you." It comes from the shallow mindset that, "I am more if you are less than I." In competition success is based on one person's success over another's. It is not based on the belief, "If you are successful, I am successful." Competition prevents partnership.

Competition becomes evident in the councils when the group's members start to see themselves as more accomplished than their peers. In some ways competition is more insidious than fear because it can be disguised under the pretense of trying to improve someone. In the initial phase the council realizes that members are making inroads with communication, relationships, and a new understanding of the importance of their work. Then they look at those outside the council and make comparisons.

Competition is reflected in statements such as, "It's going to take a whole lot of work to get them to understand this concept. What do we need to do to get them where they need to be?" It is a "power over others" mindset that will alienate those not considered a part of the group. It creates a we/they and a comparison mindset, not a helping mindset. Competition generates judgment--which is another strong barrier to partnership. The poem on the following page summarizes the effects of competition.

Judgment

Judgment is a common barrier and is engrained into a hierarchical culture. It creates distinctions between those who judge and those being judged. It is the heartbeat of a boss/subordinate culture. It has no place in partnership. In the initial stages of forming councils, the members, will often unconsciously flip into judging others who do not sit on the council. When the council's conversation becomes centered around making sure colleagues are thinking, relating and doing things the right way, judging has surfaced.

During the first phase of development the council has the potential to become the new boss who will judge if the others are doing it right. Of course, the right way is the council's way. It becomes evident in statements such as, "When will they get it? How do we get them to catch on, come along? What do we need to do to get their buy-in? How can we make sure

A Community of Competition

Some say motivation and progress
reign in a community of competition.
That it breeds the best for all
and helps us fulfill a vision.

But there is another side
to this community of gold,
it's dark shadow noticed
we may not wish to hold.

With competition also comes
an satiable, gnawing thirst.
One that drives the best of us
to selfishly prove we're first.

It becomes a game to win
and ego must take all,
pitting people against people
the outcome anyone's call.

Relationships do suffer
as the casualties of fight,
we make each other look bad
just to give ourselves more height.

The victims at the heart of this
are those we seek to serve.
They get caught in the crossfire
missing out on care deserved.

So in the end the very thing
that promised us success,
divides us from each other
where collective power manifests.

- Laurie Shiparski

Used with permission: © Shiparski, L. (1997)
Change Is Life. Poems Of Personal Transformation In The Work Place. Michigan: Practice Field Publishing

they are doing it right?" It is the "power-over" model which leads to the "all knowing council" which then determines if the work of others is satisfactory. If the council does not recognize this type of behavior, the hierarchy will continue.

The Partnership Council is not a group to replace the manager. It is not the new authority, the boss, or controller. The foundation is based on a completely different pattern of thinking. The council is a group of people willing to coordinate the work necessary to make their setting the best place in the world for a person to get care and for anyone to work. The council is about everyone's work, not just one person's work. *It is about helping every person to carry out shared work.*

Blame

Blame is another barrier to partnership. Thomas Merton (1961, p. 110) noted, "It is not that someone else is preventing you from living happily; you yourself do not know what you want. Rather than admit this, you pretend that someone is keeping you from exercising your liberty. Who is this? It is you, yourself." Blame is hard to recognize in oneself, but it is very easy to see in others. It is a common behavior in the hierarchical model. It is strongly connected to fear, judgment, and powerlessness.

Blame is a way to solve problems or to take care of mistakes that occur, by focusing on who or what is at fault. The roots of this behavior are not anchored in discovering or uncovering what happened, so to learn and improve. It is more about projecting fault on someone or something. Blame perpetuates fear and judgment-based relationships. It often is driven by the facts of the mind, separated from the compassion of the soul. It feels good initially because one can disconnect from ownership to the problem.

Blame becomes evident in councils when a decision made by the council is met with resistance from peers. This more commonly occurs in the initial phase when the council is in the throws of relationship work, both within the council and beyond, while simultaneously addressing the day-to-day problems. The following example demonstrates this barrier.

Wisdom From The Field

There were 27 members on the council. They were looking at assignments and how they impacted continuity of care. They realized it would be a tough issue because it touched the patterns and quality of every person's day. They began to uncover the major factors and the alternative ways to address the issue. There were many other issues entwined including various levels of competency, preceptorship responsibilities, new orientee schedules, seniority, pulls to cover other units, shorter lengths of stay and changing census. It was more complex than they thought. When it came time to make a decision, they did what they thought best based on the feedback of their peers.

Once it was brought back to the whole group, people began to complain. As soon as negativity toward the decision was aired at the council, blame surfaced and grew. One peer who did not sit on the council was complaining to everyone about the decision of the council and was looking for others to side with her. Carla, who was her link to the council, blamed her for all the problems.

Carla said, "I gave her an opportunity to give her input. She had no suggestions. She never comes to me, I always have to seek her out. I asked her what suggestions she had and of course she didn't have any, and laughed like it didn't matter anyway." Others began to feed into this as well. Joel stated: "The people I connect with only care about themselves and how it will impact them--they could care less for the patient." Bryce jumped in and said, "I went over and above in trying to involve everyone with this decision, half of them just said, do what you want. They don't even care enough to help."

The frustration level rose as their time together was ending. Loren then said, "I think the real issue is not the decision we made but a symptom of something else. We have become the bad guys. Why do you think that happened?" The group became silent. Bryce said, "Are you asking if we could have done something differently?" Loren said, "Maybe the next time we get together we should take a look at the whole picture, the process we used, and what this is saying about our relationships with our peers."

If blame is not recognized and addressed, the council's goal of partnership will not happen. Although at the time it does not feel like it, the situation described in this wisdom is a great learning opportunity for the council. All that is needed is one voice to break the pattern or to recognize the presence of blame, and new directions will follow. The council is a practice field, a place to learn, make mistakes and grow. To offset blame each person on the council will have to learn forgiveness. Forgiveness is the ability to let go of the past and concentrate on discovering the potential of an individual and the potential of a moment. It requires a shift from a judgmental to a compassionate mindset.

Nouwen (1974, p. 21) notes, "When we cling to the results of our actions as our only way of self identification, then we become possessive and defensive and tend to look at our fellow human beings more as enemies to be kept at a distance than as friends with whom we share the gifts of life." The principle of inquiry helps prevent defensiveness as evidenced by Loren's question in the above wisdom. Inquiry helps one move from defensiveness into a continuous learning mode. Breaking the patterns embedded into our hierarchical cultures takes work. Table Nineteen on page 117 provides some tips to break old patterns.

What helps break the old ways of being together?

Dialogue skills strengthen conversations and relationships. The Principle of Intention (See Table Three, page 16) helps us examine our reason for connecting with another. Inquiry helps us ask questions that do not put another on the defensive. Inquiry helps us to genuinely seek the voice, the perspective of another. It moves the conversation beyond the superficial words to the roots of their meaning. It is this deepening that breaks the boundaries of old thinking. *Inquiry cultivates an appreciation for diversity and helps connect seemingly polar perspectives.* This leads to new knowledge and deeper understanding. The Principle of Silence helps in personal reflection. In reflection we stop jumping in to fix, rescue or answer the questions of others which often ends exploration. Silence is also an invitation for another to continue. Kornfield and Feldman note (1991, p. 210) that "The noise created through our busyness deafens us to the words of silence."

TABLE NINETEEN

Tips to Break Old Patterns of Communicating and Relating

The first and most significant step is to NOTICE PATTERNS OF INTER-ACTIONS AND BRING THEM TO THE TABLE.

- **When defensiveness or blame surface:** Use inquiry to stop the process and to consider what learning is available. Inquiry helps move from being threatened by information to uncovering new insights.
  What are other ways of thinking about this?

- **When judgment surfaces:** Call for the group to stop and look at the other perspectives or voices not present in the room.
  What are alternative perspectives?

- **When competition surfaces:** Shift the group from comparing to uncovering approaches that tap the potential in others.
  What approaches would help us tap into the capacity of others?

- **When diversity leads to polarization:** Notice that opposites are often part of the same truths. Ask the group to explore how these opposites might be connected.
  What connections are present in opposite perspectives?

What is the nature of the work in the new paradigm of partnership?

The following exercise will help bring the nature of the work to the forefront. Think of a person, by name, with whom you have a very healthy relationship. This is a person you trust, one with whom you have a sense of unconditional acceptance whenever you are with them. This person helps you, not by fixing things, but by helping you see the potential that sits within yourself. When you are with them you are energized.

Now think of a person, by name, with whom you do not have a sense of trust. There is a feeling of being judged or strong competition. You watch your words when you are with them. You feel drained, not energized, in their presence. Once you have the names, read the following quote by Henri Nouwen (1974, p. 40), "Every human being has a great yet often unknown, gift to care, to be compassionate, to become present to the other, to listen, to hear and receive. If that gift would be set free and made available, miracles could take place."

In what way do you think this quote relates to the people you named above? Did you find it natural to think this statement was true for the person with whom you have a good relationship? Is it hard for you to see the person with whom you do not have a good relationship, within the context of Nouwen's words? Yet Nouwen notes that these gifts, these potentials, are innate in all human beings. The miracles he refers to come from the type of relationships that connect at the soul where the strengths and capacity of every person sit. What would help us see, or maybe first of all believe, that every human has all the potentials, all the gifts, of which Nouwen speaks? It is only with the eyes of our own souls that possibility becomes reality.

When did we stop expecting miracles?

The "stopping" was an insidious evolution that paralleled with the movement to focus on the work to be done. It was a gradual process starting with the soul being ignored. Then, more obviously, there was encouragement to ignore it, over time there was expectation to ignore it, and then even rewards for ignoring it. How do we stop this cycle? We must become aware of the fact that we have a choice. We consciously choose to honor the souls of all who walk with us in our work. We can choose to encourage the soul's presence, in the same way we choose to stifle it. First we welcome the soul's presence, then reward its presence, and then expect its presence. We know this process works.

The work of honoring the souls of others begins at a personal level. This work begins with the decision to recognize the patterns that eat away at personal identity and purpose. Every day we are surrounded by committed, caring people, who, in the words of David Whyte (1995), "Are desperate to belong to something larger than themselves." We learn to connect with each other, to sharpen our skills in relationships, with the same intensity with which we sharpen our other performance skills. It calls for great courage and a deeper understanding. It calls for us to respect first ourselves and then others.

The Partnership Council is a formal, outward message that the choice has been made within the setting to create new norms and expectations about relationships. Commitment is evident by the support given to those who volunteer to lead this work as council members. Chapter Eight gives examples of the support which helps with both the personal and the professional work needed to create a healthy work place.

The purpose of the council is not to protect others from the experience or personal work of change. The moth story warned us of that activity. It is in the work of relationships that we learn ways to help others to do their own work. It provides the space to learn to be together differently. It requires learning new patterns of relating and conversing. Partnership Councils do not eliminate the noise; they welcome it and turn it into music. Success is dependent on the personal relationships, first with self, then within the council, and then with those outside the council. As the relationships on the councils are strengthened, they help strengthen the relationships with all who are connected beyond the council. The following Wisdom From The Field is an example of the outcomes of living the principles of partnerships and what it looks like when noise is turned into music.

Wisdom From The Field

Jan was discharging Mrs. Keen from the Orthopedic unit to the Rehabilitation Center. Mrs. Keen, an 80 year old woman, had been admitted with a broken hip following a fall in her home. Before this hospitaliza-lion she had been the primary care giver for her husband who was ter-minally ill with cancer. The same day she fell, he was admitted to the Oncology unit with intractable pain.

Jan and Mrs. Keen had decided on the best time for the Ambu-cab to pick her up for transfer. They had allotted time for Mrs. Keen to go to the Oncology unit to spend extra time with her husband before she left the hos-pital. Because his condition was deteriorating rapidly, she was asked to con-sider the type of life saving measures they desired. This was a difficult time for her.

Jan returned to the Orthopedic unit while Mrs. Keen said good-bye to her husband. Two people from the transport company had arrived to pick up Mrs. Keen and were told she was on the Oncology unit saying good-bye to her very ill husband and would be down shortly. After about five minutes of waiting, their impatience became evident.

Although Jan did not know the people from the Ambu-cab service she immediately established a partnership. She introduced herself as Mrs. Keen's nurse and said she was sorry to be holding them up. One of the men noted that she was just one of many people they needed to transport today and they had a tight schedule. Jan did not judge the men, but in fact listened to their concern and responded. She suggested saving time by going up to the Oncology unit and having Mrs. Keen leave from there. She offered to go upstairs with them and on the way to share Mrs. Keen's story so they could understand the situation.

As Jan shared Mrs. Keen's circumstances, both of the transporters were touched. As they stood by the door, one noted Mrs. Keen was having diffi-culty getting close enough to her husband to kiss him good-bye. He imme-diately went in to help her position herself better and said they would be out-side when she was ready to leave and there was no hurry. As they were escorting her down the hall, one said, "I am a volunteer and you can call me anytime and I will pick you up and bring you here to spend time with your husband." He explained how she could do that.

The principles of partnership and outcomes of partnership come alive in this Wisdom. Jan **intentionally** connected with these two gentleman as partners. She knew she shared with them the same **mission** to positively influence the health of another. She did not judge their concern for the time they needed to get their work done as a lack of caring, but recognized their **accountability** to transport not only Mrs. Keen, but others. She knew that the **balance**, the harmony of her relationship with them was important in the ultimate care of Mrs. Keen. She honored their work, listened to their concerns, and supported them by offering a suggestion to save time and **potentiate** their work. She offered information that gave insight into the importance of their work for the life of another. She **trusted** their intention, respected them and provided information that helped them do their job better. Her invitation to others is part of the "shared work" of creating a healthy work place which is the focus of the next chapter.

Chapter Five

Shared Work: What is each person's accountability for a healthy work culture?

*"The outcomes of shared work can never be explained
by the individual ability of any member in the group."*
- Bonnie Wesorick

Everyone is accountable to create a healthy work culture. It requires work on the part of every person who has chosen to be present in the work setting. Each person is accountable regardless of position, education, role, or professional responsibilities. No one has more accountability to a healthy work culture than another. We call this accountability shared work. Shared work includes every aspect that influences the success of the mission, the purpose of the work, and the relationships of those who carry out the mission. It is the heartbeat of the second phase of creating a Partnership Council.

Shared work is a major shift in thinking. It is a commitment to stop the cycle of dehumanization. It emerges out of the conscious decision to connect the souls of all who have chosen the work at hand. No one will be seen as insignificant or simply there to perform as told. Each will be honored for their choice of contribution. Each will be respected and seen in their wholeness. Therefore, each will be expected to be an integral part of the shared work to create a healthy culture. This expectation is the first step of recognition and respect for everyone.

This concept goes beyond the isolated personal accountability to be competent in the services of the profession or role one has chosen. The concept goes far beyond the mindset to come and do "MY" daily assignment. It is not about just doing but about living and becoming by connecting with others around the choice of work. This chapter will focus on the various ways to shift from individual isolation to shared work in the day-to-day practice setting. Because this book focuses on the Partnership Council, it would be easy to think that those who sit on the council are solely responsible to create and sustain a healthy culture. That is not the intention. The council coordinates the work, but all are involved. There are many on the team and all are busy. That will not change. So what can change? The change will be in how we work together.

The partnership infrastructure is designed in such a way that every person on the team is linked to the council. This linkage is fundamental to achieving the goal of shared work. There are different ways each person can contribute to shared work. We will look at those who choose to contribute to shared work by being on the council and those who make other choices. As described in Chapter Three, one of the fundamental responsibilities of those who sit on the council is to connect with their peers. We call this One-on-One and have a visual representation of it in Figure 3 on page 91.

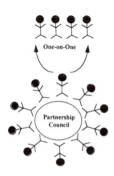

What is One-on-One and why is it important?

One-on-One is the term used to describe the manner in which every person is connected to the council. It is through this connection that the concept of shared work becomes reality. It is not just a communication link. It is far more. The primary purpose is to establish a *partnership* with a co-worker. The Principles of Partnership are the foundation for this interaction. It is a conscious approach to connect with our peers around something they value, something that gives them purpose and meaning in life and something that all of us have in common, the mission. It is very different from the typical relationships that evolve around the jobs, the tasks, the things to be done. It has nothing to do with competition, judgment, power or control. *It is a conscious attempt to stay connected with each other around the real purpose and beauty of our work.*

The goal of the One-on-One is to build relationships that connect two people around purpose and establish new ways of being together in the practice field. It is a system support that is designed to prevent the tendency to get so caught up in what needs to be done that we disconnect from each other. Confucius noted, "The nature of men is always the same. It is their habits that separate them." One-on-One is a conscious attempt to change the habits, the routines, the policies, and the daily patterns which interfere with us connecting as human beings. It is easy to get caught up in the busyness of the day, and lose sight about what really matters.

One-on-One is a conscious way to prevent dehumanization of a very busy work place. It is a way to respect others by developing a partnership and seeking their voice. It is a reminder to peers that their presence, their contribution and their perspectives and thinking really matter. It is what keeps the council from becoming another breeding ground for hierarchical behaviors.

The council is not the group everyone looks to for purpose, vision, inspiration, or final say. It is the group who looks to each person and helps connect them in the work of shared mission, vision, accountability, learning, and decision making. The heartbeat of the council's success with this goal is One-on-One. It is the personal linkage that reminds others how important their part is to the whole. It is a reminder that no one is alone, we are all connected, and whatever one does, influences others.

The council members are not the teachers coming to the student, or those who have the knowledge bringing the way it should be to others. It is a two way street where there is communication back and forth between two colleagues. *The council members are not the carrier or the protectors of the truth but are the seekers of the truths that help us deal with constant change. Being a member of the Partnership Council is a conscious decision to be a part of the continuous work to sustain healthy relationships that help achieve the mission.*

What are tips for successful One-on-One connections?

Tools, such as the ones shown in Figure 10 on page 127, help council members with One-on-One. One-on-One uses such tools to bring back the thinking and the wisdom of others on issues of concern and can be used immediately following the council session. Figure 11 on page 128 shows the format of minutes which serve more than one purpose. Minutes in this format help the members bring an overview of the work which took place at the council, share the process of decision making, report outcomes, and remember what feedback is needed from their peers by the next session. Sometimes the minutes in this format are also used as the tool to capture peer feedback if the minute turn-around time is quick. The depth of insights which the members bring back to the council is directly in proportion to the nature of their relationships with their peers.

One-on-One begins with learning another's story and connecting with him/her around what matters most. The personhood of each individual encompasses BodyMindSpirit. Roach (1997, p. 18) notes, "Our bodies, minds and souls are groaning for a deep sense of belonging. The body craves touch, food and being held. The mind craves understanding, clarity and a sense of meaning. The soul searches for inner peace, joy and a deep perception of wholeness." One-on-One is a form of touch. It is being present with another. If it was just information rendering, notes or minutes could be sent. One-on-One is a personal connection. It is sensitive to the mind as evidenced by the discussion and clarification of what matters most. It honors the soul by seeking another's voice and centering on the purpose, the joy of the chosen work.

The personhood of an individual is not one thing at work and one thing at home. Our personhood is who we are, not what we do. If the work place is insensitive or does not honor the personhood, there will be no inner peace, joy or perception of wholeness for the individual. To honor the personhood of another means connecting with him/her as one human being to another, or as one spirit to another. It is at the spirit or soul level where purpose and meaning emerges and healthy relationships and meaningful conversations are rooted. One-on One is a conscious decision to connect with the spirit.

The skills for One-on-One need cultivation. It takes practice. Where do council members begin? They begin with themselves. Learning to honor oneself as a learner with room for growth and continuous learning is a good starting place. *Cultures only transform as individuals transform.*

FIGURE 10

Partnership Council One-on-One Communication

During the month of _____I was able to discuss the following issues with my peers. Their input is noted below.

Issues	**Peer Feedback**

Figure 11

SAMPLE
PARTNERSHIP COUNCIL MINUTES
Date:_____ Time_____

Present:

Absent:

Topic/Issue	Discussion/Decision	Follow-up/Peer Feedback

Respectfully Submitted,

To be successful with One-on-One requires a great deal of personal work. There is no getting around it. That is why the resources and supports need to be available in the culture. Chapter Eight gives insights into the system supports that help individuals transform.

Until the council members respect and love themselves, it is hard to reach out to others. The following tips help: First, trust self, be honest with self, respect self and be compassionate with self. The behaviors needed for successful One-on-One are so different from those old behaviors described in Chapter Four, Table Eighteen. One-on-One is successful when the council members:

- Learn to become comfortable enough to connect with others as they are, and meet all peers where they are at as individuals.
- Show compassion, do not judge others but care for them and tap into their potential.
- Seek synchrony by connecting with peers around shared meaning of work, not just tasks or things to be done.
- Practice forgiveness of the past and discover the potential in the present and future.
- Motivate by connecting with others around their purpose and passion.
- Seek diversity by uncovering different perspectives and connect them without dominance of one way of thinking.
- Trust others without needing proof of their worthiness.

What do you do when One-on-Ones are not working well?

What do you do when those to whom you reach out reject or mock you? How do you connect with someone who does not want to get involved? Where do you begin with people who have never thought about their purpose, or how their role relates to a bigger picture? All of these circumstances require seeking common ground. It starts with knowing them, their story, and what matters to them. First "seek to understand." Some council members need help to connect with peers around their story. Exercises such as "telling our stories" found in Chapter Eight support this type of learning.

What do you do when there is a lack of motivation or low morale?

Have you ever heard someone say in desperation, "How do we get these people motivated around here?" "The morale is at an all time low." What do we mean by lack of motivation or low morale? Is low morale the absence of the soul's expression? Is it a call to set free or tap into the gifts, the capacity of each person? Low morale is a commonly heard phrase which is often used to describe people who appear apathetic, withdrawn, or showing little enthusiasm, joy or peace in their work. These are the same people who often reject One-on-One.

What is behind lack of motivation or low morale? Some people show up at work every day. They do and do, but do not connect with others. They become focused on tasks, procedures, rituals and routines, and a pattern of withdrawal emerges. They can hide behind the doing and not connect with others. Day in and day out they return and carry on the work. Therein lies one of the barriers to healthy work cultures. Much of the work, the tasks, the doing can get done, regardless of the nature of the relationships.

A pattern has evolved in the typical work setting: come, do the work, and leave. It sounds reasonable for a while. It can even be reasonable for a while--until the culture becomes one of doing, not becoming. What does that mean in a practical sense? We innately seek respect, dignity, purpose and meaning in our life. We desire to express our uniqueness. We are not parts: a body, a mind, or a spirit. We are BodyMindSpirit. Our joy comes when we express our wholeness, our personhood and work together. It has been said that you can take the best people and put them into a bad system and the system will win every time. The system needs to be changed. We are the system. One-on-One is the beginning of changing the patterns within the system.

When One-on-One is rejected, consider the other's perspective on connecting with you. If a person is not connected to their own heart, they cannot connect with others in their wholeness. We need to stop pretending this is not the case. *In a healthy work culture withdrawal is not ignored.*

Healthy relationships are valued, seen as a priority, and therefore worked on. They are nurtured, developed and sustained. In a healthy work culture, people ask, "How do we help?" "Where do we begin?"

One-on-One begins in a very difficult place-it starts when one human cares for another. Caring can be very hard because those without motivation are often not open, fun to be with or welcoming of your concern. However, the further the non-motivated get away from others, the greater the need for someone to care for them and let them know it. It is not about "putting a fire underneath them"...that could burn them. It is about helping them go inside and find the fire within. It is only when they feel the warmth, the concern of another, that they are reminded that this same human capacity sits within them. This is the purpose of One-on-One. Fox (1941, p.61) reminded us, "The door of the soul opens inward. The answer to motivating environments lies within the person."

We are shifting the mental mindset about work, about life. Work life is more than surviving. It is about thriving. The following Wisdom From The Field is an example of One-on-One related to motivation.

Wisdom From The Field

Fran has been a nurse on a medical-surgical unit for ten years. She comes to work, punches in, does her work, and goes home. She often comments that the work load is getting out of control. She is a master of the rituals, patterns, and routines of the unit. She does not ask for help or offer help. She does not bother anybody, and they do not bother her.

One practitioner commented that Fran wasn't always like that. When came to the unit she was more outgoing and involved. Something happened, but she didn't know the details. Fran has let it be known that she doesn't want anything to do with the politics of the unit. This type of thinking was not uncommon on the floor and became more the norm than the exception. Fran was labeled as negative and most of the people just let her do her own thing.

The unit had a history of "low morale." There was a group who had worked there for years, and another group in which there was more turnover. Over the last two years, a group of Fran's peers made a decision to improve the culture. They volunteered to form a Partnership Council so they could improve relationships with staff and patients and work on improving the care. There was much work to be done.

There was consensus that the care on the unit was very institutionalized, the focus was on medical care, not body, mind, and spirit and the culture was bureaucratic and hierarchical. The quality of care was inconsistent and it varied with whomever took care of the person. Joy and celebration were rare, complaints were frequent. The council realized that overall they had lost sight of why they were there in the first place. The focus on mission and relationships necessary to achieve the mission was foreign.

The council members began with learning how to first be partners among themselves. There was little trust among staff, between staff and manager, staff and educator, or discipline with discipline. They found the work of relationships and caring for one another very difficult. They were bound in the chains of judging or ignoring one another. They struggled with talking to each other about what really mattered. Talking about the purpose, the greater picture of their work, and their professional accountability was not as easy as talking about the daily tasks that needed to be done or who failed to do what should have been done. The type of communication and sharing within the council was new to them. Once they began to share their feelings with one another, they were surprised at how similar their desires and beliefs were related to important issues. It was great learning.

The council learned that the work of developing relationships necessary to help each other live the mission was not going to be easy. They began to understand that transactional relationships were easy because they centered around getting the task done. As a result, they did not have to talk much with each other. In fact, they really did not even have to know each other.

The council realized that partnering relationships were of a transformational nature and would require work on the part of everyone. They struggled with where to begin. They decided that the work they were doing as a group would need to be done with the whole team. Each person on the council was accountable to do similar work with his/her peers. The goal was to establish partnerships based on mission across the team.

When it came time to reach out and develop partnership with their peers, no one wanted to work with Fran. "You take her." "No, you take her." It was during this discussion that they learned a lot about themselves and noted they had much to learn about partnership and relationships driven by mission. They talked about how to begin building new relationships. They decided to share their learning and insights with each other as they carried out the work with their peers.

In the end, it was Mickey who said she would be willing to work on establishing a partnership with Fran. In the initial contact with Fran, Mickey explained what the council was attempting to do. Fran let her know immediately that she wanted nothing to do with it. "I've been here ten years and, believe me, nothing is going to change this place." Mickey found it difficult to know where to begin, or how to even talk with her. It wasn't easy being with Fran. There were times she wouldn't even talk with Mickey. She had "much more important things to do than waste her time with this useless talk."

Mickey struggled with her preconceived ideas of Fran and her own lack of ability to establish a relationship with Fran. Then she realized there could be no nourishing relationship unless she really cared for Fran. She realized that she didn't even know her. She sought help from the council and found that most were struggling with the work of partnership. They respectfully shared insights and learnings which helped each of them grow in their understanding and commitment.

Because of the work that was done in the council, Mickey knew that she needed to learn from Fran what was important to her, listen to her, learn from her. As a group they realized how important it was to connect with their peers at a place that was important to them. If they knew what gave each person purpose and meaning in life, it would be the opening to connect with him/her on the common purpose they shared as professional colleagues. It was this learning that helped Mickey change her relationship with Fran.

Mickey was frustrated that over the last five months her relationship with Fran was not growing. She decided to be openly vulnerable with Fran. Mickey shared with Fran that she had decided to join the council and be a part of this work because she found the unit to be a very difficult place to practice. She felt herself becoming robotic and losing compassion. She was becoming judgmental, competitive, and losing her focus on the patients.

Mickey explained that she felt very alone and knew that for patients to receive quality care, she would have to work closely with the team, and personally she didn't like most of them. She didn't like w/hat she was becoming and was thinking about leaving. She shared how she had become confused and lost sight of what really mattered to her.

Fran replied, "I know what is most important to me in life, and it isn't this place!" Mickey asked her, "What is it that is most important to you?" Fran said, "My children," Mickey learned that Fran was a single mom and the only thing that mattered to her was being a good mom for her kids. *It was then that Mickey asked her if she felt that the stress, the day-to-day distant and often disrespectful relationships, along with the robotic practice patterns, impacted her ability to be a good mom?*

Fran was silent. Her eyes moistened. Mickey said, "That is why I think this work we are undertaking, to have our unit be the best place for people to get care and the best place for anybody to work, is so important." This was the beginning of a partnering relationship between Fran and Mickey. They had connected on purpose.

Caring cannot be an act. Meaningful conversations are not scripted. There can be no alternative motive, or desire to save the other person. Roach (1997) gave beautiful insight into the approach for successful One-on-One when she said, "A person is not a problem to be fixed, but a mystery to be contemplated." One-on-One cannot be an assignment. It must come from the person's heart, the place of compassion. It begins by connecting with another where they are at.

One-on-One is not about fixing someone. It is not to bring them "into the know." The purpose is to be there with them. As Mother Teresa (1996, p. 61) said, "It is not how much you do, but how much love you put into the doing that matters." Humans recognize compassion, love and caring, even if they cannot reciprocate. The reason this is so important is that when they see it, it reminds them of their own capacity to be the same. Compassion is hopeful because it connects with the soul of another. Williamson (1993, p. 185) noted, "The soul thrills at the reminder of what we all already know." One-on-One is the beginning of building a bridge to connect everyone to the shared work necessary to create a healthy culture.

What is the role of those who do not sit on the council in shared work?

Everyone is accountable to create a healthy work culture, not just those who sit on the council. It is not an option for a few, it is an expectation for all. What does that mean from a practical sense? It means that coming to work and doing the task at hand or the assignment for the day is not enough.

Have you ever experienced the following? You come on the unit and the first thing you do is look at the assignment sheet. You notice Carol is on tonight and you find this uncomfortable knot-like feeling coming in your gut. You do not like working with Carol. She seldom interacts with anyone. She punches in, does what she thinks she should do, and punches out. It isn't that she does not do her "assignment," but she never interacts with others or offers to help anyone else get things done. In fact she acts very bothered if anyone interrupts her, asks her for help or tries to connect with her. She tells people, "I do my work, I get the tasks done and I do not want to get involved." When she is working, there is tension in the air. If something out of the ordinary happens where you need to help one another, you cannot count on her and you feel very alone. There is no relationship, there is no partnership.

What is a peer's accountability to Carol? If everyone is accountable to create a work space where each of us can evolve to be more human, more loving, and become people of purpose, what does this mean in a practical sense in relating to Carol? In a culture only focused on getting things done, the accountability is to work around Carol. She is seen as a productivity barrier, not as a person disconnected. She is seen as a weak FTE (full time equivalent), a body. In a healthy culture Carol's behaviors would not be ignored. She is a lost partner. It is disrespectful to her and others to ignore the situation. Someone needs to care enough about her to address this serious relationship issue.

When a person disconnects, and it is ignored over the years, it is a challenging situation, but it must be addressed. Everyone who works side by side with Carol is impacted in different ways. Carol's situation is an insidious but powerful daily message. The message is that disconnecting from the place of purpose, the soul, is not only acceptable, but may in fact be tolerated and even rewarded. It then becomes easier for others to disconnect in the same way.

It is a major shift to think that each person is equally as accountable to relationships as to the delivery of tasks or services. Competency is often focused on the services a person provides, not on the person's relationship skills. In addition, we have observed that many do not see themselves accountable to global work, that which relates to the overall integration across a unit, department or division, and is discussed in Chapter Seven. This is often seen as the job of the manager, the quality team, the educator, or the researcher. Connecting with the work beyond the tasks to be done is foreign in the old ways of thinking. Connecting one's work to the whole is not a norm in the old institutional or hierarchical paradigms.

Somewhere along the line, the accountability to respect each other as human beings got lost in the madness of getting things done. It appeared as though there was a choice to have one or the other, that is, to do the work or have healthy relationships. The lesson learned from Carol's story is the importance of relationship work. If there is no conscious effort to maintain a healthy culture, it will become a breeding ground for the evolution of colleagues living as Carol. People will continue to perform and do things, but the toll on the quality of life for them and those who share the journey with them will deteriorate. Every person is vital in a healthy work place. Every person must see that they have a part to play to create and maintain a healthy work place. One-on-One is the proactive approach to make this happen. It is the beginning step to get everyone connected.

What are some other ways to begin connecting everyone with the shared work?

The concept of shared work naturally leads to shared work distribution. What is the work and who does the work? Everyone is accountable for relationships and the shared mission. Often the shared work around mission or services such as patient care is familiar. However, competency calls for the continuous development of skills requiring diverse resources such as fiscal, education, research, and quality.

Partnership brings forth a recognition that not just one person is accountable for service outcomes. For example, fiscal and operation resources are inherent in any setting's structure. Every person on the unit impacts the fiscal outcome just as every person on the unit impacts the quality outcome. Each person is a resource for the others. In the words of Leland Kaiser, (1994) "You are the problem, the solution, the resource." In the old paradigm, the focus was on one person's accountability, not shared accountability.

The Partnership Council coordinates the integration of work. Each person on the unit participates. There are many ways to participate in the work of the unit. Work distribution is done in various ways. There are short term and long term shared work teams. Common shared work teams are education or resource work teams which support continuous learning needs; quality work teams which look at the structures, processes and outcomes of work patterns; and administrative teams which look at fiscal and system work. These are examples of long term shared work teams. Short term work teams arise as the needs of the unit change, for example, work teams to address merger issues, changing work loads, or specific goals the unit is working on.

There are many choices available to people to volunteer for and opportunities to contribute to an area of their special interest. Although all the work of the teams is connected to the council, the work is done by the whole team as shown in Figure 6 in Chapter Three. There are equally important ways to be involved in shared work distribution, other than participating on work teams. There is fundamental shared work that relates to the continuous day-to-day accountability for maintaining a healthy work culture. Table Twenty gives examples of shared work that is done by individuals on a daily basis.

TABLE TWENTY

**SHARED WORK WHICH CONTRIBUTES TO
A HEALTHY CULTURE**

- Accountability to competency in personal scope of practice.
- Integration of the Core Beliefs into daily practice.
- Role model Principles of Partnership.
- Incorporate dialogue skills in daily work
- Read the council minutes and give feedback.
- Suggest ways to improve care and relationships.
- Connect with council linkage.
- Read professional literature and share learnings with others.
- Volunteer for shared work teams.
- Help cover for those who attend council.
- Participate in telephone tree.

The ideal place for the concept of shared work to begin is with the job interview. When you look at an advertisement for "job openings," it often focuses on the talents of the individual that parallel with the work at hand. It is a time for the individual to think about talents he/she can personally bring to the work place. Often the person being interviewed is not thinking about his/her accountability to others in the work setting nor is this individual aware of the concept of shared work. The actual interview is a critical time for clarifying expectations.

It is the accountability of the people interviewing to give examples of those expected behaviors that support shared work to create healthy work cultures. If there is no conscious attention given to what these behaviors look like or what it means in the practical sense to be accountable for a healthy culture and shared work, it will be difficult to determine if the person is the best fit for the setting. Examples that show the day-to-day ways in which accountabilities for healthy relationships and cultures are presently demonstrated are shown in Table Twenty. These examples should be reviewed during the interview process.

Wisdom From The Field

A person was being interviewed for a staff role. She had 15 years of experience in two similar settings and felt comfortable with her practice skills. When the concepts of culture, relationships and shared work were brought up, she outwardly seemed a little tense. She wanted to know what accountabilities she would have, especially if any were beyond the typical daily assignments. She said, "I have never thought of being accountable to the units global work or the team's partnerships." She thought that was the role of the manager, and therefore, wondered what this meant to her specifically.

Her questions led to a conversation about the Partnership Councils and about how this structure supports the unit to develop partnerships and also coordinates the work to make this a good place to practice. She said she had never been exposed to this type of thinking, was never on a unit that had a Council, and asked if this was like some task forces in which she had participated. She stated, "I have a tight home schedule and there is little flexibility in the number of hours that I can spend here outside my scheduled working hours. Coming in to a lot of meetings is not something that I can commit to." It was at this point the conversation evolved around the shared work opportunities as listed in Table Twenty.

What supported the interview process was the system infrastructure designed to facilitate each person carrying out his/her accountability. That is what the Council structure helps to achieve. For example the person can see how the present structure involves all people in the shared work. In addition, it gives the interviewer a chance to explore with the person the strengths he/she has and how he/she might enhance the potential of the work and culture.

Although the concept of partnership was new to the person being interviewed, it made her excited about the possibility of working at this setting. She noted the accountability to competency was familiar but said she would need help to develop her partnership skills. After she had a clearer understanding of shared work distribution and what that meant for everyone on the unit, she began to see the possibilities for herself.

The above scenario is common. The work field is in a great transition from the old ways of working together to the new ways. Starting at orientation makes the work easier. Starting One-on-One right at orientation strengthens partnerships very rapidly. The following letter was received by a new orientee from the person who would be her One-on-One.

Wisdom From The Field

"Welcome? My name is Jean Jones and I will be your link to the unit's Partnership Council which you just learned about in orientation. I was one of the people that you met during your interviews. By now your mind is probably swirling with all of the new things. The good new is, we will have time to sort through it together once you start working on the unit. The questions you may have about the work of the council, your accountabilities, and mine as your link will become clearer later. I will find you on Tuesday, your first day on the unit and hopefully we can go to lunch together and start to get to know one another. I'm looking forward to having lime with you following the next Partnership Council meeting which is built into your orientation. The meeting is Tuesday, July 8th at 3:45 p.m. After the meeting, we can take time to explore whatever is necessary. I close with great anticipation of getting to know you and working with you."

The initial contact is an important part in bringing the theory of partnerships into reality. It is best if One-on-One begins right away. Often the new council members are concerned about how to introduce themselves and initiate the partnership. A key learning is that meaningful conversations are not prescripted. The appropriate words, the most personal words, cannot be planned or scripted. The single most significant criteria is that they come from the heart.

Over the years we have found the greatest challenge during the transition to shift cultures is related to the many people who have been working in the field and living the old ways of being together. When the Partnership Councils begin, they only know what has been, and often are skeptical about what can be. That is why the design of One-on-One is so important in council development. The following quote by Wheatley and Kellner (1996, p. 50) speaks of the importance of how the One-on-One linkage is approached: "We encourage others to change only if we honor who they are now. We ourselves engage in change only as we discover that we might be more of who we are by becoming something different." The fundamental premise of linkage is to honor the mission we share and each other as we are; and not fix, rescue, mold or simply share information. The linkage is another way of engaging in the connections to expand our capacity to serve.

The concept of shared work is a natural path when we realize that we are all connected. It calls for us to work closely together, not just to do, but to think and become together. Shared work connects each person to shared decision making which is an important component of partnering relationships and the focus of the next chapter.

Chapter Six

Shared Decision Making:
In what way can Partnership Councils
expand their capacity?

"Our decisions generate ripples
that touch the lives of many for all time to come."
- Laurie Shiparski

What are some of the phrases we currently hear about decision making in our work settings? "Individuals that make decisions are dictatorial." "It takes too long for groups to make decisions." "I expect people to come to the meeting with data and solutions for the problem or they need not come at all." "All I have to do is sell the rest of the group on my idea." "There are clearly identified boundaries, therefore, certain decisions are my accountability." "Don't make waves, you have to be a team player here." "In raising issues polarization and conflict surface that hold up our progress." "This issue is just too complex; will someone just take control and make the decision?" "We have found a new way to make decisions and from now on all decisions are to be processed this way."

Each of these statements have surfaced in Partnership Councils an work settings. These words offer clues to many of our experiences with group decision making. In this chapter we will explore some of our understandings and methods pertinent to individual and collective decision making. Questions that will be explored include: Who makes what decisions? When is the appropriate time to make a decision? Does shared decision making really take longer? What is our basis for making a decision?

Some of the current barriers to making effective decisions in our work places will be addressed. These include hierarchy, buy-in, power, competition, blame, apathy, fear, superficial versus deeper resolution of issues and long term effects of our short term decisions. These barriers are an outgrowth of our beliefs about decisions that we have developed through-out our lives. In working with many Partnership Councils, certain patterns have emerged. In naming these beliefs and discussing them we can move beyond their limits. The barriers can be overcome when we know the thinking behind them. Table Twenty One is a summary of these assumptions about decision making and it is followed by in-depth discussion about each one.

TABLE TWENTY ONE

Shifting Assumptions About Decision Making

Current Thinking ————————➤ **New Thinking**

Current Thinking	New Thinking
Only a few should make decisions or we should all be involved in all decisions.	Honor each others capacity for decision making by synchronizing individual and shared decision making.
There are set boundaries for who can make what decisions.	Explore moving boundaries
Questions and conflict get us off track.	Seek inquiry and diverse views to obtain collective understanding of issues and increase alternatives for decision making.
There is only one right way to make decisions.	Draw from a variety of methods of decision making.

Assumption #1
Only a few are to have decision making capacity in an organization or everyone should be involved in all decisions.

This first assumption is like a two-sided coin. On one side of the coin is the belief that only a few have the capacity to make decisions in an organization and the other side is the belief that everyone should be involved in all decisions. Throw the coin away--we can never get it to land right in a toss! It is not one or the other, but both aspects are worthy of consideration as we seek a deeper understanding. This assumption needs to be replaced with the belief that we all have capacity for decision making, and we honor each other as human beings in the process. The principle of potential speaks well to believing in each others abilities. We can explore current boundaries of decision making together. A Partnership Council can be a place to begin this exploration.

Assumption #2
There are unchanging, clearly identified boundaries for who makes what decisions.

We each make hundreds of decisions every day. Some are easy and some more difficult. We advocate our views, ask others about their perspectives and use our best judgment in making our immediate and long term choices. At times, decision making has been exhilarating and other times terrifying. It has always been a part of our lives.

As we grow and mature, we gain more responsibility and along with it comes a higher level of decision making. As toddlers just learning to talk we begin to show decision making abilities in our own self-centered ways. We have been in training our whole lives to be decision makers because as human beings we desire to facilitate our becoming and evolving as a person. Margaret Wheatley in her video, *Leadership and The New Science* (1993), compares humans to sub-atomic particles. She notes that we are like waves of potential that don't know who we are until we bump up against someone else or some new idea that we then interact with in new ways. So why have we supported having certain people make most of the decisions?

Let us explore a way of thinking that helps us move beyond these two assumptions.

A common request from councils is to have a black and white list of who makes what decisions. This is indicative of normal transition for a council from hierarchical to partnering relationships. The question frequently asked is what decision making boundaries are there for the council. There is a simple but often unpopular answer to this question. The council begins with the boundaries that exist and as part of their evolution. Council members question and expand the boundaries together. They explore shared decision making together. This conveys trust in the intentions of their colleagues who are making decisions related to their role expertise and every day accountability.

To explain this more clearly we have diagrammed the idea below. Each person makes decisions on his/her own and within groups. Consider these situations as being part of a person's area of decision making to improve care and relationships. The question always presented is, "Who makes what decisions?" Individually, each person makes decisions every day related to his/her roles and expertise. This freedom of decision making is appropriate but does need to be synchronized with others.

Decision making between two people, such as a staff member and a manager, illustrates an area of individual decision making and an area of shared decision making which has boundaries. Each has accountability to outcomes with different responsibilities.

The ultimate partnership is when people can explore this gray area of shared decisions and question the boundaries together. There is no blame, resentment or mistrust, only genuine exploration. In partnership the emphasis is less on who makes the decision and more on determining if the decision is aligned with the values of the group. The result is that the decisions are more likely to be congruent and understandable to people who have developed shared understanding around Core Beliefs.

In Figure 12 on page 147 consider the gray Partnership Council circle as an exploration field of shared decision making. This is an area where individual and collective decisions are welcome. Each person brings their own unique expertise such as the nurse, pharmacist, non-licensed staff, manager, educator, social worker, volunteer, and researcher.

Figure12
Synchronizing Individual and Group Decision Making

Group Decision Making

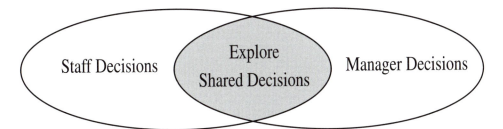

The council is a place where individual decision making can be synchronized with others and shared decision making can expand.

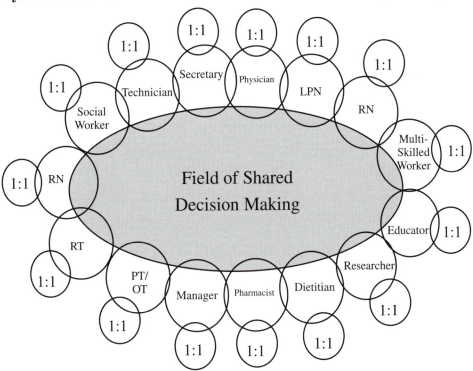

Individuals bring their 1:1 linkages and enter a corner of their circle into the area of shared decision making and the boundaries are explored together.

When the council evolves their shared decision making overlap grows but individual decisions are also preserved. A balance and synchrony emerge as members help each other uphold their agreement to live the principles of partnership in their decision making.

As individuals bring their own beliefs about power to the field, some of them perpetuate hierarchy and block shared decision making.

We have to ask ourselves how the many voices of authority in our lives have influenced us in receiving decisions from others and exercising our ability to make decisions. In what ways are we perpetuating a "power over" culture? Many individuals and councils believe and act as though certain people in their work environments have power over them and then wonder why those people have power over them. The following is an actual experience of how one Partnership Council broke its pattern of perpetuating a power over relationship.

Wisdom From The Field

I was warned as a new manager in an intensive care unit that the surgeons would be difficult to work with and that they had power and control over the unit--that they were not interested in partnership. All they wanted was what was best for themselves. Many staff and managers had treated the surgeons with this thought in the back of their minds. A behavior that stemmed from such a belief was to distance ourselves from the surgeons. Don't ask them, just do the changes and they will never notice. Another approach was to make a detailed plan of how to get the surgeons to buy in to our latest change. It is not surprising that reactions from the surgeons included mistrust of our motives and rejection of our desired changes. The Partnership Council had made decisions that evoked anger and resistance from the surgeons. The surgeons believed that managers and staff on the unit were trying to exert power and control over them. We were perpetuating this negative cycle of hierarchy.

As a new manager I had an opportunity to begin differently with the surgeons. It was my choice not to heed the warning. Instead, I met with the surgeons and made my intentions of partnership clear. I extended an invitation to them to become partners with me and the Partnership Council. After all, we were all there for the same reasons: to give the best care to people and make this the best place to work. I saw them as my equal and respected them for their contributions. In turn, they reciprocated the same treatment toward me.

A new cycle began. The Partnership Council started connecting with physicians in many ways. Members began helping their peers to build partnerships with physicians in daily interactions around patient care. All physicians (including new house staff) \were invited to partner with us during the first month they came to the unit. Council members invited a physician to join the Partnership Council and found ways to inform the other physicians of its purpose and use. The shift in relationships was quite profound. Physicians and care providers perceived a change from power and control to partnership by intending to develop partnership and treating each other accordingly.

During the process of shifting this cycle many personal beliefs around power surfaced as the Partnership Council dialogued. Some of the care providers believed that the physicians were supposed to be the directors of care, never to be questioned. They had learned that in school. Some believed that because some of the physicians were older and wiser, they must know the right thing to do. Gender and cultural issues also surfaced.

For Partnership Councils to be effective it is vital to discuss key questions that help make our thinking visible to us. When we find ourselves in situations of blame, mistrust, and conflict, we can ask ourselves: How are we perpetuating this situation? What views might the opposing people have? Are we centering on what is best for those we serve and care for? What is our real intention here? What thoughts do we have about "them" that need to be checked out with "them?" What is the nature of power and control? How does all of this affect our ability to make decisions? In seeking deeper understanding of these questions, conflict may arise within the group. This leads us to a third assumption.

Assumption #3
Questions and conflict get us off track or slow us down.
This assumption is responsible for keeping individuals and councils at superficial levels in their relationships. Some people would say, "So what!

We like our work relationships at a superficial place." The temptation to keep opposing views at arms length has devastating effects on productivity and time. Many councils spend an inordinate amount of time revisiting the same issues over and over again. This is a sure sign that the real issue has not yet been uncovered and addressed.

Questions and conflict are to be expected and welcomed in effective decision making. We must move through conflict and end up with stronger relationships and better decisions. If there is a conflict, it means we have different views of the situation. Would our decisions be better if we considered many possible views? We can learn ways to respectfully question others, expose our own thinking and seek the wisdom of all views. These ways will be discussed more as we consider dialogue principles and methods later in this chapter.

In some Partnership Councils, members have had to acknowledge that disagreement was not always welcomed. We know it takes courage and patience to learn in the midst of our disagreements. Many have chosen to work through disagreement because the alternative is even more difficult and detrimental to our long term effectiveness. If we choose not to work through conflict we will have apathy.

Apathy occurs when we perceive that what we think or do no longer matters. Apathy blocks individual and shared decision making. It is hopelessness, withdrawal and survival only mode. Think about a time when you experienced apathy in a group. How was it? Did it drain you? Most would say they could not wait to get out of the experience. Even experiencing conflict is better than apathy because at least we still feel alive in disagreement. Partnership Councils having apathy is like contracting a disease. This does not have to be a terminal condition. The following Wisdom From The Field tells of Partnership Councils that diagnosed apathy and implemented a treatment plan.

Wisdom From The Field

In an organization where Partnership Councils had been in place for two years the council members were gathering for an annual retreat. It was to be a retreat of relbeusing on their progress and next directions. Each council spoke of realizations, disappointments and accomplishments. During this process one Partnership Council revealed that it was in an apathetic slump. There was low attendance at meetings and members that came could not seem to make decisions. As the group inquired into their circumstances it became apparent that a series of difficult changes within the past six months may have contributed to their current state. The council lost its manager and its council chairperson, both of whom members respected as effective leaders. The new manager came to the council and made it clear that members could not bring problems if they did not have a solution to offer. The meetings had turned into problem-solving meetings versus a place to work on partnerships. Members had also withdrawn from conflict with physicians in their unit around critical practice issues. The pervading feeling throughout the unit was one of isolation and defeat.

As members of this council spoke, the others listened and learned. One member said, "If I could just find our pulse again." She implied that it felt dead on the unit. She believed that life still existed but it was just dormant now. As the members joined in to ask questions and to reveal their thinking around the issues of that unit, something happened. Disagreement emerged and passion surfaced from members of the apathetic council when a practice issue from their unit was questioned. It was inquiry from others on the issue of not getting daily weights on their patients every day as the physicians had requested. This sounded like a small issue but it had far reaching implications regarding nurse-physician relationships. It looked like a compliance issue when. in reality, new research had surfaced that indicated a practice change but they were so apathetic no one had discussed it with other units or the physicians. It was in this meeting that they realized they were not alone in their circumstance. The other councils had experienced some of the same things and perseverance had helped them make it through tough times.

They realized that because they had not sought differing views in their issues they became overwhelmed and gave up. Issues were not being brought because no one person had the answer. The possibilities of their collective wisdom was shut down. It was a relief to have disagreement surface for it was better than suffering through the apathy. The member who spoke earlier shouted, "We have a pulse!" The realizations that day offered the troubled council a place to begin revitalizing their efforts. Never again would they feel alone. Never again would they stifle the voices of disagreement. They had learned that there was always a collective action to take.

Assumption #4
There is only one right way to make decisions.

The Partnership Council members described in the previous Wisdom From The Field addressed multiple choices in the face of their complex issues. They taught us the importance of welcoming problems and issues that need careful consideration by a collective group. The cultures that reward only one person's greatness are dissipating. Partnership Councils grow collective greatness. They use a long list of ways to invite diverse perspectives and make decisions. There is not just one way to make a decision, and we have learned that the process of coming to a decision is critical. In the aftermath of a disruptive decision *we have learned that it is usually not the decision itself that caused unrest but the process used to make the decision and how the decision was communicated.* Partnership Councils provide a place for the unrest to be aired and resolved. It has been most effective to evaluate the process of decision making in order to improve the next time and to highlight our continuous learning.

What methods facilitate shared decision making in Partnership Councils? William Isaacs, in the *Fifth Discipline Field Book,* by Senge et al. (1994), tells us that the Latin word for decision literally means "to murder alternatives." Though it is not our intention to murder alternatives, our agendas, time constraints, and lack of patience drive us to quick fix ways. These types of decisions can hinder continuous learning. In the old way of thinking, once the person of power made the decision it was final.

Sometimes we find ourselves in critical time constraints that legitimately warrant quick thinking and decision making. Even in those situations it is helpful to review the decisions made and how we could improve them for the next time. As noted by Michael Jones (1995),"! wonder how the rush to completion has short-circuited our capacity to move in harmony with these deeper cycles of creation, cycles which by their very nature tend to be patient and slow."

What are we really trying to accomplish in shared decision making? Relationship building and continuous learning are the achievements of shared decision making. It is a never ending process. We make decisions that help us, one way or another, to choose our next directions. The long term goal is to increase our shared understanding. *This supports us in moving decisions closest to where the service is being rendered and tapping expertise/rom all involved.* In the paragraphs to follow we will explore the issues that come to councils, common decision making scenarios, and methods of shared and non-shared decision making.

All issues are welcome at the council. What the council does when an issue arises is what really matters. There have been organizations that have tried to limit the issues brought to the council. This has not worked well. It has raised the suspicion that the Partnership Council is another figure head group that is just doing what management wants anyway. It is usually a symptom of fear that a group questioning and changing boundaries will be like a "loose cannon." Those with this fear think that restrictive boundaries will keep the environment safe from disruption. Those who think they have control do not yet see that it is an illusion. This control will stifle the resolution of issues and send a message that will perpetuate mistrust.

When the issues brought to the council are limited, members will think that organizational leaders do not see them as capable of handling information. It has been best to openly welcome all issues and trust that issues can honestly be worked out together. In organizations where all issues are welcome there has not been anarchy but these organizations have experienced an increase in trust and accountability through the Partnership Councils. This is not to say that councils would not spend time struggling to resolve issues. *We have learned that in the collaborative struggle, trust and relationships grow.*

The only exception to this may be in some settings where unions are present. Most unions have welcomed decision making by councils as long as they stay focused on practice improvement and avoid issues of wages and hours. Partnership Councils have flourished in union settings by seeking partnership with union leaders and deferring these issues to the appropriate union group.

A common occurrence in the initial phases of Partnership Council development is to load agendas with operational issues or decisions that were previously made by the manager, such as scheduling, finances, and staffing, because members may have felt less control of these in the past. It is often a symptom of a lack of trust and sometimes a testing ground for the partnership between managers and staff. This occurrence should trigger us to ask the question: are we balancing operational issues with practice issues? Though operational issues are important and do impact the service we render, it is key to equally focus on decisions regarding continuous improvement of care. Another key question would be, how can we increase trust and enhance our partnerships?

It may be helpful to explore common decision making scenarios in councils. The following are among the four most common scenarios.

1. A decision is already made and brought to the council (such as with the closing of a patient care unit). The council is engaged in planning the transition but may not be able to change the decision. This scenario also provides an opportunity to clarify rumor mill stories related to communication of such issues.

2. An issue within a council's current field of shared decision making arises and members cooperate to make decisions. They always question how their decision might affect other areas and link appropriately to other Partnership Councils and groups. *An example of this occurred*

when an Emergency Department (ED) Partnership Council decided to stop transporting patients to inpatient units. As ED council members brought this up at the centralized council where all the Partnership Council Coordinators met, they realized their decision impacted many areas and they needed to plan with those areas.

3. Someone or some group makes a decision that the council believes could have been better addressed in the council infrastructure. Members explore the possibilities, seek clarification and give feedback for either this decision or the next time it occurs. *One example was an organization revised job description without using the council infra-structure. A task force was convened that had staff representatives on it. There was poor attendance but the project moved on without the input. When the Partnership Councils were presented with the final changes, they recommended additional changes and called for the leaders to utilize the councils when the job descriptions came up for revision again. Their recommendations were accepted.*

4. Councils themselves proactively plan new directions and involvement. An example is expanding shared accountability in finance and budget issues. *Managers can proactively teach staff about budget reports and issues with the intent of having staff become more involved with deci-sions regarding finance management.*

In every case successful Partnership Councils have learned to ask two key questions in the face of every decision: how will this support patients who seek our services? In what way will this impact our relationships and practice? Keeping this in mind, the following methods have been used in councils for decision making.

Partnership Councils have experimented with decision making methods including voting, discussion, and consensus. We will explore each of these methods and, in addition, discuss the use of dialogue. Though dialogue is not considered a decision making method, dialogic principles can be used very effectively to support decision making.

Dialogic principles strengthen our collective understanding and pave the way for shared decision making.

Voting has been used frequently in organizations prior to the initiation of Partnership Councils. Some councils began using this method of decision making only to find it a quick fix. Voting does not compel us to carefully consider the outcomes of our collective decisions. It is an easy way out for many who can cast their support for one option and later complain that their choice was not selected. In voting, options are narrowed to a limited few and majority rules. We do have to weigh the consequences of our vote, but not as a group. In this method we are not tapping our collective wisdom. The following Wisdom From The Field describes how a Council decided to break its old pattern of using voting as a decision making method. A council member describes the process.

Wisdom From The Field

In one of our Partnership Council meetings we were discussing our staffing and skill mix. Two scenarios emerged as possibilities to address some of the current issues we were facing. Our manager offered her expertise as the operations resource and then it was up to the entire council to decide. We had already gone 1:1 and gathered our peers input on the issue and shared those perspectives.

It was suggested that we do a secret ballot and make it a vote since that would be a quick and easy way of doing it. Someone else suggested that we should try to get consensus on the issue instead of the voting. We were skeptical that consensus could be reached on such a passionate issue, so we decided that if we could not reach consensus we could always vote as a last resort.

We advocated our different views, and listened with respect to all who spoke. It was definitely a learning discussion but no obvious decision emerged. Finally at the end we asked every person around the table to share his/her final thoughts. It was clear after this that a vote would not be necessary. We were amazed how the collective perspectives came together to give us direction. We were all comfortable with the outcome and no one felt like a loser. We knew we could always revisit the decision later after implementing it. This experience was a confidence builder for us and I don't think we will ever choose voting again.

We have learned that voting does little to build relationships. It carries the risk of promoting competition as constituents rally to have others vote for their proposed option. The only circumstance where voting is helpful is in the selection of council members and coordinators. It is a way that many can voice their choice when there are more volunteers than council seats.

Consensus was introduced as an effective way for Partnership Council members to surface their collective wisdom in shared decision making from the very beginning. It continues to serve many councils well, yet it is not without its limitations. William Isaacs (1993, p. 26) notes that the word consensus means "to feel together." He states, "Our goal is to find a view that reflects what most people in a group can live with for now. This assumes shared action will arise out of a shared position." This definition does offer insights into the nature of consensus but in some ways it seems too narrow a description for the consensual process that has occurred in councils.

Over time, many Partnership Councils have evolved the art of consensus through practice. As people seeking healthy work settings, members have expanded their efforts in consensus building. They have learned the principles of dialogue and are using them in their consensual conversations. This is a way of using the dialogic principles of intention, listening, inquiry, silence and advocacy while having a specific intended outcome in mind. It does not matter what you call conversations of this nature but is important to have them.

Paula Underwood (1997) describes consensus in the following way. "It is nothing you sit down and gain before set of sun. It is an ongoing process that is never begun because it never ended. Only from time to time particular foci are necessary. When consensus toward certain decisions is required, a council may be called and all invited to speak." *This describes consensus in the Partnership Councils. Ongoing relationship building is part of consensus building.* We change our thinking and being as we continuously learn and grow. Then, on a consistent basis such as in a monthly Partnership Council meeting, all members come together to use consensus related to a particular topic.

Consensus has been an effective method for us to use in making shared decisions. It is a higher level of decision making than voting. It invites diverse perspectives and calls the group to collectively consider the consequences and outcomes of decisions. Consensus calls for each voice to be heard which builds relationship. It is an agreement process that may call for compromise on the part of those who are not sure of the group's direction with the decision. The process of consensus brings life back into the work place because it requires and values each person's point of view. In Partnership Councils, even the voices of doubt have been valuable in helping to flush out the possible problems with the decision at hand.

You may be asking how consensus actually occurs. Once an issue or idea is brought to the council, everyone has a chance to contribute his/her perspectives. Then others begin to question and offer insights that generate alternatives for solving the issue at hand. The group considers the alternatives and discusses the consequences and benefits of each one. At the end of the discussion a collective direction emerges. There may be a few who still have reservations but they are willing to try the decision that was collectively identified. There is a group commitment to evaluate the decision as it is implemented. There is a willingness to alter the decision as concerns are identified The following Wisdom From The Field offers a look at how this works.

Wisdom From The Field

An issue was brought to the Partnership Council one month by Jim who was speaking on behalf of his One-on-One link, Ian. He was concerned about the quality of patient education that was occurring as well as how they were connecting with other care provider teaching prior to and after the patient came to their area. As the discussion ensued it was clearly a passionate issue. The form required the documentation of the person's level of understanding of what was taught, not just what information was given. It also required that the patients story be known by all providers so that appropriate teaching methods could be used.

There was defensiveness, blame and shame all present in the discussion. The group was divided on what action to take from here. Some wanted to use corrective action to force people to assume accountability while others wanted the form removed. The council recognized their situation and called for a moment of silence. Jim asked the council to shift off of the issue of the form. He suggested they use dialogue. The council agreed. The group began to use inquiry and advocacy skills to uncover the deeper issues. They explored the question, "What do we believe about our teaching and patients' learning?"

This conversation was very revealing. The critical issues that surfaced were that the differing views on teaching and learning impacted how people carried out this aspect of their role. They also discovered that there were some who felt inadequate in this new approach and were resisting it because they needed more education to educate others. This was enough insight for the council to reach consensus on what the next actions would be. They devised a list of questions to go One-on-One with as they were seeking even more clarity before rushing to fix this problem. Jim also volunteered to ask Ian if he would lead a shared work team in researching more information.

The next month people returned with their One-on-One feedback. Jim brought Ian and they both had further information on the topic from the shared work team. After all listened to the information at hand a discussion ensued to flush out benefits and consequences of the emerging choices. The whole picture became clear to the council and a plan was developed. As a follow up each member took the plan out One-on-One and explained why and how this was the outcome of their discussions. The plan did not include corrective action or removal of the education form. It did include time for more dialogue on the topic and education for the care providers on teaching and learning. The issue was not one of accountability and compliance after all. This issue represented a call for support, understanding and clarity on how education fit with their mission.

The initial steps of this plan were received well by peers and it was consensually decided to move forward while listening carefully to the voices offering feedback and evaluation. There was a commitment to modify the decision as needed.

Partnership Councils sometimes find consensus difficult to understand at first. It requires practice and a comfort with trying something new. The group needs patience and perseverance in learning this method. Giving clear information on what it is and how it works when beginning to experiment helps decrease the frustration. It has also been important to validate at the end of the meeting what has been decided through consensus. When major issues are presented Partnership Councils help members go One-on-One by using the worksheet in Figure 9 on page 121. In shared decision making all involved must have adequate information to offer their input. We have learned that being very clear on what you are asking others has been important to a successful outcome.

At times those that compromised feel coerced into trying something they are unsure will work. We have learned to be flexible in decision making. If a council decides on something through consensus there is a commitment to address issues as they arise. Figure 13 on page 161 shows a follow up loop that ensures issues can be revisited and addressed in Partnership Councils.

In following this diagram we can see that an issue comes to the council where it is discussed and a decision is made to either go One-on-One with the issue for feedback or a shared work team is asked to bring more learning back to the council before One-on-One is conducted. Once the One-on-One feedback is gathered the council member brings it to the Partnership Council for discussion, dialogue and consensus decision making.

FIGURE 13

Shared Decision Making Via Shared Work
How Do Issues Come to Council?

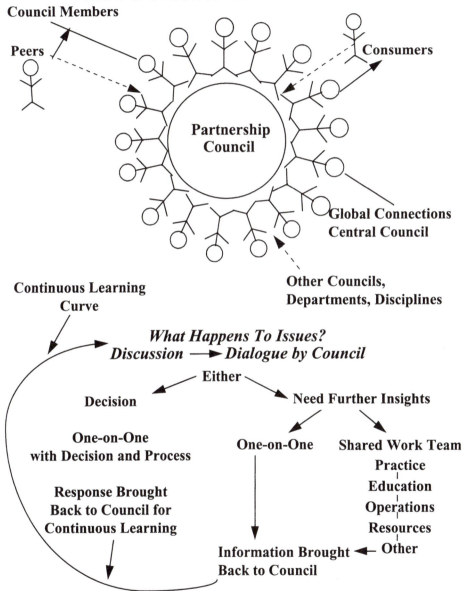

Council Members

Peers

Consumers

Partnership Council

Global Connections
Central Council

Other Councils,
Departments, Disciplines

Continuous Learning
Curve

What Happens To Issues?
Discussion ⟶ *Dialogue by Council*

Either

Decision

Need Further Insights

One-on-One
with Decision and Process

One-on-One

Shared Work Team
Practice
Education
Operations
Resources
Other

Response Brought
Back to Council for
Continuous Learning

Information Brought
Back to Council

The outcome of this is then taken back through their One-on-One linkages to explain how this outcome was reached and how their feedback helped. As the actions from the decision are initiated, consequences and progress are monitored by the council so that adaptations can be made and outcomes identified. In the continuous learning mindset of decision making, these observations are brought back through the top of the loop to cycle through again as needed.

Wisdom From The Field

I am a Patient Care Assistant and as a Partnership Council member I link One-on-One with other Patient Care Assistants and the Housekeeping Technicians in our area. One month we were exploring ways to make patients feel more welcome upon admission to our area. An idea came up that required us to go One-on-One with our peers. We were seeking feedback on the feasibility of placing a welcome sign with important information on the bedside stand. When I connected with Jim our housekeeping technician he responded with, "Gee I'm surprised I'm even getting asked for my feedback on this one. I don't really like the idea because it will just be one more thing to try and keep clean around here." I explained that I would bring his feedback.

At the meeting we went around the room and listened to all of the One-on-One responses and then had a learning conversation. By the end of our time a collective direction became clear. We decided through consensus to implement the use of a welcome/information sign. It was then important for me to return to Jim with information on how we had arrived at this decision. I explained about the different perspectives brought and the consequences considered. I said, "I know your feedback was not selected as the final decision but it did offer a perspective that none of us had thought of and it added an important piece to keep in mind as we moved forward. How do you feel about the outcome?" Jim could see how his feedback added to the options considered and he felt he could try this idea out. I asked him to please be alert to anything else we should be aware of as we went forward. I learned a critical lesson with that interaction. Sometimes people just want their views considered and they appreciate being asked. When the process is respectful of them they can usually consider a decision they did not support in the beginning.

Consensus continues to be an effective option for Partnership Councils to achieve shared decision making. The following table has quotes from council members who have used consensus.

TABLE TWENTY TWO

Council Members Key Learning About the Use of Consensus

"With consensus there have been no losers."

"Consensus always leaves us respectful of each other."

"Consensus gets the collective 'they' out"

"Feedback from our One-on-One linkages is crucial to the consensual process."

"Coming to agreement through consensus is more difficult than voting but it yields better outcomes."

"Trusting relationships must be developed before consensus can happen."

"First we had to learn to really listen to all perspectives before consensus could be reached."

"Consensus takes time and patience but it sure makes a difference. It took us three months to arrive at consensus on one difficult issue but there was no buy in work to do after the decision"

"Consensus requires communication between members and calls on collective group wisdom."

Dialogue

Partnership Councils have been experimenting with dialogue as a way of building relationships and shared meaning. Many of them have reported dialogue as being the way they have learned more about their collective circumstances. This learning has been like cement that holds a foundation strong and stable. It has strengthened relationships and has contributed to the ongoing building of consensus. In dialogue the goal is to uncover truths and deepen meaning; it is not to make a decision or resolve an issue.

Dialogue has been used by many people over the centuries but is a new way of being together in the work place. Work places have pulled us toward fast communication, and quick decisions. Dialogue slows down our interaction and provides space for listening and reflection. It shifts the time and work to the front end from the back end of decisions.

Dialogue is another form of conversation in which we genuinely inquire into the thinking of others as well as our own. It is a time for us to listen, explore and reflect. The purpose of dialogue is to tap into the groups collective wisdom. The goal is to become aware of our deeply held assumptions and beliefs and to listen for deeper understanding. There are principles that can help us practice dialogue.

Many Partnership Councils have learned and are using the principles of dialogue; intention, listening, inquiry, advocacy and silence. They have already been introduced earlier. Dialogue offers conversation that is free of judgment, and rich with respect for diverse thinking. It is a process that enhances the emergence of truth. Dialogue is very different from discussion. Table Twenty Three shows the distinctions between discussion and dialogue.

TABLE TWENTY THREE

Distinctions Between Discussion And Dialogue

DISCUSSION	DIALOGUE
Defend	Explore
Certainty	Uncertainty
Competence	Vulnerability
Know	Learn
Separation	Connection
Stating	Uncovering
Expert	Beginner
Opinion	Truth
Judging	Searching

As mentioned there is not an agenda to follow, a decision to make or an issue to resolve at a dialogue gathering. However, there is usually a topic, question or other stimulus for reflection in dialogue. More experienced groups may not need such a beginning, but we have found it helpful in earlier phases of learning dialogue. Examples of questions that Partnership Councils have used include; What is the nature of change? What is equal worth in the work place? What is the essence of power? What is our purpose and meaning in work? What would it be like to bring our whole selves to work? What have I learned about myself during change? Reflection on a poem or verse has also been effective. Two verses recommended are words from Ghandi, "Each of us must be the change we want to see in the world" and "My life is my message." These topics help us to identify our underlying beliefs that drive our decision making and actions.

The third book in the Wisdom From The Field Series is a very good reference for learning more about using dialogue in Partnership Councils. It is entitled, *Can The Human Being Thrive In The Work Place? Dialogue as a Strategy of Hope* (1997, Wesorick and Shiparski). Table Twenty Four on pages 166-167 is a worksheet that comes from that book and offers a format for councils to follow as they begin to explore the use of dialogue.

TABLE TWENTY FOUR

DIALOGUE INTROSPECTION

Dialogue is a process that enhances the emergence of truth.

What is Dialogue?

How is dialogue different from other forms of conversation?
- Debate - "To beat down."
- Deliberate - "To weigh out."
- Discussion - "To break apart."

Most of our meetings are like ping pong matches in which the participants bat their opinion around the room or like merging traffic in which there is little listening, just waiting for an opening to get one's opinion inserted. Discussion is not bad. It is often how we make decisions and get things done.

Dialogue: "A flow of meaning."

Dialogue is another form of conversation in which we genuinely inquire into ways of thinking that we take for granted. It is not about trying to come to consensus or make a decision, but rather to explore and reflect, to listen to everyone's thinking as just as valid as my own, to be willing to examine my own thinking and be influenced by the thinking of others.

Examples of distinctions between dialogue and discussion:

Discussion	Dialogue
Defend	Explore
Certainty	Uncertainty
Competence	Vulnerability
Know	Learn
Separation	Connection
Stating	Uncovering
Expert	Beginner
Opinion	Truth
Judging	Searching
Dependent/ Independent	Interdependent

Share some of these guidelines.

Guidelines for the emergence of dialogue:
a. Leave our roles and positions outside.
b. Display and genuinely questions our assumptions and those of others.
c. Suspend certainty and judgment.
d. Slow down, leave space between comments.
e. Have a willingness to be surprised and influenced by another.
f. Not here to fix, manage, or process.
g. No hidden agendas or perplexed outcomes.
h. Allow for silence.
i. Speak from "I" and listen to the "WE."
j. Allow multiple perspectives to surface without needing to resolve them.
k. Consider others' perspectives/opinions as just as valid as your own.

Thoughts, Realizations, Wonderings, Learnings
(FACILITATOR HINTS)
Note: This two page handout can be used by participants as a format to facilitate dialogue in their settings.

Table Twenty Four, continued

Dialogue Introspection. Page Two

A Process for Dialogue to Emerge	**Thoughts, Realizations, Wonderings, Learnings** *(FACILITATOR HINTS)*

1. Developing the Practice Field.
The purpose of the practice field is to establish an environment where the conditions are prime for dialogue to emerge. A place where participants can practice the art of dialogue. It is really a list of considerations for the group that addresses how they wish to be together.

Sample practice field:
a. Keep confidentiality.
b. Speak from "I."
c. Listen deeply to others and yourself.
d. No side conversations or interruptions.
e. No assuming--check each other for understanding.
f. No agendas, no leaders, no judgments.
g. Value each person's contribution.
Additions from group:

2. Check-In.
A "Check In" is an invitation for each individual in the group to share his/her thinking. It is a way for other group members to practice listening skills and gain insights. Check-In sets the tone for being together in a different way.

3. Dialogue Question, Statement, or Quote.
Facilitator will read the question, statement, or quote and offer a moment of silence for participants to reflect.

4. Dialogue Experience.
Invite anyone to begin speaking as they feel moved to do so.

5. Debrief on Dialogue Experience.
a. Participants to write key learnings on 3x5 card and give to facilitator.
b. Invite participants to share their experiences and learnings with the group.

6. Closing Poem.

Facilitator Hints column:

1. *Share purpose and examples. Ask for additions from the group. They can record them on their individual dialogue introspection sheets.*

2. *There will be a question provided for each person to answer during Check-In.*

3. *Starting the Dialogue. Before we begin, it might be helpful to realize that what we are about to engage in may feel awkward because the pace is different. Sometimes there are moments of silence which we are not used to in the fast pace of our regular meetings.*

4. *Introduce the Question. To stimulate our thinking for the dialogue I(we) would like to first share the following questions, give you time to reflect, and then provide an opportunity for you to share your thinking with the person next to you.*

5. *After hearing the question, take a few minutes to think about your own questions and thinking with regard to this issue. Think even deeper and ask yourself what is behind that thinking? The question is:*

6. *As facilitator, feel free to share any realizations, observations, energies, and/or noticings you have about the dialogue experience.*

Thank everyone for participating. Note that speaking is not the sole indicator of participation. Many people participated by listening and experiencing internal dialogue, all of which are contributed to the experience and wisdom gained.

Dialogue is a time to practice relationship building skills of intention, listening, advocacy, inquiry, and silence

As an example of how a Partnership Council might experience dialogue we offer the following Wisdom From The Field.

Wisdom From The Field

Only a few people on this patient care unit had learned and experienced dialogue, but they realized it would be a key strategy for the others to learn. They brought their learning and recommendation to their Partnership Council and a consensus was reached for all to learn more. They developed strategic goals for the unit that included a plan to introduce dialogue. The goal was to grow as a continuous learning group. A year's worth of education, exploration, and discussion culminated at their annual unit goal setting session. This was a time when the strategic initiatives were determined with staff, manager, and educator all in attendance. This year they were not going to brainstorm and list goals and objectives as they usually did, but they were going to use dialogue to deepen their collective understanding before the planning.

The brainstorming format and subsequent multiple vote and rank ordering processes were perceived to have been very successful at previous retreats. There were concerns by the members that they would not accomplish the same objectives with the use of dialogue. However, they were willing to give it a try.

Articles on dialogue were distributed to members in advance of the retreat to refresh their thinking and expand their knowledge. Much time was spent selecting a poem to read for the dialogue opening, and even more time was spent discussing what the opening question should be. It was decided to have the dialogue outside in a setting far removed from the hospital environment. A park with wetlands was chosen, and box lunches were ordered to create a picnic like atmosphere.

Council members met at the park and were escorted on a ten minute hike back into the wetlands where dry ground and picnic space were located. Blankets were placed on the ground and members sat around in a circle eating their boxed lunches. A few key concepts of dialogue were reviewed, a check-in was completed, the poem and question presented, meditation time honored, and the dialogue began.

The dialogue lasted for two hours and all members were actively engaged in the process. In keeping with time commitments, the dialogue was summarized and concluded within the two hour time frame. The themes that had emerged and gave guidance to future council initiatives during the dialogue included the following:

- Strengthen and enhance partnering relationships with patients, families, co-workers, and the multidisciplinary team.
- Create an environment where each team member is positively affirmed and encouraged to let his/her light shine.
- Continue the journey with dialogue.

Feedback from the council members about the dialogue experience was overwhelmingly positive. The environment for the dialogue was peaceful. The earth brought out their sense of spirituality. During the dialogue, a jet flew overhead, and it reminded one member of the importance of keeping in touch with reality and remembering what they have available to them with the use of technology.

Other learnings included:

- The initial dialogue question did not make a difference. They learned that the important questions and wisdom emerge without the need to carefully craft an opening question. One person reflected on a question she had heard recently when participating in a team member interview. The question centered around asking the interviewee to think of a shift they had worked in which they had gone home feeling especially rewarded and glad that they had chosen health care as their career. Others quickly picked up on this and much personal sharing occurred.
- Nature played a significant role in creating a learning atmosphere. Leaving the sheltered area by the parking lot and taking a ten minute walk to the destination gave each person time to debrief.

- It was important to summarize the key themes in the dialogue at the conclusion. This was surprisingly easy. There was a clear and common understanding as to what those themes were.

- The prior experiences with goal setting were also very productive, but the goals were rather superficial. Dialogue took them more to the heart of what they were about. It was easier to take the message back to unit team members.

- Dialogue saved them time. They accomplished their dialogue in two hours. The year prior, the brainstorming and decision-making processes took four hours.

- The interdisciplinary team member expressed great appreciation for the use of dialogue and was awed by the wisdom she had gained from the experience. She presented the council with a stone for use with future "check-ins" and remarked on how she had not experienced anything like this in her time at the hospital.

- Experiencing dialogue time together bonded the council members in a new and different way. Learning to listen to each other generated a higher level of respect and awareness of their interdependence. It was a profound event which touched their souls and left each of them better for having had the experience.

In summary, it may be helpful to see the methods just described and consider how they all fit in shared and non-shared decision making fields. As Figure 14 shows, Partnership Councils and work settings will experience and use all of these methods. However decision making can be more effective if a council chooses methods in the shared decision making field. It is important to consider decision making as a continuous learning process no matter what method is used.

Debate, deliberation voting, and discussion are often used to analyze issues but have outcomes of win-lose. In these scenarios people may feel that their input is not adequately heard or that the loudest voices will rule. Individual preferences and analysis of the pros and cons are the goal.

Figure 14
Differentiating the Fields
of Shared and Non-Shared Decision Making

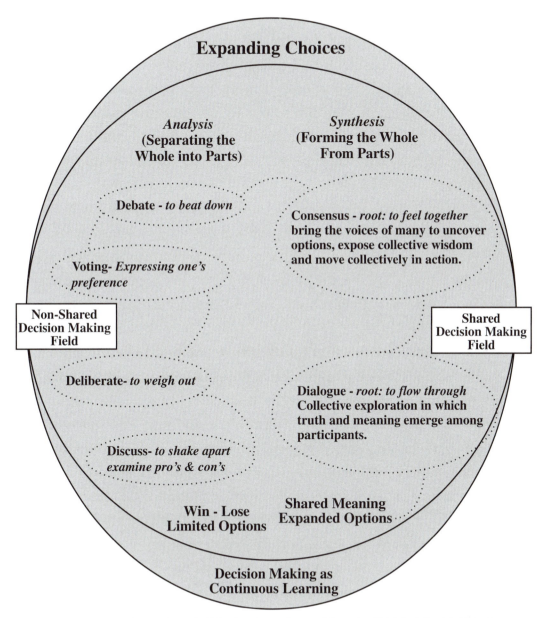

The root meanings of the words are italicized and are referenced from the fifth Discipline Field Book (Isaacs, 1997).

Partnership may be present but these methods do not require or encourage it. *The non-shared field also is limiting in the generation of choices* because it's methods do not have the intention of seeking deeper meaning or shared agreement.

As issues become more complex it is important to move to methods that evoke deeper insights. Consensus and dialogue are to be used to develop shared understanding around complex issues in the shared decision making field. Synthesis, or connecting a whole from its parts, is the goal in this field. Shared agreement is an outcome of consensus and shared understanding an outcome of dialogue. They both offer win-win scenarios and expanded choices. They are methods that require and enhance partnerships.

As Partnership Councils find themselves revisiting the same issues over and over, dialogue is indicated to uncover the real issue that is being masked by more trivial issues. With issues or topics of high passion and polarity councils have been more successful using dialogue and consensus building. Movement through these various methods should be fluid and flexible.

What can a Partnership Council do in addition to practicing the above methods of decision making in hopes of enhancing their capacity to deal with complex issues? In addition to strengthening relationships while in the midst of every issue and decision there are also foundational ways to strengthen a group's connection. Many Partnership Councils have done initial and ongoing work that has increased their shared understanding. Chapter Eight offers an in-depth look at these specific strategies. For example. Partnership Councils have identified the following processes as invaluable in collectively preparing for decisions and learning to come: mission and vision work, learning each others stories, and living Core Beliefs.

Evaluating the outcomes of our decisions requires constant attention. In evaluating our decisions it is imperative that we consider the decision and the process. Partnership Councils that have experienced negativity around their decisions have most often found the negativity focused on the process not the decision. In other words, people can live with most decisions if the process is respectful. They desire to be involved, to have their perspectives heard and to be informed of the process and outcomes. Honesty of information shared has been a key factor in building environments of integrity and unity. The following table offers questions to evaluate the outcomes of decision making.

TABLE TWENTY FIVE

Questions To Evaluate The Outcomes Of Decision Making

The Process	**The Decision**
1. Were the Core Beliefs and mission used?	1. How is it supporting those we serve?
2. Were all voices heard, One-on-One linkages?	2. How is it supporting us in living mission and Core Beliefs?
3. Did follow up communication occur with One-on-One links to explain decision making process and outcomes?	3. What are the favorable and unfavorable impacts--are we responding?
4. Were shared decision making methods used and consensus reached?	4. In what way will the decision impact relationships?
5. Was there continued evaluation and feedback and flexibility in altering the original decision as needed?	
6. What are the perceptions of others--is further clarification needed?	

When shared decision making is perceived as going well we must take the opportunity to celebrate and realize what we are doing to perpetuate this positive cycle. This does not mean that decision making will be easy, it means that we can begin to see the long and short term effects of our decisions. Council members have to continually point out these long term outcomes to others as they reinforce the purpose and focus of council existence. *It is in the act of shared decision making that we actually strengthen our partnerships with each other.* We are challenged to live partnership principles and stretch our thinking as individuals and as a group.

We continually learn, and shape our next responses based on the results we see. So what about failures? What is a failure in a continuous learning mindset? There are no failures but there are decisions that are better than others. There is no such thing as a perfect decision. We can become paralyzed if we wait to begin with the perfect decision. The Partnership Council strives to make the best decision possible knowing that shared decision making can produce more options than individual decision making. The process of shared decision making helps avoid the paralysis of perfect and provides the opportunity to experience the joy of continuous learning. Remen (1996) reminds us of the importance of this perspective when she said, "Perfection is the belief that life is imperfect."

There are consequences to our decisions and actions. Good and bad the consequences have to be flushed out as completely as possible in the beginning. It has been necessary to find ways to stay centered during shared decision making. It decreases the possibility of negative consequences and transcends the lure of quick fix decisions while promoting principle centered, long term outcomes. The Core Beliefs in Table One on page 11 have served as a compass to many councils during these times. Also staying focused on their collective mission and vision has aided in effective decision making. Councils constantly consider who is affected by their decisions? They think and act in local and global ways.

There are growing pains as normal movement forward and slipping back are both experienced. This is the result of Partnership Councils who are willing to experiment, practice, and grow. They are experiencing a positive change cycle and expanding their boundaries. They exhibit the flexibility to change decisions midstream. In some organizations such change might be considered indecisive. Effective decision making requires a fine balance of knowing when to forge ahead as planned and when to adapt a new direction. The Partnership Council structure and processes offered in this book are meant to assure this balance.

Every experience we have in decision making, either as individuals or collectively, offers us great learning. We have found ways to acknowledge learning as an outcome. Partnership Councils call it key learning. Whenever we desire to know what we have all learned from a decision making experience we ask our council to write their key learning on a 3x5 card. We then collect the cards, type them for all to read and receive a second waive of learning. This important activity helps councils keep their perspective on their circumstances. It also helps the participant to engage and consider the proceedings in light of their own personal learning. No matter what the outcome the learning always offers direction.

A final note on making decisions from our wholeness BodyMindSpirit. After considering all of the above in our decision making we must always be aware of what parts of ourselves we are using to make them. We often sell ourselves short by merely using our minds to logically make decisions. In Partnership Councils we have learned to call upon our whole being. This means using our body, mind and spirit to continuously learn, grow and make choices. Our decisions look different when made from this integrated place.

Ram Dass in his presentation *The Path Of Service,* offers a clear example of what a decision from only the mind renders. Consider how the people working for the U.S. Government must have come to the decision to store atomic waste in New Mexico. They had research experts tell them that the life of atomic waste was three times as long as we have known life to exist on this planet. They said they tested the waste containers and results indicated they would probably last that long. How did they rationalize endangering the people of that area? They decided that the lives of the people there could be sacrificed, after all they were mostly people of poverty. So, the waste was buried deep beneath the land. The land today is unusable and unsafe. It will never be salvageable. The people there suffered as well. A decision such as this came from the mind and was not balanced by the soul.

For Partnership Councils and work settings who exist to continually improve health care and relationships, decision making must be made using bodymindspirit or else they will risk consequences that could be devastating to our humanity.

Chapter Seven

System Thinking:
What are the outcomes of connection?

"In our exploration of what's possible, we are led to search for new and different partners. Who we become together will always be different than who we are alone. Our range of creative expression increases as we join with others. New relationships create new capacities."
- Wheatley and Kellner

The greatest evidence of a successful Partnership Council is the realization that their potential has been enhanced by connecting with each other, and they seek to expand their partnerships. The lessons of healthy relationships rooted in purpose and nurtured by meaningful conversation are not easily forgotten. The desire to uncover new, expanded linkages comes with the realization that without linkage, we are alone, our capacities are limited and our boundaries restrictive. Isolation is no longer acceptable because connections deepen personal and professional capacities. Merely surviving is intolerable. Growing, expanding and thriving become the norm. Partnerships end the fear of being alone and the fear of connecting with others beyond the comfort zone.

Partnership Councils bring the concepts of systems thinking alive at a local level. The council provides the fundamental structure that naturally leads the group to desire connections at a global level. Members learn that there are more perspectives and more possibilities than one person could ever see or know. One member compared the experience to a puzzle, knowing that no one person can know the whole picture without each person bringing their piece of the puzzle to the table.

The realization that we are all more when multiple voices and connections are made within our immediate area, prepares us to move beyond the boundaries of our setting/unit/departments and seek a more expansive, complete picture. One person may have a picture of a tree in his/her mind, and without the others perspective will miss the surrounding forest and the rivers and mountains beyond. It is the success at the smaller table, the local level, that ignites the passion to journey beyond the familiar territory and link beyond.

The Partnership Council provides the fundamental structure necessary to create a systems thinking culture. Systems thinking according to Senge (1991) is the "Discipline of understanding the dynamic rather than the detail complexity of systems--seeing the whole, interrelationships and patterns of change." The Partnership Council brings colleagues together to experience the whole of their present and local reality. The council learns in a practical way the concepts of system thinking due to the nature of their existence. They create a place to develop and enhance relationships, meaningful conversation, and expand linkages to achieve shared mission and vision. Max Depree (1989) notes the first accountability of a leader is to define reality. The council defines their reality. It is this successful leadership that propels the group to reach beyond to become a part of a greater reality.

What does shared work at the Partnership Council look like?

To effectively organize shared work efforts, some Partnership Councils have found it very helpful to define the current reality. Great insights have come to councils who have revisited the initiatives and groups previously developed to carry out shared work. They assess for system connections and simplify the structure. The following worksheet (Figure 15) can be used to link current work to the Partnership Council. This will assist with decreasing fragmentation and redundant efforts.

An example of how this transition looks is illustrated in Figures 16 and 17. Figure 16 is an actual example from a Respiratory Care Department who had put on paper a visual representation of their structure and connections. After establishing their Partnership Council, the council mem-

Figure 15
UNIT/DEPARTMENT SHARED WORK LINKAGE PLANNING SHEET

As a Partnership Council, one of your first priorities is to identify your current unit/department structure or how shared work is organized and accomplished. The council is the central place where all initiatives and people are linked. Please fill in your council members in the large circles below and key initiatives or people that are linked to your council through it's members. If a key initiative such as quality improvement is not linked, find a way to link it to the council.

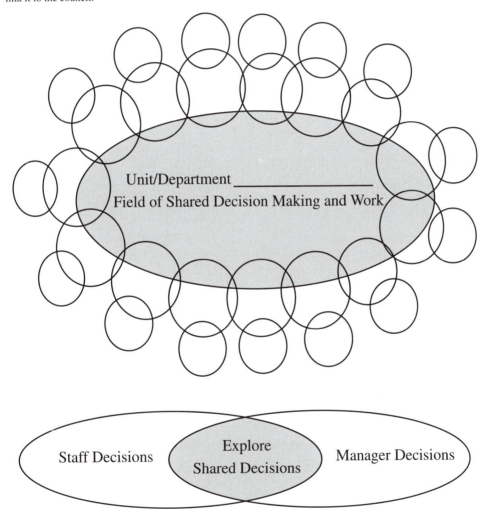

The council is a place where individual decision making can be synchronized with others and shared decision making can expand. When the council evolves their shared decision making overlap grows but individual decisions are also preserved. A balance and synchrony emerge as members help each other uphold their agreement to live the principles of partnership in their decision making and shared work.

Figure 16
ORGANIZATIONAL CHART

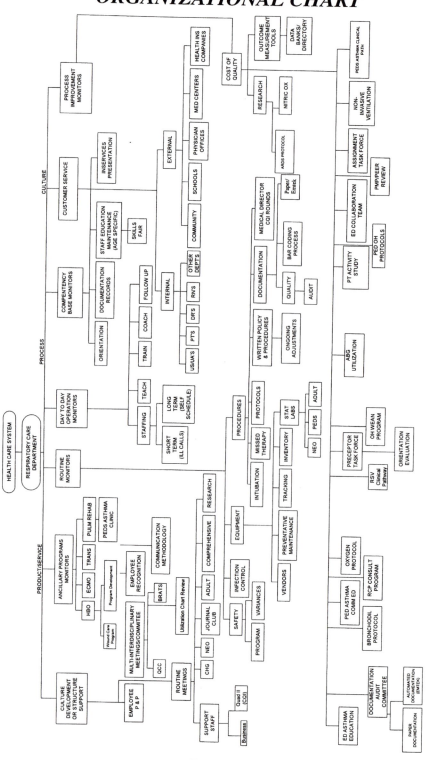

Figure 17
Respiratory Care Department

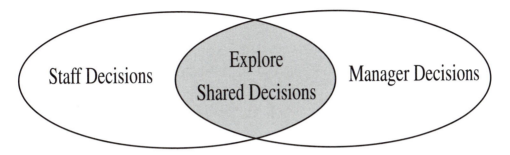

The council is a place where individual decision making can be synchronized with others and shared decision making can expand

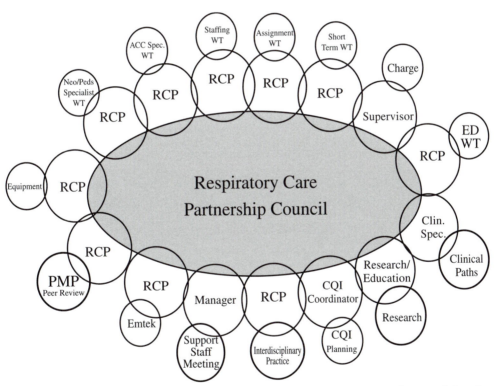

Individuals bring their 1:1 linkages and enter a corner of their circle into the area of shared decision making and the boundaries are explored together.

When the council evolves their shared decision making overlap grows but individual decisions are also preserved. A balance and synchrony emerge as members help each other uphold their agreement to live the principles of partnership in their decision making.

bers worked with everyone in the department to ensure that the council was the central place where all work and people connected. Creating a place for linkages and shared decision making created a whole different visual representation to the work in the department as seen in Figure 16. In fact, it was only after this change that there was a sense of "shared" work--because the work was now connected to everyone in the department.

What is the importance of systems thinking in a healthy work culture?

No one person, no one profession, no one unit or department can assure an individual or our society quality health care. The understanding of the complexity of the whole of health care, the interrelationships and the patterns of change are essential to assure quality care. Linkages via partnerships are the heartbeat of systems thinking. Duplication and repetition of services are the outcomes of a disconnected system. Most providers and recipients of care have experienced the repetition of questions, the same questions over and over again. This wastes many hours of time and therefore millions of dollars which could be used to improve care. This common problem cannot be eliminated without systems thinking.

What is the connection between systems thinking and quality?

The design of the system or structure is capable of having a greater impact on relationships, culture, and the outcomes of care than the effort and competence of the individual. The majority of all health care providers are committed and competent people. They desire to give quality care. Individually they are doing their best. Systems thinking has taught us that individually we can work as hard as we want--faster then ever, and increase our personal competencies, but without partnerships and systems connections, there will be no quality. For example, duplication or repetition can only be prevented with effective linkages. Quality rests with the ability to create system supports that establish strong linkages of the people within and across systems, communities and society in order to live the core beliefs. **We must create new system supports.**

Under normal day-to-day situations, the system can enhance or interfere with the ability to give quality care. Can you imagine then, how important the system supports become when the providers and recipients of care are attempting to change their old habits, the real evidence of continuous learning. Each person will benefit from a system that supports the change and rewards the new behaviors that correlate with the Core Beliefs, principles of partnership, and shared decision making/leadership. That type of system emerges within Partnership Councils.

The system is a catalyst for each person's work and the work of the team. Before we can change the system to support the quality of the work we must first know each person's work and how the system impacts the work. It also requires understanding the system well enough to make changes at the right point, called the leverage points. Leverage points are those invisible critical places that, when changed, bring lasting long term positive outcomes. Systems thinking helps us to see the invisible components of the system. It is the invisible forces that have the greatest impact on everyone in the system. These invisible forces are the patterns of interactions and interrelationships that occur constantly.

Archimedes said, "Give me a lever and a place to stand and I will move the world." Leverage points are not about doing something faster or better but doing things differently, more wisely, in order to carry out and sustain the mission. It is not about finding out what needs to be done, it is about finding a new way of doing what needs to be done. Partnership Councils and global linkages are not only major leverage points, but they are the place where leverage work is done and new leverage points are uncovered.

In what way does the Partnership Council create the foundation for system linkages?

Partnership Councils form the foundation to build further connections. Russell Ackoff (1986) defines a system as a whole that cannot be divided into independent parts. He notes that no subgroup in the system can have an independent effect on the performance of the whole. The council structure provides the means and process to connect every person to the whole. Moving beyond Partnership Councils to centralized councils and other expanded linkages creates a natural bridge to connect with the whole.

What is the nature of systems thinking linkages?

Systems thinking linkages expand the leverage points of partnership and shared leadership by creating new patterns of interaction. Linkages are not hierarchical in nature, they create networks for new ways of thinking, relating, and continuous learning/improvement. These linkages occur at a local and global level. Local linkages are connections with colleagues within the immediate surrounding work place such as unit, department or geographic area. Global linkages are connections with colleagues beyond the local boundaries. Linkages provide infrastructure to align values and coordinate, integrate and expand shared work within the whole.

The previous chapters addressed three different types of **local system linkages:** *Partnership Councils, the One-on-One process, and Shared Work Teams.* Every person and all point of care service (place where care or service is rendered) is connected locally to the Partnership Council via One-on-One and Shared Work Teams. There are two broad types of **global linkages:** *the Central Partnership Council linkages* which connects all Partnership Councils and the *networking linkages of Shared Work Teams.* The purpose of global linkages is to assure that all parts are continuously connected with the whole. Both are extensions of the fundamental Partnership Council structure. The concept of global linkages is nothing new, what is different is the purpose of it. See Figure 18 for examples of local and global systems thinking linkages.

What is the purpose and structure of the Central Partnership Council (CPC)?

The purpose of the CPC is to connect all local councils and create global linkages across the setting that evolve around the heartbeat of the system: the point of care or service. It is an essential step to link and create

Figure 18
Local And Global Systems Linkages

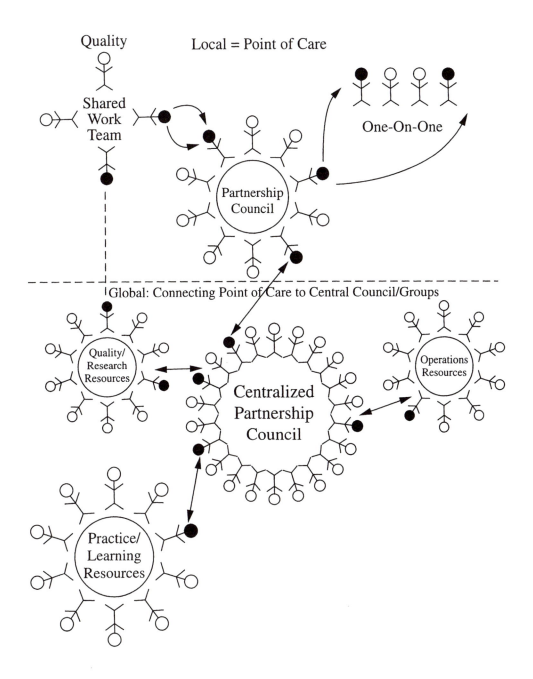

Quality

Local = Point of Care

Shared Work Team

One-On-One

Partnership Council

Global: Connecting Point of Care to Central Council/Groups

Quality/ Research Resources

Centralized Partnership Council

Operations Resources

Practice/ Learning Resources

a systems thinking work place. The Coordinator from each Partnership Council becomes the link to the central council. Since the principles of partnership are the same, the connection is not of a hierarchical nature, but is a continuum for learning and linkage. The central council connects the voice, learning, struggle, and realities across the setting.

The central council is a mirror of the diverse units/departments, specialties, service lines, disciplines and roles that comprise the setting's whole. That is why some global resource networking groups as seen in Figure 18 also connect at the council. That is the only way the central point of care can achieve the diversity of roles. As evident in Figure 18, the centralized Partnership Council needs the expertise and connection with the operations or managers, practice/learning resources, and quality/research resources. Since they commonly have global networking gatherings, a representative can connect all of them with the centralized council.

The following structural design and principles have been found to be successful in supporting the work and learning of the central Partnership Council.

- Links all global work to the point of care. Therefore it is a mirror of the diversity of the setting/organization.
- Meets each month to strengthen partnerships, expand vision and carry out shared work.
- Has the same person attend from each of the Partnership Councils or global networking groups/shared work teams. This provides consistency needed for relationship building within the group. We have found that a two year rotation deepens the learning and creates a familiarly of global issues that can be built upon.
- Carries out membership accountabilities which are inclusive of the Partnership Council role as defined in Table Eleven on page 83, as well as assuring the council links with all other colleagues throughout the system.
- Closes the loop between councils by sharing feedback and learning across the setting.
- Seeks collective wisdom and supports shared work.

- Participates in leadership activities for continuous learning.
- Determines collectively the appropriate linkages beyond the system into the community, country and world.

A historical note may be helpful here related to the diverse nature of the CPC membership and linkages. Within the health care system, especially in hospitals, nurses are the largest group of care providers. The concept of a "central place" to gather nurses was initiated in many clinical settings in the early 80's and was often referred to as a Shared Governance Council. A common name for this central nursing group was the Professional Practice Council or Professional Nursing Council. As the Partnership Council paradigm evolved over the last 14 years, some significant lessons emerged. Although there was a strong need for staff nurses to link, that was not sufficient enough to optimally enhance the quality of services at the point of care. Nurses, although the largest point of care professionals, are one of many diverse disciplines and/or specialties.

For true partnership and systems thinking to be achieved, there would have to be a more inclusive point of care council, both locally and globally. That is why local Partnership Councils and central Partnership Councils have evolved into interdisciplinary councils. The historical Professional Practice/Nursing Council is really nothing more than a global Shared Work Team for nurses, similar to the global operations or managers group, educators and quality/research teams. With the emergence of the council to a true centralized point of service council, the nurses are still largest in number because they are the coordinators of many local Partnership Councils.

In the transition from a "nursing only" centralized council to an interdisciplinary council, nursing as a discipline needs to find a way to connect to do their shared work. Nursing is unique in a sense that there is not one department Partnership Council that connects all of them like other disciplines are more likely to have. An example of this is a Respiratory Care Department with a Respiratory Partnership Council that links all respiratory therapists throughout the setting/organization. One example of how nurses can connect to their discipline-specific shared work is for the nurses on the Centralized Partnership Council to meet before the entire council gathers.

The following perspective of a central council member gives insight into the purpose and outcomes of this council.

Wisdom From The Field

"When I think about linkages I always come back to think about the house wide Central Partnership Council. I will never forget when I first started going to these gatherings--I was very new at Professional Practice Councils and relating to anyone outside my unit. I did not trust anyone outside my unit, didn't really know what other units did and didn't really care. It never occurred to me that there was wisdom to be gained from these gatherings and that if I could listen, I could learn a great deal. It didn't take me long to realize that going to these council meetings was like sitting at the table with a professional from every specialty in my hospital. There are many areas where the care of the patient overlaps and patient care is what the council is about. How does what we do affect patients and families? It is a safe place to explore issues and to learn from one another.

One of the things that impressed me most was the realization that every unit doesn't have to re-invent the wheel every time something new comes up. We can build upon each other. We discuss what others have learned along their journeys and what they recommend. Two examples are doorside charting and merging of units. The first unit to implement doorside charting began the learning process and then it was built on by others. Another example is the merging of units. There is much wisdom to be gained by listening to the voice of experience. By listening we learned from each other resulting in smoother transitions for the rest of the units and new relationships were built along the way. What had previously been painful experiences were now a time to consciously learn, grow and challenge ourselves in a less stressful way.

We now have a resource to develop relationships and consult with each other for present and future changes. When our periop area began preparing

OB patients pre-operatively for cervical circlage surgery, we consulted with our peers from Special Care OB. They helped us with fetal monitoring and we helped them with issues related to sending patients to surgery.

The connections are invaluable. It is wonderful to know someone in surgery, pediatrics, orthopedics, and in the other departments such as environmental services and now even beyond the walls into Home Health. We have a web of two way communication that can either go out from the council or come in from the various system entities. Every individual present represents their particular area at the centralized council. These individuals have the resources of the One-on-One communication system in their areas. This network is invaluable for all of the team in serving patients, families, and each other."

The Central Partnership Council provides the foundation to link across the setting and creates a systems thinking approach. Integral in the sharing of local learnings are the leverage points at the point of care such as capturing the person's story, mutually identifying the individual's health needs, mutually planning and coordinating individualized care, clarity on scope of practice, and professional exchange/communication. CPC also proactively looks at leverage points that are more global in nature such as shared meaning and purpose across areas and disciplines by facilitating the Core Belief Review Process every two years. There is always a conscious connection related to what is happening at the local level (Partnership Councils) and what is happening at the global level (Centralized Partnership Council) which generates learning and expansion that never stops going back and forth.

What does shared work at the Central Partnership Council look like?

The shared work is not around approval but connecting and integrating the work to uncover inconsistency of care, repetition, duplication and identify fragmentation. The specific work evolves around the structure, process and outcomes of the day-to-day practice and its synchronization with the common mission, shared vision and Core Beliefs. The following Wisdom From The Field adds clarity:

Wisdom From the Field

The director from the cardio-thoracic telemetry unit brought an important systems thinking issue to the Central Partnership Council related to family visiting. The issue came in the form of an actual patient/family situation (as most of them do). Mrs. Lake had been staying overnight in her husband's room during his hospitalized stay. When Mr. Lake was transferred to another unit, one of the nurses told her that she was not able to stay overnight. Mrs. Lake was very stressed about this since it did not make sense to her that the determining factor to stay with her husband was based on which unit he was on versus his unique needs. The significance of inconsistencies in practice across the system were explored and council members consensually agreed to share the work of this global issue. The CPC designated time on their agenda every month to continue the work.

The first step the CPC members took was to look at the issue from a systems thinking perspective by using a systems thinking loop diagram which portrayed reinforcing loops. It showed how quick fix decisions that are not mutual with the patient and family reinforced their dissatisfaction and how alternative decisions could reverse the negative feedback loop. Not only was learning happening about the issue, but also about systems thinking dynamics and relationships.

After some initial learning, council members went back to their own Partnership Councils and explored some key questions related to patient/family visiting on their units/departments. The questions and conversations then continued via the One-on-One process to seek thoughts from every patient care provider.

While the One-on-One process was occurring, the CPC members spent time at their next meeting reviewing existing published research about outcomes related to family visitation. Research articles were critiqued and findings were shared. The findings and recommendations discussed revealed patterns that added to the learning.

Wisdom emerged from the research and then the collective feedback/wisdom of all providers via the Partnership Council. The conversation focused on how decisions about family visiting should rest on what is best for the patient, not typical rituals, routines or habits of the patient care area.

The conversation then centered on how the Core Beliefs and clinical tools were designed for mutuality. The patient history or "story" provides the framework for care providers to learn important things that impact visiting from family and friends such as sleep patterns, coping mechanisms, relaxation patterns (whether they include being with others or being alone), and patient/family preference for involvement in care.

In the end, the CPC designed a visual tool that captured the many "options" care providers have when it comes to family visiting as well as how the clinical tools help to establish and maintain mutuality with each patient and family. This also was taken back to each council and then One-on-One to further refine before it was used and shared with others as a teaching tool.

Just as in Partnership Councils, sometimes it may be best to establish a shared work team within the CPC to do some ground work, investigate, learn and make recommendations about a specific issue that will stimulate conversation. The next Wisdom From The Field is an example of how a shared work team was developed as a result of an issue raised at CPC, how it integrated it's learnings and recommendations back into CPC and then tapped the thoughts/input of every Partnership Council member and care provider in order to implement the most effective system wide change.

Wisdom From the Field

A Clinical Coordinator, Mary, from one of the patient care units asked to be on the agenda of the Centralized Partnership Council to discuss lost patient belongings. She had noticed an increasing trend of lost patient belongs in her area and also noted that many times the problem seemed to come from items being lost as patients moved from unit-to-unit throughout the system. By bringing the issue and her perspective to CPC, she knew she could validate if it was a system-wide issue, capture insights from providers throughout the organization, as well as gain collective wisdom on how to best go from here in addressing the issue. After Mary presented the issue and her perspectives at CPC, focused discussion followed with the eventual realization that it was indeed a system issue and would need a global approach to resolving it. A shared work team was then developed in which Mary and one of the CPC members agreed to co-lead and a director at CPC agreed to be in the facilitator role of the work team.

The Patient Belonging Shared Work Team then took on a life of it's own and established meeting times and a membership that covered a wide variety of stakeholders throughout the organization that had key connections related to patient belongings (e.g., admitting office, volunteer services, emergency department, transport service, staff nurses, unit assistants, risk management, out-patient areas, etc.).

At key times during their work on the issue of lost patient belongings, the team would come back to CPC to tap into the collective wisdom of individual Partnership Councils and the One-on-One process. Final changes in managing and tracking patient belongings throughout the system had come after tapping the thought and input of everybody that interacted with patients and their families. Implementation and on-going evaluation is also included within the infrastructure of CPC and Partnership Councils.

As illustrated by the two examples above, the type of issues that come to the CPC evolve around the point of care or practice issues that are relevant across the system. The council members because of their common ground on what matters most engage in meaningful conversations that can address global issues. It saves time, prevents duplication of effort while expanding the capacities to solve problems and co-create a healthy work place. We have learned that it is in the "meaningful conversations" themselves, whether at the table or One-on-One, that have the greatest impact in changing patterns and work cultures.

What is the purpose and linkages of global networking and shared work teams?

In the old hierarchical paradigm, the global gatherings were often to make decisions and keep the local groups, such as staff, on track. Within the partnership paradigm the global networking is not hierarchical, but simply a linkage which enhances learning and assures the connections necessary to strengthen relationships and carry out the work.

It is very much the norm to have managers within settings meet on a routine basis. In addition educators, researches and quality leaders commonly establish formal networking sessions. The need to have meaningful conversation, relationships, sharing and learning time within disciplines, role, specialties and those having similar accountabilities or shared work makes sense. In the partnership paradigm, the purpose of a shared work team has nothing to do with controlling another group.

Global linkages are essential for continuous learning, prevention of duplication and replication and the uncovering of an abundance of options for effectiveness. Once the human infrastructure of Partnership Councils is established, various global networking groups will emerge. *Partners do not need permission to connect with others to improve their work.* Therefore different networking configurations will unfold as needed.

One example of shared work linkages is purposefully connecting all of the perioperative areas. As seen in Figure 19, the Inpatient Surgery, Outpatient Surgery Center and Post Anesthesia Care all have their own Partnership Council. Although these councils connect at the Central Partnership Council for global mission and vision work, their shared accountabilities for the surgical specialty creates a need for them to also connect solely with each other in order to more effectively carry out their work. This is just one example, in some settings a similar example may be connecting product line groups.

Figure 19
Shared Work
Specialty Linkage Options

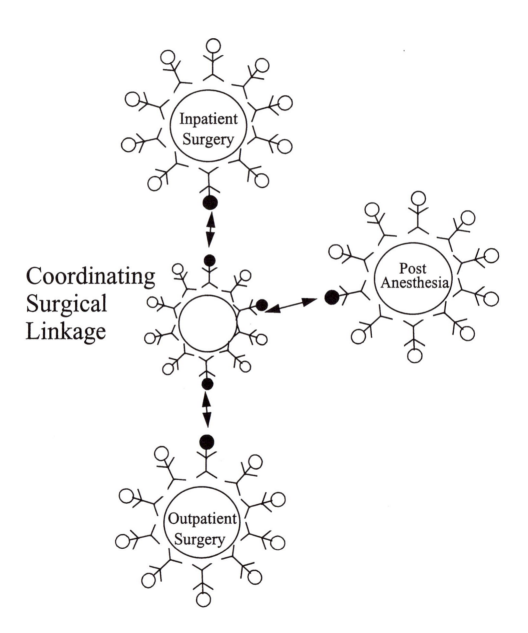

Coordinating
Surgical
Linkage

Figure 20
Partnership Council Core Linkages

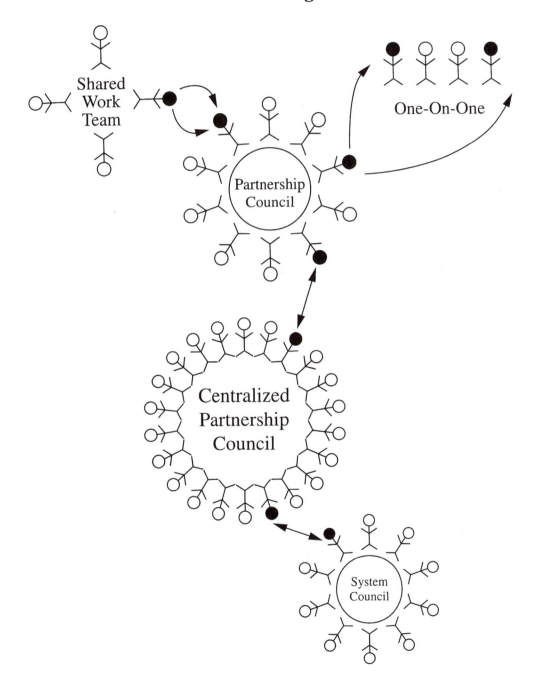

What are ways to create systems linkages for networking and continuous learning?

A major paradigm shift is occurring in health care systems. There is a need and call for integrated health care. For a system to provide health care from conception to death will require a diverse connected group of providers and Partnership Councils that reach beyond the walls of the present fragmented health care system.

The mission of health care has no walls, just as the people we serve are not confined by walls. Once health care providers experience the outcomes of partnership and shared leadership as listed on Table Seven, the fear of connections beyond familiar walls to the system will naturally unfold. See Figure 20 on page 195 which visualizes the movement of partnership across the health care system. Once again, this is not a hierarchical connection but one of linkage, networking, and learning.

It shows that all entities within the system have a mechanism for partnering within a systems thinking framework. Figure 21 on page 197 gives an example of possible systems connections and what a Systems Partnership Council may look like. The importance and need for system linkage is clearly illustrated in the following clinical scenario.

Wisdom From The Field

Sue was the primary caregiver for Kris who came to the community OB clinic in her third month of pregnancy. Kris had contracted HIV from her husband and had not known about the diagnosis when she became pregnant. Sue noted that Kris was an inspiration to many of the mothers in her support group. Over the last months Kris often volunteered to be with the mothers during difficult times. Sue stated Kris was a rare person who cared intensely and spent no time blaming anyone for her circumstances Her great concern was for her child, as well as the other mothers and their unborn children.

Kris went into labor at the beginning of her eigth month. She delivered at a local hospital. Following the hospitalization she returned to the clinic

Figure 21
System Council

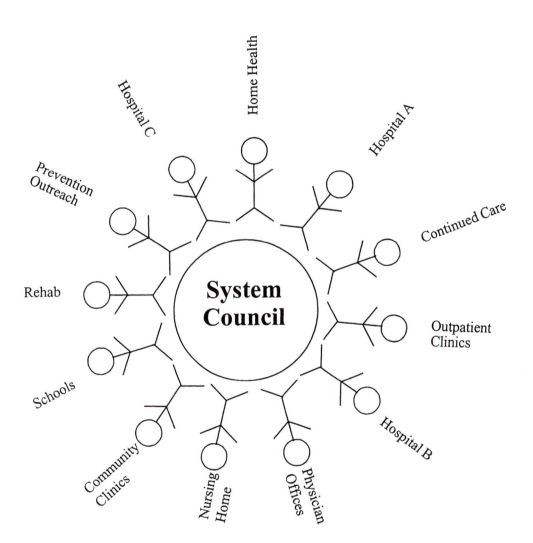

very upset with the care she received. She shared with Susan how rude and disrespectful the staff were. Kris felt like she was "on trial and being judged." Sue's immediate reaction to Kris's story was great anger towards her peers at the hospital. She wondered how they could treat this gentle, loving person so disrespectfully. "What have we become?" she wondered.

Sue thought if they had known Kris's story, known her as the special person that she was, it would have been different. She pondered what to do. She realized that all the people in the clinic were at risk like Kris. What was her responsibility? She remembered what she had learned from Kris. It would do no good to blame those at the hospital. Then it dawned on her that she needed to link with the caregivers at the hospital. She needed to share and be the connection. She knew Kris's story, they didn't. It was the beginning of partnership across settings.

So often we hear that we cannot give the kind of personal or individualized care because there just isn't enough time. Most healthcare settings are very busy. In Kris's case one setting knew her story and yet when she went to another setting no one knew her story. It seems logical that if we form partnerships across settings we will create a way for the story to be passed on. It will save time, stop duplication and repetition and obviously improve the quality of care.

What are outcomes of systems thinking connections?

The concept of shared work beyond walls becomes increasingly valued as the rewards are experienced. Interdependence becomes the norm. Connecting diverse perspectives helps to see the big picture. No one individual or group can see 100% of the big picture from their vantage point. Individuals and groups represent their own experience and perspective no matter how broad or narrow that may be. Paula Underwood (1997) states, "When walking through the trees on a path--always look at the trees around you and where you are. Don't just look at the path, if you do you'll get in a rut." Being linked helps us to always see the forest and the trees so that we become accustomed to the experience of seeing the big picture of the landscape and the world around it.

Outcomes based upon a foundation of shared values/beliefs and a system which addresses identified leverage points will be different than outcomes based upon old patterns of thinking and behaving. When each professional knows their accountabilities, establishes mutuality to determine desired outcomes, and integrates services with all members of the health care team across the lifeline, quality emerges. This begins with providers having personal clarity and commitment to partner in order to stop repetition, duplication, and fragmentation between providers and within systems. Energy can then be focused on assuring that services rendered are appropriate for the individual and match the individual's health need. The desired outcomes are based upon the merging of the provider and consumer's perspective.

The desire for expanded linkage is directly proportionate to the existing council's ability to form partnership, experience the outcomes, and have the courage to step across unfamiliar boundaries. Once positive outcomes are experienced, the members have the courage to step across another unfamiliar boundary and then another... on their continuous learning journey. It is hard to believe in the initial phase of partnership development that the desire to reach out to unknown peers will happen. Wheatley and Kellner (1996, p. 52) speak to the outcome of this transition, "We seek out one another. Separate beings unite to create more complex beings. The separateness we thought we were creating melts into the unending dance of co-adaptation and change as we become ever more aware of those from whom we cannot be separate."

The systems thinking structure is only as strong as the individuals who create the linkages. The work needed for personal and professional transition are part of the every day continuous learning that must go on to initiate and sustain a healthy work culture. Chapter Eight provides insights into the tools and resources as well as the approaches that facilitate the continuous learning necessary for success.

Chapter Eight

Continuous Learning:
What helps people grow in partnership?

*"Learning sleeps and snores in libraries, but wisdom
is everywhere, wide awake on tiptoe."*
- Josh Billings

In many work places there is neither time or space to even consider what our learning has been and how it will impact our future. Often this is because the idea of continuous learning is not fully understood as a way of life. There must be a commitment and systems in place to support continuous learning if creativity and innovation are to emerge. In this chapter the essence of continuous learning and system support will be addressed in theory and through practical applications. This chapter will offer direction on how to begin and sustain the work of connecting continuous learning with the concepts of Partnership Councils.

Partnership Councils provide an ongoing space to tap into the wisdom that is in every work place and in the souls of everyone who works there. This wisdom is generated from cycles of continuous learning. *Continuous learning is the ability to experience each moment as a learner and teacher for the ongoing growth of self and others.* This kind of learning can be considered the very reason that Partnership Councils exist and even the reason that we as human beings exist. To live is to learn. Learning is about living and evolving, not just being alive. As human beings desiring to live our full potential, experiencing each moment is not enough, we must have a willingness to be changed by each moment. In a healthy work place, continuous learning is not focused on knowing but rather this kind of discovery.

What is the nature of learning in councils?

Partnership Councils provide a framework for building the capacity of individuals and organizations. Developing the skills required for partnership is a continuous process. The partnership principle of potential acknowledges the inherent capacity of each person to continuously learn, grow, and create. The ongoing journey of becoming "all that we can be" requires understanding the self. This means a clear picture of who we are, what we believe, and who we want to be.

A positive attitude, goals, and resolutions are not enough to change our behavior patterns and habits. Stephen Covey (1994) notes that we are not our habits and do not need to be victims of our conditioning. To replace old ways we need to understand ourselves. He recommends that we assess ourselves, our principles, areas for growth/change, make a commitment, get feedback and establish a process for follow-through. Partnership Councils provide the space for this process to take place, both individually and collectively. The members work with their peers to set expectations and new ways to think and be together. As familiar barriers arise we have discovered that embracing continuous learning behaviors offsets them as shown in Table Twenty Six.

What are examples of living continuous learning in the work place?

In researching what made progressive companies such as Intel, Khow, and Scandinavian AFS able to thrive while others couldn't even survive, authors Ghoshal and Bartlett (1997) uncovered patterns. The patterns all led to the development of their theory which hinges on the strong belief that it is individuals that make the difference, hence the title of their book, *The Individualized Organization*. In addition to developing a relationship of mutual faith between individual and company, another cornerstone of these companies was their expansive view of continuous learning.

These companies see continuous learning as an end in itself. It is beyond a commitment to support individual development; *it is the decision to foster the outcome of collective learning*. Within the major corporations

TABLE TWENTY SIX

Barriers	Continuous Learning Behaviors that Counteract Barriers
Competition	Everyone is a teacher and a learner. We are unique individuals with unique strengths and talents which we should celebrate. It is very limiting to always uphold our contributions as better than others. Many perspectives are needed to foster innovation.
Judgment	Seeking to understand others in their wholeness rather than judging them opens up new possibilities of thinking and being.
Fear	Fear can either paralyze or propel our actions. It is our choice to welcome fear as a friend that catches our attention as long as we then question, "What is the fear here to teach us?" Through understanding we as individuals and groups can recognize fear as energy, new direction and action.
Blame	There is an attitude of learning from our mistakes rather than finding someone to blame. We must always ask ourselves, "In what way have I contributed to this situation and what have I learned?"
Entitlement	Our greatest rewards come when they are not expected. As individuals we produce our own reward and recognition from within and show our gratitude to others because that is how we want to be as people. Giving with no expectation of receiving can free us from the bonds of entitlement.
Rescue	When there is shared meaning for continuous learning, it is understood that everyone is responsible for their own learning. Each circumstance is happening in order to teach us something. If we rescue others from this learning we are inhibiting them, not helping them to grow.

that are able to transition with change, the managers and executives have a focus of being a teacher and learner. This meant much more than an occasional seminar or ad hoc training. One company, KHOW, wanted to shift from hierarchy and islands of individual expertise, to developing a structure that linked people horizontally for learning and generation of wisdom. This same effect is created through the Partnership Council framework.

The experiences of these companies also address the assumption that you can't teach old dogs new tricks. The people that engaged in continuous learning were able to embrace change and transform themselves as the company and world changed. In other words, how long a person worked at the company was not an indication of whether that person could drastically change their leadership or learning style. This reiterates for us that we should not prejudge a person's ability to change with the times. *All human beings have the potential to change if they choose.* The following Wisdom From The Field offers a personal experience of changing oneself within a continuous learning mindset.

Wisdom From The Field

A Partnership Council had been in existence for nearly four years and had truly embraced the concept of continuous learning. The staff, manager, and educator had evaluated how they carried out many aspects of their current jobs in order to align them with the principles of partnership. Each of them asked, "How would my relationships need to change if I lived the principles of partnership? Each person on this council had made personal changes and they had grown together as a leadership group. They assumed accountability for helping each other live the principles of partnership. This meant their conversations were built on caring for each other and valuing each individual's continuous growth.

This had been particularly hard for the manager who had learned to be successful in her role by being the one to direct and control the work of the department. Though she knew the work of partnership would be difficult she realized it was the right thing to do. In working with the staff, she believed the principles of partnership in her heart but found it easy to be distracted from living them in the midst of day-to-day issues. She shared this vulnerability with the Partnership Council members and they agreed to help her as well as admit that they faced the same situation themselves. All members needed help from each other.

During one meeting, the manager was to propose the implementation of a hospital wide project to the other council members. It was the implementation of a combined role of direct care assistant and housekeeper called Patient Support Associate (PSA). The manager felt fear and uneasiness as she pondered how to present this issue to the group. She had been told by an executive that this project was not an option, it must be implemented house wide. The executive told her that her credibility rested with the ability to sell this project to her department. The manager acted out of fear, rationalizing to herself, "This is a smart group, they'll see the benefit, accept it and never know it was mandated "

Half way through the meeting the council members were airing their concerns with the project being implemented in a large intensive care unit. They realized the manager was back pedaling and a caring council member raised the question, "Has the decision to implement this in our unit already been made?" The manager answered, "yes" and went on to explain her fear of being honest with the group. The member who spoke up said, "This does not fit with our agreement to partnership." The manager admitted her mistake and stated that she had learned a valuable lesson; she would not be afraid of the groups reaction in the future. The other council members reassured the manager that they considered this experience one of learning and were not going to judge her. Many council members came up to her after the meeting and patted her back. They said things like; "It's O.K., we are all learning together, this is a great sign of progress for our council because we see each other as human beings capable of mistakes but willing to help each other," and "I appreciate you showing your vulnerability and being honest, we could see your good intentions."

This situation would have been disastrous in a culture that did not embrace continuous learning. It certainly would not have been considered a positive outcome since the group had been working on partnership for four years and this kind of thing was still happening. Our patterns of thinking help us make meaning and bring context to our experiences. This example shows the potential for thinking to be productive or destructive.

What patterns of thinking promote continuous learning?

Continuous learning is inhibited in task dominated and hierarchical cultures. Partnership Councils create the space to *shift* these long-lived patterns of thinking, relating, and practice. Goethe said, "Treat a man as he is and he will remain as he is. Treat a man as he can and should be and he will become as he can and should be." Though we realize that continuous learning is greater when an individual chooses to be on a path of personal transformation, there are implications for cultivating an environment that invites growth. The health of individuals in the work place is potentiated when a work place is designed to evoke full expression of his/her potential through continuous learning. Shifting from the current ways of being together requires opportunities to learn new skills and new insights. Everyone will need to continually change. What are the shifts in thinking and relating that promote continuous learning?

TABLE TWENTY SEVEN	
Shifts And Thinking That Promote Continuous Learning	
Current Thinking ⟶	**New Thinking**
Knowing	Learning
Doing Things Right	Doing the Right Thing
Certainty	Questioning
Defending	Explaining
Power Over	Power Releasing
Judging	Searching
Limitations	Expanding
Opinions	Truths
Sameness	Diversity
Predictable	Surprise
Mechanistic	Dynamic Connectedness
Analyze	Explore
Patterned	Creative

Celebration of changes in thinking, practice, and relating is a key reinforcement for continuous learning. Acknowledging lessons learned from mistakes recognizes that growth emerges from all situations, the negative as well as the positive. Is there such a thing as a *mistake* in a continuous learning environment? Many would say no and even go on to admit that they have learned their most valuable lessons in their so-called "mistakes."

We must recognize continuous learning in the day-to-day experiences, realities, and relationships with others. It is an inherent component of a part-nering relationship. Synergistically, partnership is the ultimate strategy to support continuous learning in an organization. A relationship is not an activ-ity. It is a process of self-revelation. It helps one be clear about what he/she personally values. It frees one to explore and connect. It releases us from the fear of the unknown and welcomes learning and growth. The following poem captures the essence of continuous learning.

Learning To Live In The Gap

The Gap is where
We now live and breathe
A place between
Current and desired reality.

We've tried to live
In this gap so wide
trying to predict, measure,
and sometimes hide.

When will we get there
arrive at the end?
How will we prove it,
our dreams to defend?

It's not about achieving
An end in sight
for as soon as we reach it
we see a new field of flight.

It is about being.. .living
on this eternal continuum
learning and growing
For now and to come.

- *Laurie Shiparski*

Used with permission: © Shiparski, L. (1997).
Change Is life. Poems Of Personal Transformation In The Work Place. Michigan: Practice Field Publishing.

By now the concept of continuous learning as a way of life should be more clear. Some understanding will take place just reading about learning in Partnership Councils, but actually doing the work of councils offers far greater learning and growth. Thus far there have been discussions around personal, council, and cultural growth toward healthy work places. Throughout this book strategies to accomplish this learning and growth have been suggested and there are even more to come. You may be thinking, this all sounds great but where can one begin in applying the concepts presented in this book? Some strategies can be implemented on a personal level and others require a carefully thought out plan to implement in a work setting. Over the years, there has been much learning by those who have embarked on this journey.

What would a plan for initiating and sustaining Partnership Councils look like?

The foundational work of initiating Partnership Councils is the same work needed to sustain them. It is work addressing ongoing relationship building and practice improvement. The following processes and strategies are system supports to achieve our vision of having the best place to work and the best place for people to come for health care services. If there is no support for this foundational work, there will be much time and money wasted on addressing the symptoms of much deeper unrevealed problems. Ironically, what some might call the "fluff work" is actually the relationship work that makes healthy, productive work places a reality.

We will begin with a strategic plan to use as a guideline for initiating Partnership Councils. This generic initiation plan is always modified in an organization to meet circumstances and address unique needs. Ongoing efforts to plan, track and communicate progress are critical no matter if you are initiating or sustaining a council. Before beginning, a few words of caution around using such a plan should be considered.

It is imperative that the principles be upheld in the process. This is more difficult than it may appear because our tendency is always to implement in the familiar ways we have done with other projects or programs. This is not just another program--it is installing ongoing structures and processes for continuous learning via partnership and shared practice. The processes offered in this plan are intended to be experienced differently than the way we've always done things. In fact, conducting the processes often reveals issues and patterns that have long been buried in a culture. This uncovering of real issues should be celebrated as progress even though they may cause a chaotic feeling at first.

Another caution lies in sticking to the plan to a fault. This commonly happened in hierarchical cultures. When we get so fixated on adhering to a plan, we are blind to the emerging wisdom of the moment that actually moves us toward our desired outcomes. There must be a respect for both pre-planning and changing midstream. One or the other alone will slow or block progress. Sometimes councils have gotten so entangled in their well-meaning plans that they have stifled creativity and perpetuated environments of "doing to death." The concepts of patience and persistence are invaluable assets in this kind of "people work."

Finally, initiating Partnership Council concepts offers a way to reinforce and advance work in progress at a setting, as well as to introduce new ways of strengthening practice and relationships. This is an evolving, living journey, and all learning experienced to this point is valuable. Some of the ideas in the plan may not be new information but validations of what we have all believed to be the right things to do and ways to do them. This is indicative of the common ground we all share. It may even be the reason you have chosen to read this book. We are connected in our efforts to create healthy work places through Partnership Councils. At this time, it will be helpful to review the following strategic plan.

TABLE TWENTY EIGHT
Plan For Initiating and Sustaining Partnership Councils

Phase I. Establish Support For Proposed Transition

A. Introduction to Partnership Council framework given by person or group to identify key stakeholders. Include ways in which Partnership Councils support the work in progress and vision of organization including purpose, structure and desired outcomes.

B. Total administrative support including executives and board members.

C. Identify global coordinators) of Partnership Council work.

D. Identify global interdisciplinary work team to guide progress.

E. Identify stakeholders.
   - Physicians
   - Professional Disciplines: Nursing, PT/OT, Respiratory, Lab, Radiology, Pharmacy, Speech, Dieticians, Social Worker
   - Case Managers/Utilization Review
   - Medical Records/Health Information
   - Pastoral Care
   - Support Services: Engineering, Housekeeping, Admitting, Business Office, Finance, Computerization
   - Consumers
   - Executives, Directors, Manager, Clinical Coordinators
   - Education Resources
   - Research Resources
   - Academic Settings in Community
   - Home Care, Extended Care, Clinics, Physician Office and all affiliate sites
   - Leaders of major organizational initiatives, e.g. service line, managed care

Phase II. Establish Common Foundation

A. *Conduct overview of Partnership Councils for all participants and stakeholders. Offer alternative ways for those unable to attend, e.g. videos, books and tapes, 1:1 conversation.

B. *Assess current organizational status in the following areas: mission, vision, Core Beliefs, use of dialogue, structure and processes to

Table Twenty Eight, continued

enhance relationships and point of care practices as they relate to the implementation of councils. Identify linkage needs.

C. Use assessment to write a proposed plan for initiating councils which will be revised with global centralized council.

D. Begin to identify ways to track and communicate progress, identify and utilize current measurements as well as new ways.

E. Budget and plan for fiscal resources, local and global.

Phase III. Establish Partnership Council infrastructure for practice ownership, continuous learning and interdisciplinary collaboration and innovation.

Global:

A. Call for Partnership Council members from each department.

B. *Conduct one day Dialogue Workshop focusing on the art and skill of dialogue for council members and other stakeholders.

C. *Conduct two day Partnership Workshop: Clarifies roles and workings of a council. Prepares members for leadership and partnership.

*These workshops have been provided by skilled facilitators from the CPM Resource Center and are available upon request.

Local:

D. Unit/Department/Council/Area (First Six Months)

1. Lay the Foundation
   - In the first meeting (and all meetings to come) introduce and use "Check-In" as the beginning and close with having each person write and share their "key learning." Schedule subsequent meetings monthly, at a consistent time.
   - Discuss learning from the Partnership/Dialogue Workshop.
   - Present purpose and format of Partnership Council. Include how this will be different from other meetings.
   - Select a coordinators) if not already done.
   - Establish consistent meeting times - monthly.
   - Council should review current structure and organization of their work. Discuss needed linkages, complete shared work worksheet, go 1:1 with completed worksheet.
   - Assign and communicate 1:1 links to each member, make sure there is a process in place to assign new staff as they are hired.

<u>Table Twenty Eight, continued</u>

- Contact your 1:1 linkages on how you will connect from here on out and explain how this council system will work on your unit. Invite them to use the council by submitting issues or feedback.

2. Engage in relationship building (exercises to connect in shared purpose):
   - Sharing our stories exercise.
   - Mission, vision. Core Belief discussion.

3. Lead proactive planning, include ways to track and communicate progress.
   - Schedule a four hour goal setting or celebration session for all council members to develop unit/department goals or revisit the goals already developed to assess for the integration of new ideas around partnership and practice. This will help provide a foundation for developing future agendas. This plan should represent a syntheses for organizational goals and vision with unit-based/department goals and vision. Revisit, re-evaluate in future meetings.
   - Communicate progress and learning, seek feedback and collect ideas from 1:1 linkages.
   - Keep running tally of council ideas addressed and outcomes; this can be done through minutes.

Global:
E. Establish global council.
   1. Includes all PC Coordinators
   2. Operations resource representation
   3. Practice-learning representation
   4. Research/QI representation
   5. Assess other necessary linkages and stakeholders to assure systems thinking connections.
F. Determine long term New Council Member Workshop (one day) for those joining throughout the year. (Table Thirty Nine in Appendix A.)
G. Revise organization orientation to include Partnership Council information.
H. Use this infrastructure! Teach others in the organization to use it.
I. Track and communicate progress.

Table Twenty Eight, continued

Phase IV. Clarity on the Essence of Professional Practice
A. *Schedule one day for centralized council and identified stakeholders to learn about an interdisciplinary professional practice framework.
B. *Each discipline to clarify their scope of practice.
C. *Evaluate whether clinical documentation system supports professional practice - philosophically and practically.
D. Use global Centralized Partnership Councils (CPC) and local Partnership Councils (PC) to address practice issues that arise.

*Workshop and/or more information available through the CPM Resource Center.

Phase V. Ongoing Focus, Support, and Progress

Global & Local:
A. Communicate outcomes and progress.
B. Continue to assess progress, vision future, support people in the work, and continue the learning/growth cycle.

After reviewing the initiation plan for Partnership Councils you may be thinking that it looks like a lot of work! It is, but it will be the most rewarding work you have ever done. Usually, in today's organizations, there are many initiatives occurring at one time which create confusion as to how they all connect or support the mission and vision. This is not a plan or program to fix a problem. It is a commitment that must be made to ongoing learning and growth. By design, the plan includes a continuing cycle of: 1) assessing current status and planning, 2) identifying interventions and taking action, and 3) recognizing and communicating outcomes and progress. All of these phases offer learning imperative for directing us now and in the future. Remember, this book provides the detailed information needed for this plan to be carried out as we now discuss some of the processes used in each phase.

Phase I: Establishing support for the transition to Partnership Councils.

Many of the ideas presented in this book can be implemented by individuals in any work setting or life situation. This phase focuses on sharing information about Partnership Councils and healthy work cultures so that a shift of even greater magnitude can occur. One or two people can change a work environment to an extent; however, a mass of people can shift the environment even more quickly and effectively.

Engaging a critical mass of people in this vision can also reduce the risk of individuals losing enthusiasm, persistence, or even burn out. The history of Partnership Councils began with masses of direct care givers but has wisely expanded to include all tracks. This is why the key stakeholders must be identified and invited to participate early on in the process. The approach of invitation is key here. An empowering process such as Partnership Councils is less effective when mandated.

It has been our experience that it only takes few people to ignite the interest of others. As the wave of interest travels across the organization, partnership potential emerges that far exceeds what was originally imagined. Invite many to the initial introductory sessions and you will be amazed at the interest and positive response. As for those key stakeholders who are not interested, keep inviting them throughout the process, but do not let a few voices stand in the way of what is being called for by the many voices.

In organizations currently utilizing Partnership Councils there is a person designated as the **Global Practice Partnership Coordinator** (called CPM Coordinator in some settings). This person is a resource, integrator, and liaison with multiple disciplines and groups within a health system. They are key communicators and facilitators of practice and relationship enhancements. This role may also be shared by two people. Typically, one of these people is a Masters prepared Registered Nurse because of the broad scope of practice that nursing assumes in patient care. The other person is a colleague from another discipline.

Those in this role are experienced in large scale organizational change, building partnerships, and cultivating the leadership in others as well a themselves. Foremost, they have a vision and passion for actualizing a healthy work place through continuous learning. They can be people already in the organization or can be recruited from the outside and they usually have other job responsibilities like system integration, quality improvement, or education.

Together, the Global Coordinators mobilize others such as the interdisciplinary coordination team to weave the concepts of Partnership Councils into everything in the organization. They are always positioned at a system-wide place so they can support this work at a global level. A risk presents in that Partnership Councils can be perceived as only the Coordinator(s) project. It must be continually clarified that they are a resource and leader but are not the only ones responsible for doing the work required. This is shared work by everyone. The CPM Resource Center connects these Global Practice Partnership Coordinators across the continient to further enhance the work and nature of learning.

Phase II. Establishing A Common Foundation
Councils have used an atypical mission and vision process to build a field of shared meaning.

Shared mission and vision are the compass for us to use during our planning, decision making, and actions. <u>Mission</u> focuses on what is meaningful, what is the purpose of the work. The purpose gives us the courage to act or live the mission. The <u>vision</u> refers to what it would look like if we lived our mission, our purpose fully. Margaret Wheatley offers a definition for vision in her video, *Leadership and The New Science* (1993). She describes vision as an invisible field surrounding us, a field that we can detect as we enter the organization or place. This is very different than the view of vision as something we are constantly drawn toward, yet never really attain.

The process of creating shared mission and vision is a partnering activity and a practice field for inquiry and advocacy. Expression of soul is honored in this way. Tables Twenty Nine through Thirty One in Appendix A are worksheets that can be used for personal and shared mission and vision development.

These worksheets have been developed by those who have done mission and vision work in their councils and in their work places. A personal mission statement worksheet is one tool used to facilitate personal mission development. The development of shared vision and mission will build upon individual work to create collective vision. A newly developing council will prioritize this work to occur early in their development process and an established council will review their shared vision and mission on a yearly basis to determine where they are in their journey, changes to make in their course, and what they should celebrate. This review often occurs at the yearly goal setting session which is discussed later in this chapter.

In many organizations there are people who have temporarily lost sight of their mission as well as how they fit with the organizational mission. They are often the apathetic, seen as negative, withdrawn or bored people who come to punch in and punch out. In these situations no amount of education or corrective action will really change them. For this to be an effective process each person has to come to terms with it in their own time. The choice sits within each person and the Partnership Council offers an invitation and opportunity to uncover their dormant passion through connecting and exploring purpose with them. Even when there are people who seem to live their passion in work and life, mission and vision work offers a collective energy for them to tap and grow even more. The following verse offers reflection on the initiation of this important work.

Wherever You Are--Is Where You Should Be!

Stop looking around
stop looking ahead
The answer sits in the moment.
Wherever you are
Whatever is happening
Is exactly where you should be.

Don't be concerned
about finding your purpose
You carry it where you go
It sits in your heart
It is always right there
Just waiting to be connected to the moment.

- Bonnie Wesorick

It is most important to do this foundational work of mission and vision. For Partnership Councils it has been successful to begin first with having each member create a personal mission statement and then engaging the whole group in mission and vision development. Sometimes people have not realized the value of personal mission work until they see what it does for others. This has led to people developing an interest in doing their personal mission after experiencing a good process in a group creating shared mission. The process is a powerful way to build relationships, produce positive energy, and synchronize efforts. It breaks the usual routines and patterns and begins a new way to be together.

A personal mission statement worksheet (see Appendix A) is one tool used to facilitate personal mission development. Once a person has done their work, it is key to ask if your personal mission is synchronized with the organizations. If the answer is yes, then an individual has solid awareness of this and can move forward more effectively. If the answer is no, the individual must identify their choices and act on the best ones. If an individual remains working in an organization which is out of synch with their personal mission, the personal toll can be high. It is an unhealthy situation that can harm not only that individual but also every person in the work place.

Often the words "mission" and "vision" make us think of a top down activity in an organization. The processes shared thus far have been developed and used by thousands of people to break traditional thinking about these processes. The words are the same but these processes facilitate individuals from all levels coming together to have conversation about their personal purpose or mission, their department mission, and the organization's mission. They assess synchrony between these missions and are encouraged to dream a future. They may end up with written mission and vision statements but the true outcome is the shared mission and vision that is developed through having the conversation itself.

Some interesting cultural issues have surfaced during this process. In some settings managers have become anxious having staff create the vision, because they think people will come up with things that are inappropriate or unattainable. This fear is more harmful than letting people speak from their hearts as to what matters most for them and their work. This is merely a symptom of hierarchy and control.

In other settings people may feel uncomfortable or resent the time set aside because they are not used to discussing purpose, they usually meet to solve problems. The most common response after having conversations around mission and vision is "We have never talked about this before and I think that's why I felt isolated. Now I feel connected, synchronized with those I work with." The following Wisdom From The Field is one person's experience with this process.

Wisdom From The Field

In a home health setting where an organizational mission and vision had existed for over 100 years, people were excited about having a discussion around their collective mission and vision. There was great passion already around mission to serve the community. There was desire to continue finding ways to personally live the mission from whatever role a person held. As I worked with one group, the Finance Department, it became clear that some of them had given the mission a lot of thought, and some, very little. As the mangers, educators, and staff began to discuss and dialogue about their desired mission and vision, it was apparent that the end result of words on a paper did not reflect the full value of such conversation.

A staff member led the discussion and was honest enough to reveal her discomfort since the managers usually led the meetings. Throughout this process hierarchical ways were being identified and changed. As the discussion ensued some people felt that their role was merely to work at a computer or answer a phone inquiry about a bill. Others embraced the mission and vision but were frustrated with the inability to live it.

Finally a man who had been quiet, spoke up. "I know I don't deliver clinical care, but I think my contribution to the clients experience is critical to improving their health." "Every time I am on the phone with a client

I know I can either add to their burden or reduce their anxiety just by the way I show I care." "I also know that those numbers I crunch day in and day out can make or break a community support project." "My work is much bigger than just me. I know I am making a difference in peoples' lives." After his words there was a silence. Someone spoke saying she had never really thought about it in that way before. She realized that clients could probably tell how we viewed our jobs just by how we conversed with them. Another person remarked on how we all used some of the same words but that we each had our own unique meaning for them.

They went on to write a mission and vision statement for their Finance Department which they planned on sharing with the other departments in an upcoming Partnership Council. Their mission statement looked like this: "Our mission as the Business/Finance Office is to serve the patients and their families, as well as support co-workers and others, so to have a positive impact on the quality of life." Their vision was a list that included things like "educating others on financial information, maintaining understanding and developing empathy for the patients and families as well as ourselves and co-workers, seeking accuracy in data, being accountable, and learning more about other departments."

At the partnership workshop when all of the departments presented their mission and vision statements everyone got a sense of their uniqueness but more importantly they realized their oneness. Using different words or representing a different aspect of the business came together like the pieces of a beautiful puzzle. To hear the words from each other was important as they shared their written words and the learnings from participating in the process itself.

What are the outcomes of this process? The following words reflect key learnings experienced by those who have engaged in this process of shared mission and vision development.

Key Learning From Participants In A Shared Mission-Vision Process:
"I was struck by the honesty of my colleagues."

"It is refreshing to focus on patients."

"I was surprised by the controversy; it felt difficult but necessary."

"Discussion started as a chaos of words; by the end I felt like I knew each person a lot better."

"It feels like an invitation to have more conversations like this--before now we have never talked about our purpose here."

"I realized that our words often get in the way of our relationships and collective work."

"This is a unifying process, I could feel our excitement grow."

"On paper mission and vision was not alive. It comes alive in discussions and then in action."

"At first I complained that this seemed to be another task or useless exercise; after experiencing it I realize that it is the process not the paper that connects us."

"I always thought our department was unique and different; now I realize the common threads we share with many other areas."

"I felt very alone in my work and did not believe anyone else cared; after hearing others I know I am not alone."

"I was surprised at how difficult this was for our department; I thought we had arrived as a cohesive group but found that discussions about our purpose were different."

"It was refreshing to validate our common ground."

"This was not a discussion we normally had; it was very difficult to put our beliefs into words."

"Ideas emerged in our group that could not have individually."

"As we became clear collectively we realized that together we could find the time and resources to do what mattered most to patients and ourselves."

"I noticed walls coming down."

"Learning what each other believes helps me become more clear individually"

In these discussions the question that usually arises is, "This all sounds great, but how can we ever hope to live it?" Once connected on common mission and collective vision everyone's efforts are about closing the gap between current and desired reality. It provides a sense of direction for the Partnership Council. *The process connects the council and the paper reminds them to revisit their conversations of meaning.* Laurie Beth Jones, in her book. *The Path: Creating Your Mission Statement For Work And For Life* (1996), offers the following insight: "If your mission holds no personal passion, it is not your path. Once we set our feet on a path, we will be corrected and guided as long as our hearts stay focused."

Using dialogue in Phase II to break the old patterns in meetings and interactions.

Dialogue has been discussed throughout this book as a foundation for relationships and meaningful conversations. In the plan, methods are found to teach and learn about dialogue. A <u>Dialogue Workshop</u> with interactive exercises to practice the principles of dialogue around current circumstances offers an introduction. <u>Practice dialogue sessions</u> can be set up by posting a time and place open to all interested people. These have been held in various settings such as outside in a park or in a conference room. Topics can be predetermined or decided by the group at the session. The format for dialogue was introduced previously on pages 166-167 in Chapter Six.

Each <u>Partnership Council meeting</u> should offer time for dialogue. There are simple, but effective ways to consistently bring dialogue to council meetings. Using a "check-in" at the beginning of council meetings establishes a good practice field to hear each voice and invite each member to share their whole being. It also provides a transition from the busyness of the day and helps one be totally present in the meeting. Councils that use check-in routinely have found that as they understand where the individuals stand, they are less judgmental and more accepting of individuality and diversity.

It is essential to plan time for dialogue into the agenda especially with topics that are complicated or filled with passion. End each meeting with Key Learning. Remember continuous learning means we take notice of our learning along the way. If each member writes and verbally shares their key learning from the meeting, another level of learning is revealed. These learnings are often typed up, included in minutes, and redistributed for others to read. The following Wisdom From The Field is an example of how a council began the process to use dialogue.

Wisdom From The Field

Our goal setting session for our Partnership Council was scheduled. The co-Chairs valued the use of dialogue and wanted to expose the council to the continuous learning that dialogue brings. The concerns regarding the need to be cost effective and accountable for the time together weighed heavily. Would the inexperience of dialogue within the group alter the outcomes? Would our goals for the year be clear enough that plans could be implemented?

We decided that careful preparation was necessary to make the experience successful. How do we set the tone? What information will the participants need to be successful? We chose the theme "Planting the seeds of our future" and prepared communications focused on growth individually and collectively to all partners. We chose the video. *Law of the Harvest (Covey, 1988)*, to focus on our mission.

On the appointed day, while the co-Chairs were preparing the room, one of the members entered the room. She was clearly bothered by something. When asked, she remarked, "I hate dialogue; it just does not accomplish anything." However, she agreed to participate in the experience. Our time together began with a check-in, assisting us to acknowledge where we were at the present time and allowing us to let go and be fully present.

We shared information on capitated care and the merger that would affect our next year. Dialogue principles and guidelines were explained to the group and ground rules were displayed for reminders. Emphasis was placed on the importance of listening for the deeper truths and inquiry into what was behind the thinking. Allowing silence and being comfortable with it was also reinforced.

We started with a paraphrase of a Ghandi quote, "I must become the change I wish to see on our unit." It was very silent for what seemed to be minutes, but slowly members spoke. The atmosphere changed from slightly tense to intense listening and respect. Truths came and deeper wisdom emerged.

When we finished, we focused on our key learnings individually first, then shared with the group. One of the key learnings evident was that we had reached the truth of the matter in a way never before accomplished. Our key learnings were clear and our goals flowed from them. Participants were fully invested in them because they came from the deeper truths they had shared. There was a peace with the knowledge that what had taken place was the emergence of collective wisdom.

The member that started with negative feelings about dialogue previous to this session shared how the session had changed her feeling about dialogue and was thrilled with the wisdom that had emerged. The group felt that this format was one which would assist us in future plans and reaching goals set forth in this day. The group later shared the excitement of the session with the peers they represented.

The skills of dialogue are foreign in our typical day-to-day work patterns and gatherings. It requires a conscious intention to successfully integrate them during our time together. The use of dialogue changes the whole manner and outcomes of our work together as experienced by this council. The skills are not only important during the times the council meets, but are fundamental to establishing strong One-on-One connections. Initiating partnership and meaningful conversation through One-on-One has been described previously and is mentioned here as a reminder that the One-on-One connection is a time to enhance meaningful conversation. It is a time to practice listening, expand thinking, see through another's eyes, learn to celebrate the uniqueness and diversity of peers. It is a time to have learning conversation, and grow shared meaning as well as develop healthy relationships. It is a process which celebrates the outcomes of meaningful conversation.

Phase III: Establishing Council Infrastructure

The information in Chapter Three addresses the fundamental structure for initiating a Partnership Council. Assuring the infrastructure enhances practice ownership, continuous learning and interdisciplinary collaboration and innovation requires resources. There is a need for local and global resources, especially those that relate to relationship building.

Continuous learning resources for meaningful conversation and relationships are essential during the transition to partnering relationships. There are many different supports and processes that help the shift. One example is the process of "telling stories." In her writing on reinventing relationships, Charlotte Roberts states, "Two leverage points for dissolving barriers to collaboration are promoting intimacy and shared authority." Intimacy is referred to as the act of opening yourself to others by sharing your true feelings. (Senge, Roberts, 1994, p. 70). The concept of shared authority relates to shared ownership and accountability. Both of these are components of developing partnership.

Telling our stories is an interactive exercise to practice sharing about ourselves and milestones in our life. This intentional act of intimacy and disclosure can be a powerful partnership building activity which is also a practice field for meaningful conversation. In addition, the experience is a tool for self-introspection and reflection about one's health, BodyMindSpirit. Table Thirty Three in Appendix A provides an overview of this exercise.

Stories precipitate a call for different types of resources to support transition.

One of the greatest lessons of partnership (and the cecropia moth story) is that each person needs to do their own personal work. Learning a person's story does not mean the listener needs to "fix" the uncomfortable, unexpected or challenging situations that every person experiences as a part of living. Within our past cultures we often had readily available resources to help learn new task skills or practice issues, but few to help with individual work related to personal and professional relationships.

We recognized the need for self reflection and created tools to help each person carry out the process. Personal reflection time has been helpful for individuals to get in touch with their beliefs and behaviors. The reflection tools provide a self-directed activity to guide the learning process. They help each person identify where they are and to develop their own learning goals and plans accordingly. Individuals and groups have gained great insight from using these tools and meaningful conversations have been stimulated. Some of the tools used include:

- Beliefs that support an empowering or "power releasing process" (Table Thirty Four in Appendix A). It addresses personhood, interrelationship, process issues, and beliefs that we as providers may have about ourselves.

- Self-reflection of leadership behavior (Table Thirty Five in Appendix A). It looks at personal understanding, values, beliefs, and behaviors that relate to personal leadership skills.

- There are also worksheets that address council member accountabilities and expectations (Table Thirty Six in Appendix A) and council success factors (Table Thirty Seven in Appendix A).

The reflection tools help people to bring their knowledge, thoughts, expertise to a conscious level. They are not a test or a negative reinforcement but rather are a learning tool which reinforces current knowledge and does not seek to find out what someone does not know for evaluation purposes. Principle centered support recognizes that individuals are all at different levels, will grow at their own pace, and cannot be compared with each other. The tools facilitate introspection about personal beliefs, values, attitudes, and practice.

The challenges come from the uncovering of self-information. The words of Rabbi Heschel spoke to the real support when he said, "Now we have to help you know what you see, rather than see what you know." Often in the work place resources to help each individual with their personal work or issues were scarce. This fact led to the initiation of different types of continuous learning resources in our setting such as:

- Resolve: an employee assistance program that offers availability of counselors to help with personal issues.
- Close Enough To Care: resources to help those who need earned time off for personal or family reasons. The available money comes from colleagues in the setting who donate via money or some of their earned time off to be used by those in need.

Our typical continuous learning resources in the organization supported the knowledge of their professional services but little to support their relationship with self or others. Cultures will not be healthy without both.

Continuous Learning Processes In Healthy Work Places.

Creating a healthy work culture is ongoing work. Enhancing the process of continuous learning and growth is done in different ways. Support for ongoing work is coordinated throughout the system by consciously designed activities that engage people in meaningful conversation. One example is the Core Belief Review process.

Process: Core Belief Review

We created a new learning tradition which gives us permission to deepen our conversations and come together to clarify those things we believe matter most. We call this activity The Core Belief Review Process. The Core Beliefs are listed in Table One. The following Wisdom From The Field gives further insights into the nature of a system process that supports continuous learning related to what matters most.

Wisdom From The Field

Jan was new to the Partnership Council and was struggling with her One-on-One relationships with some of her peers. She did not feel connected with them as a partner. When she mentioned her concerns at the council, Lori said that she thought the timing of the Core Belief Review Process would really help her strengthen her partnerships. The Review Process formally takes place every two year across the whole organization. Jan had only been at this setting for a year and although very familiar with the written Core Beliefs, had never experienced the review process. She was confused as to what it was about and how it could help her situation. Lori went on to explain it to her in the following way.

The Core Belief Review Process is designed to deepen our insights, our understanding of what matters most about caring for patients. The Core Beliefs on this card are the result of a process that has gone on over 20 years. The purpose is to uncover the words that capture the common underlying knowings or belief within the hearts of those providing or receiving care--words that describe what really matters about the nature of health care. These words become a visible reminder of what really matters and are used to give us direction to continuously improve our care.

Lori went on to say that every council member goes One-on-One with peers, recipients of care and community people to seek their insights into what they think is most important related to quality health care. It leads to very meaningful conversation. It is a window of opportunity for Jan to talk with her peers about what they believe. Lori noted to Jan that the nature of the conversation will give her an opportunity to connect with her peers differently. Following Lori's comments everyone was stimulated to share how the review process opened the door to better partnership with at least one of their peers. Each example that was shared gave Jan helpful suggestions as to how to lead into the conversation, what helped deepen it, and what type of questions and responses enhanced the communication. Many commented on how they expanded on the outcomes of the Core Belief Review Process over time with their colleagues.

The Review Process takes place over at least a six to 12 month period of time. It is one of the most powerful global learning activities that takes place in the organization. The outcomes far exceed the updated list of Core

Beliefs that unfold. Values clarification about the Core Beliefs related to mission is part of personal and professional transformation. What matters most for patients and the team is reflected in the Core Beliefs. The council plays an active role in the review process of the Core Beliefs by interviewing others to find out what matters most to them and asking if the Core Beliefs are congruent with their mission and values. This is a way for personal disclosure and mutual sharing.

A Core Belief worksheet has been used to stimulate personal thinking and has been used as a values clarification for individual and group learning. This worksheet (Table Thirty Eight in Appendix A) lists the Core Belief, the intended meaning, and then asks the learner to give examples of how this is practiced in daily work and relationships.

Phase IV: Clarity on the Essence of Professional, Interdisciplinary Practice.

Once councils are established, their focus and learning regarding practice issues heightens. In this phase there are global and local opportunities to examine and to progress professional, interdisciplinary practice. The plan speaks to conducting a day of learning related to developing a professional practice framework. This has typically been a workshop where specialists from the CPM Resource Center have presented the philosophy and leverage points of an integrated health care system. This includes a documentation system that focuses on giving wholistic, individualized care by an interdisciplinary team. It also centers on care providers being clear on their scope of practice.

Scope of Practice Process

Just as the Core Belief Review Process strengthens Phase III, so does the scope of practice process strengthen Phase IV. It is a continuous learning process that has system supports to bring interdisciplinary colleagues together in order to clarify scope of service and integrate those services at the point of care. The process is designed to uncover similarities and difference of practice. It leads to an integrated documentation process that prevents duplication, repetition and helps each discipline build on the other's practice. It also spans the health care continuum. This work is not covered in this book but information about the process is available from the CPM Resource Center.

Phase V. Ongoing Focus, Support and Progress

Ongoing evaluation is another name for conscious learning. Although it can be done in different ways, true evaluation calls for synchronization of processes that demonstrate outcomes, learning, celebrations, things that work, and things that do not work. This requires strong linkages within the infrastructure especially between councils, shared work teams and network linkages. The following considerations can help sustain and grow the people and the work of Partnership Councils.

Continuous learning begins in orientation. Mutual sharing regarding purpose, meaning, and vision of work begins during the interview process. The Wisdom From The Field in Chapter Four told of Carol's story about how, 15 years in practice, she discovered that there are work cultures that value and support being accountable for the work of partnerships and of the area served.

A foundation is built to stimulate personal values clarification, and understanding regarding the professional practice model in a centralized orientation. This interactive learning time addresses: Purpose and Goals, Core Beliefs, Scope of Practice, Principles of Partnership and Partnership Councils. During orientation, a designated peer from the council introduces him/herself to explain the council's role, and invite the new person to attend a council session. Some council members have given a letter to their new designated peer in order to clarify their role as a link to connect the new person with the council. See Wisdom From The Field on page 140.

What system supports are in place for *new* Partnership Council members?

The strategic plan for initiating Partnership Councils outlines essential processes and content for preparing people for their roles on councils. Equally important is developing and maintaining a system support that provides the same opportunity to learn and connect for new council members; one, five, or ten years down the road. Having new council members join the council without having the same foundational information and experience is a sure way to weaken the effectiveness (or existence) of a council. We have provided quarterly Partnership Council Workshops to prepare all new council members for their new role. This includes all newly hired managers, educators, clinical nurse specialists, etc. The diversity of the participants (from different units, shifts, departments, disciplines, roles, etc.) creates a wonderful learning experience and supports the purpose of the workshop. The purpose is to gain common understanding on the purpose and infrastructure of councils as well as clarity on the principles of partnership, dialogue, and systems thinking.

A sample content outline of this eight hour workshop is found on Table Thirty Seven in Appendix A. Also included in Appendix A are worksheets that are described below and included in the workshop syllabus:

Communication Barrier/Enhancer Tips: A tool to reflect on personal communication style and to consider as One-on-One is initiated and sustained with peers.

What Makes One-on-One Work? Collected tips from experienced council members. Facilitates great discussion about participants own experiences that everyone can learn from as well.

One-on-One Role Playing: A facilitated fishbowl technique in which volunteer participants read directly from the script and the group as a whole shares perspectives on the One-on-One discussion/dialogue.

The workshop always closes with writing and sharing key learnings from the day. This has been a successful strategy for participants to bring their personal learning to a conscious level and provides a wonderful check-out process. The wisdom that is shared reinforces the learning of others and takes learning to a different level. It is a living example of collective learning and serves as a practice field for sharing in a group setting which provides an opportunity to practice vulnerability.

If members are "recruited" to join the council and then are not supported to understand the true essence of a Partnership Council and their role as a member, the council is at risk for losing its purpose and credibility. Providing a workshop where all can come and learn together has proven to be one effective way to support the Partnership Councils and their outcomes.

What systems supports are in place for the continuous learning and development of the Council Coordinator?

The Partnership Council Coordinator's role is critical to the successful functioning and continuous learning activities of the council. Since Council Coordinators change, it creates a need for an ongoing mechanism to orient them to their role. The practitioners who serve in this role enter the role with great diversity in terms of personal strengths, talents, leadership experience and education. There was inconsistency in the resources necessary for the Coordinators to be successful in their role. Because there are consistent role expectations and accountabilities for Council Coordinators and members as discussed in Chapter Three, we found it is necessary to provide resources for their orientation and continuous learning.

A shared work team consisting of individuals from each track, including Council Coordinators and a CPM Coordinator, explored creative approaches to this challenge. They determined that the desired outcomes of this process were as follows:

- Provide a framework for consistent and comprehensive orientation/learning process for all new Coordinators.
- Enhance partnerships between Coordinators and key leaders in their work culture/setting.
- Delineate role accountabilities for the initial and on-going development of Coordinators.
- Strengthen individual councils and outcomes of councils.

- Strengthen synergistic interactions and outcomes of the Centralized Partnership Council (CPC).

The work team looked at tools and processes commonly used for orientation and continuous learning in order to determine an approach to meet the identified desired outcomes. Competency Based Orientation (CBO) was the focus since it is a framework commonly used for orientation of new staff and for new skill development in health care settings. Competency plans are based upon established performance criteria, involve learner input with self-evaluation, and are individualized to meet the learners needs. A competency plan is a learning plan and is not simply a "check off" for a list of tasks accomplished. The Competency Based Development Plan (CBD) is a tool to facilitate self directed learning. Thus, a decision was made to develop a competency based learning and development plan for council coordinators.

The CBD for the Partnership Council Coordinators is found in Table Forty Three in Appendix A. It consists of core competencies, performance criteria, learning activities and validation methods. The core competencies identified on the CBD are:
- Demonstrate professional accountabilities in the role of the Coordinator.
- Demonstrate effective leadership of council sessions and processes, and daily activities within the partnership paradigm.

Performance criteria delineates common expectations which facilitate role clarification. When looking at the CBD in Table Forty Three, please note that the learning activities are self-directed and the validation method most commonly used is self-report and/or worksheet completion. The new Coordinator evaluates which performance criteria they meet upon entry into the role and then plan activities to meet the unmet learning needs/performance criteria. This self-directed learning activity involves self-reflection and personal exploration regarding a plan for new learning as well as reaffirmation of leadership strengths necessary to develop.

Developing partnering relationships and practicing the communication skills of this interactive process are facilitated by a learning activity which involves the use of a partnership worksheet. (Table Forty Four in Appendix A.) This worksheet is designed to be used in an interactive discussion during which each person will address each question to begin to build the foundation for their partnership. The questions relate to what each individual needs from the others and what others can expect from them. This is followed by discussion regarding how they will stay connected in their work. This intentional partnering activity is part of the continuous learning practice field which nurtures communication and partnering skills that will be used on a daily basis with patients/families/members of the team and in all aspects of life.

Two new Council Coordinators made an appointment to meet together with one of the shift managers in their work area. Prior to this discussion they did not perceive that they had a partnering relationship with this individual. Using the worksheet facilitated their discussion about what can be expected from each individual and what they need from each other. After a short time they perceived "the walls coming down" and they co-designed the dynamics of their desired working relationship. Subsequently, their relationship has been congruent with their verbal discussion and all participants have acknowledged satisfaction with their relationship and with knowing what they can hold themselves and each other accountable to.

Another partnering learning activity is to meet with others from various roles and to attend the networking linkage gathering of their specific track, e.g. attend Advanced Practice with the CNS, Clinical Resource Council with the Educator, and Administrative Council with the Director/Operations Resource person. The worksheet on Table Forty Five in Appendix A shows that the purpose of this is to learn about the differences and similarities between the linkage gatherings of the various tracks and to enhance understanding of the unique roles of each person. This is fitting with the overall purpose of these gatherings which is a time for meaningful conversation and continuous learning.

There are many other learning activities available as part of the CBD which are described on the tool itself. One of the key variables in using the CBD is having a designated person to serve as a resource to the person using the tool. We designed the Director/Operations Resource to coordinate the process with the new Council Coordinator but this role could also be filled by a Practice/Learning Resource person. The support and coordination role includes:

- Provide time in the work day to complete learning activities,
- Assist the new Coordinator in scheduling learning activities,
- Assure that all learning activities are met within identified time frames,
- Seek out additional learning activities as indicted based upon individual needs of the learner,
- Track finances related to the CBD,
- Facilitate ongoing learning opportunities throughout the year.

The time spent in these activities supports partnership building and joint accountability for the operations of the council. One of the benefits of using the CBD is that it is a creative flexible tool which is meant to serve as a *guide* for the learning journey and personal transformation process. This provides the structure and consistency desired but also the flexibility to facilitate personal growth. The use and continuous evaluation of the process encourages the sharing of tips and learning activities which adds richness to the diverse methods of exploration and discovery. The CBD supports the coordinators in being continuous learning role models and mentors to their peers. It is a tangible system support and practice field for shifting thinking and behavior.

The CBD is a relatively new tool and although there are many evidences of how it has facilitated learning, it is still being evaluated in terms of its effectiveness. It is being shown is this book as one type of a tool which can be used in order to provide systems support, clarity, and a framework for consistency in terms of opportunities for growth. A risk would be to consider if a rigid tool that was not individualized for each learner.

Thus, continuous learning occurs when individuals relate to each other in their humanness, begin with their personal clarity and exploration, and then reach out to share the journey in partnership and shared accountability. Its success is evidenced by the realization that the only person they can change is themself. Learning is supported when its value is recognized and supported by the system. Learning occurs at the partnership council sessions, during One-on-One relationships with peers, and with daily activities and relationships at the point of care. Learning is supported by personal accountability and the commitment to be a learner, a teacher, and one who serves others.

Annual Celebration/Advancement Sessions

Annual Council Celebration/Advancement sessions help with Phase V which centers on strengthening focus, support and progress toward healthy work places. These sessions (previously called goal setting sessions) are a time when council members reflect on the previous year's progress and learning, as well as consider goals for advancing partnership and practice. Council members engage in teaching/learning activities, dialogue, and self-reflection to contemplate and plan their future. It is a time to learn, celebrate progress, set new goals, build on previous goals, and revisit mission and vision.

The Partnership Council Coordinator(s), educator, and manager usually facilitate planning for this event. At times it is difficult to support attendance by all members, but the strategic importance of this gathering is so highly valued that everyone contributes what they can to make this happen. It is one the most effective proactive planning strategies that can be done for a department, area, or organization in sustaining and progressing practice and relationship growth. There are examples of pre-session preparation, minutes, key learning, and goals in Appendix A, Tables Forty Six through Fifty.

In what way is continuous learning supported as Partnership Councils link with continuous quality improvement initiatives?

The work of partnership councils is continuous learning and improvement that occurs through linkages and shared work. Continuous learning is not accomplished just by a program or project. The depth of learning is dependent upon the diversity of methods and the integration of learning into daily activities. Continuous quality improvement is just one thread of continuous learning. They both should be a conscious part of everyday life and work as well as a part of all council work. Some settings consider their partnership council to be their continuous quality improvement and continuous learning work team while others establish a linkage between quality groups and their council structure.

Thus, continuous learning occurs when individuals relate to each other in their humanness. It begins with personal clarity and exploration, and reaching out to share the journey in partnership and shared accountability with each other...recognizing that the only person one can change is self. Learning is supported in a Partnership Council, through experiences in the council meetings, as well as through One-on-One relationships with their peers. Learning is supported by personal accountability and with the commitment to teach and serve others.

Lessons learned while creating a continuous learning culture.

The continuous learning road is very different than the typical performance expectations within the hierarchical cultures. In the past a consistent pattern with little deviation was expected and rewarded. Most organizational reports show growth or losses but not the phases or foundational work that occurred to create the growth or decline. Most graphs look at outcomes of the peaks and valleys, not the journey. **Continuous learning is about the journey**.

A pattern emerges in environments where the work to create a continuous learning culture is taking place and **it often takes the councils by surprise!** The ability to recognize this pattern is helpful in strengthening every council's journey. The fundamental pattern is similar to hills, plateaus and valleys. The length, breadth, and depth of the rise, plateau, and valley will vary within every council. The three phases of continuous learning are all normal, desired, and purposeful. Each phase is impacted by the other.

The journey of continuous learning cannot be depicted by linear graphs connecting the dots of peaks and valleys such as this: /\/\/\ The rise, plateau and valley are all connected and produce a circular pattern or waves of potential that are best visualized as a spiral movement of energy such as: 🜚 It is important to remember that all three phrases are the potential waves created by the relationships within the council.

The initial **rise or climb phase** is the period of activity and behaviors surrounding a council when members come together to do the work of partnership. The strategic plan in Table Twenty Six shows the important fundamental processes that need to be addressed in the initial phase of council development. In our old way of thinking we thought certain indicators demonstrated that councils were "doing what they were supposed to do." We valued such decisions as significant accomplishments, e.g. who makes up the council, the representation, the number and choosing of One-on-Ones, the first One-on-One connection, and when and how they meet. Such work is a visible sign of progress being made. **It is essential to realize that learning and doing are not one and the same or necessarily synonymous.** We have learned that clearly from our old cultures. In fact the doing can lead to rituals, routines and patterns that interfere with learning.

During the rise/climb phase the council will start working on the problems, issues or concerns most pressing in the setting. In recognizing the importance of tangible outcomes, the council may be tempted to get caught up in these and may not pay as much attention to the relationships, the invisible, less tangible work. When this occurs, it is reflected in the quality of the decisions the group renders. However, the stronger the relationships with one another, the better the decisions and work that emerges. There is usually much optimism and energy during this phase.

Some insidious things can happen during the rise phase. The group may become problem driven, and not relationship, mission or vision driven. It is easy to get caught up in the doing with little focus on what members are learning or the purpose of their work. The number of items addressed on the agenda, and the number of problems addressed or solved become more valued than relationships and the learning process.

The nature of the second phase, the plateau phase, will be determined by the nature of the rise phase. During the rise/climb phase, if the focus is more on doing or the number of decisions made, the plateau phase may be short or non-existent and the climb may even lead directly to a decline or retreat phase.

The **plateau phase** is the period of reflection and inquiry that solidifies learning and sets the stage for further growth. It naturally unfolds when there are less issues or things to do. It may occur following the completion of the initial council foundational work. The plateau phase is often the most foreign and uncomfortable for the council. The change in pace can produce fear within the group. Quotes made by council members who were experiencing the plateau phase, but didn't understand it, give further insight:

"We are losing our steam, our enthusiasm is declining, and we are accomplishing less."

"We don't have a unifying project going and people are losing interest."

"We've become complacent and things are just sitting still."

"We were the most active council; now many don't even come."

"We don't seem to be able to make decisions about anything."

"We have become a place to bring information, that is all."

"The morale is low; we haven't done anything lately."

"The honeymoon is over and we do not know what to do."

"We are not making progress."

The plateau period is an invitation to deepen the relationships in order to advance the work. It is essential in a continuous learning culture. It can be initiated or evolve naturally. It is a necessary experience, not a call for concern. It is normal. It is a call for **reflection** and offers an opportunity expand capacity. The plateau is where true learning is solidified. It is a conscious call to remember the lessons learned "while doing" and "from doing," and to celebrate the work. Reflection is a major indicator of continuous learning. It is similar to the silence "of awe" experienced in dialogue or meaningful conversation. It is the most foreign phase during the transition into a continuous learning culture.

If the council does not understand or recognize the plateau phase, it may lead to a **decline or retreat phase** as described in the Wisdom From The Field on pages 150-152. When the doing stops, the fear steps in and old thinking emerges. The fear that the group is failing or losing its momentum can cause the plateau to become a valley. We call this institutional retreat or slipping back into old patterns of being together. The fear opens the door and gives permission to slip back into the old patterns. It can be prevented by understanding the phase and collectively reflecting via dialogue. It is a natural time for the goal setting work to prepare for the next rise phase.

Once a council understands the plateau, they will not only recognize it, and take advantage of it, they will initiate the plateau for their own personal growth. Reflection during the plateau phase can prevent or end the decline or retreat phase. It also opens the door to discovery which places the group back into the rise or climb phase. A decline or retreat phase can be precipitated by various things. The most common are associated with the nature of the relationships within the council and with their peers. That is why the tools and resources for continuous development of relationships shared throughout this chapter are so important for council members. The simple recognition of the importance of relationship work, and the need for it, can prevent a decline or retreat period.

In the initial phases of Partnership Council development, we noted that certain events, such as a change of the manager, can precipitate fear. It is the fear of the return of hierarchy because they do not have a partnering relationship with the new manager and are uncertain whether the manager will support the work. As with most fears, this can paralyze the group sending them into a decline, or the fear can be recognized as a stimulus for the work that needs to be prioritized by the council. The goal is not to eliminate declines, for in the declines councils have experienced profound learning and progress. The lessons of the phases of continuous learning have helped councils in many ways: the rises have been greater and higher, the plateaus have been more timely, and the declines have been less severe and less frequent.

The noises of learning in the Partnership Council sound nothing like the snoring heard in libraries. The waves of potential are a constantly vacillating sound that keeps the BodyMindSoul on tiptoe, so to synchronize the ever moving dance of life, the dance of relationships.

The Waves Of Potential

It is hard to see gain
when something is taken away.
It is not the fear of reflection
It is the fear of loss
the loss of doing

It is not the fear of learning
It is the fear of loss
the loss of knowing.

Together we are waves of potential.
We can end the fear of loss
with the desire to expand capacity.
We are waves in the ocean
receding to gain force to move forward.
Together we can end the fear of loss
move to the plateau of reflection
break the silence of knowing
and welcome the noise of learning
that is present in every moment of every day.
- *Bonnie Wesorick*

Chapter Nine

Closing Thoughts:
What is our hope for tomorrow?

*"What lies behind us
And What lies before us
Are tiny matters
Compared to what lies within us."*
- Oliver Wendell Holmes

The hope for tomorrow rests in the ability to learn and act in the present. Partnership Councils provide that opportunity. The work of today is the hope for tomorrow. Life only exists in the moment, not in the past and not in the future. What is alive brings hope. Hope sits in the souls of those who are alive. This book is about bringing the soul, that which "lies within us" into the work place. This is transition work, similar to the cecropia moth's work. It is a part of the evolution of humanity to reach a higher level of being together in the work place.

We are on the brink of a new time. Some day there will be no need to create an infrastructure to support the presence of the soul in the work place. You may find this hard to believe right now, especially in the face of the common resistance to this work. What is the resistance about? Is it nothing more than fear? Ferguson, M. (1987) noted, "It's not so much that we're afraid of change, or so in love with the old ways, but it's that place in between we fear...it's like being in between trapezes. It's Linus when his blanket is in the dryer. There is nothing to hold on to." As a result of this fear, there are always people who will attempt to put a stop to this work.

Many different reasons will be given as to why we should not create Partnership Councils. For example, "This is not the right time; things are too uncertain. We can't take on another project. Everyone around here has more on their plate now than they can handle." "We can't burden the staff with another initiative." "We do not have time to do this work." "No one would disagree that it would be nice to do this work, but it is fluff in comparison to the work we must do, and you know how tight our budget is right now." These concerns make one wonder about what to do.

What Can I Do?

What can I do?
I'm drowning from so much to do.
Stop doing, stop doing
Connect with the voice within.
first within you
and then within others.

How do I pick and choose
when I have so much to do?
What Can I do
if I don't get it done?

Stop doing, stop doing
connect with the voice within.
first within you
and then within others.
- Bonnie Wesorick

It is the relationship with self and others that brings new potentials and expands capacity. Partnership Councils stop the doing long enough to connect within and with each other. This is important in order to create new insightful approaches and not just "do together" but equally important "become together."

What have we learned? There is no "right time" for the work of partnership. There is only time. The only way to escape the chains of time is to *live* in the moment, not just "do" in the moment. It is a choice as to how one wants to live. It is not a time, budget or fiscal issue. It is a choice issue.

Relationship work is not another initiative. It is not another program. It is the work necessary to create healthy work cultures that respect and honor the souls of humanity.

Many questions will surface as you begin this work. It is a sign that continuous learning is occurring. We have also learned that as the many questions go deeper, the last one asked may in fact be the answer to the previous question. We have, however, uncovered the answer to one important question often asked by those with whom we do partnership work. "Do we need permission to do this work?" Yes we do. We were surprised when we searched to find out from whom we needed to seek permission. It was not from the people we serve, third party payers, the boss, the organization or the government. It comes from the very place that is calling the question. The permission comes from within, within each person. **It is a personal choice, a personal journey.** Something that might be helpful to you as you begin or sustain the work of partnership is captured in the words of Quinn, (1993, p. 40) "The journey itself is going to change you, so you don't have to worry about memorizing the route we took to accomplish that change."

There is one more question that will surface and resurface as the work is done: "Why is this work so hard, if it is so right?" This is a question that we have pondered often. Is it hard because it is so intimately connected to the spiritual dimension of humanity? Is it hard because it calls for us to face ourselves, our purpose, our personhood? Is it hard because it is so different from our present rituals and routines? Is it hard because we are unclear about what is important to us as individuals and to humanity as a whole? Is it hard because it exposes the connectiveness of all living matter and souls? What will help us move forward in this challenging work? The following question may help: Is it One, the Other or the Same?

Is It One, The Other Or The Same?

I have marveled at the beauty
of the mountains
The opportunity to
be near the moose, the elk and the buffalo.
I stood in awe of the glaciers
reflecting the sun-while
eagerly awaiting the next whale sighting.
And then I noticed one person
reaching out to help another.
I wondered, how could I ever
take for granted the beauty, the mystery,
the potential, of one uniquely splendid
human being connecting with the soul of another?
I have been in awe of mountains but failed
to notice the vastness of one soul
the invisible but tangible presence of every
human being.
Is it one, the other or the same?

- Bonnie Wesorick

It is ironic that this book is about a human infrastructure that helps us to live, to love, to work, to care as humans in the work place. Yet the soul needs no structure to love or rules to care. It just needs a place to be expressed. We hope this book will help you create such a space. David Whyte (1995, p. 295) describes the nature of the work when he says, "Preserving the soul in corporate America means reclaiming all those human soul qualities sacrificed at the alter of organizational survival." The good news is that no one is alone in this reclaiming work. We have learned from the cecropia moth story that we cannot do it for each other. However, we can enhance the conditions for each other's transformation.

Although we have uncovered more questions than answers, we have found where you can go for the answer to such common questions as, "Why is this work so hard, if it is so right?"

The answer is within you-
The place where partnership begins.

Appendix A

SECTION I

MISSION AND VISION
DEVELOPMENT PROCESSES

TABLE TWENTY NINE

DEVELOPMENT OF PERSONAL MISSION STATEMENTS

Personal Mission Statements

Your mission statement reflects the meaning and purpose of your work.

To achieve a shared-vision and true "partnerships," we must all have a common mission in our work as practitioners and leaders. A common mission comes only after each of us has spent time developing our very own mission statement. Please come to the Leadership Workshop with your personal mission statement completed.

Tips for writing your Mission Statement   (paraphrased from Steven Covey's book: *Principle-Centered Leadership*)

*   A mission statement is a brief statement capturing the meaning and purpose of your work. Your mission statement should be short (1-2 sentences) so that you can memorize and internalize it.

*   Keep it simple, general, generic.

*   Ask yourself the following questions:
    What do I value? What is most important?
    What is my practice all about? What contribution can I make?
    What do I stand for? What is meaningful to me?
    What is my essential mission, my reason for being?
    What is being entrusted to me?
. . .therein lies the beginning of your personal mission statement that will continue to evolve!

My Personal Mission Statement

_____

_____

_____

_____

Is my mission in sync with the organizations stated mission?

TABLE THIRTY

SHARED MISSION AND VISION DEVELOPMENT

GOAL: Offer opportunity for group discussion around what matters most that leads to shared mission and vision development.

Suggestions to Facilitate Process:

1. Have the organization's mission and vision or other applicable documents for comparison/reference.

2. Development of mission and vision should involve all staff and all individuals in the various roles. All tracks and roles should attend sessions and contribute as well.

3. An area may have one session or multiple sessions to accomplish mission and vision development. It is critical that all staff and managers in a department be involved in this process. It is a learning opportunity, not a task to be done.

4. The mission statement should briefly state the meaning and purpose of the unit/department/area. Ask, "Why do we exist?"

5. For the vision, start by asking, <u>what would it be like if this were the best place for us to work and best place for people to seek service</u>? Brainstorm this question in three categories: Practitioner--Patient--Environment.

6. If there is difficulty visioning, it is helpful to take their dissatisfiers and reverse them into positive statements reflecting a vision of how things should be--example:

    Statement--"Patients have to wait too long to get what they need around here."

    Vision--An environment that supports patient needs as a priority to be met in a timely manner.

7. Compile brainstorming ideas throughout sessions. Have a staff leader condense ideas into summary statements for the vision.

8. Reiterate to all participants that this should be a team process. The manager should <u>not</u> develop vision in isolation and present to staff for input.

9. Missions and visions are meant to be re-evaluated for revision at least every year and as needed to reflect the continuous learning process.

10. After each area conducts this work, have them share outcomes in a global meeting. Ask each member to share how the process went in their area. What was their key learning about process and content?

Questions for group to consider as each area presents their work:

1. What patterns or themes do you observe?

2. What words or statements stand out?

3. Do any statements or words make you uncomfortable or push against your personal mission or values?

4. What was your key learning during the mission and vision experience in your area and/or in this large group process?

TABLE THIRTY ONE

MISSION AND VISION DEVELOPMENT WORKSHEET

The work you do as a group today will be foundational to clarifying your collective purpose and connecting the work of your team to the whole patient experience. The process of developing a mission statement is one powerful way to accomplish this. Brainstorm in your groups the following and complete the worksheet.

I. Mission Development
There are three elements to a mission statement:
1. A mission should be no longer than a couple sentences.
2. States our purpose using action words.
3. It should be simple and from the heart.

Questions:
1. What do you stand for? What principle cause or value will you be willing to defend? Write a word or phrase that represents the core of our particular section of work in home care. Examples: accomplish, serve, connect, support, believe, work, build, alleviate, nurture, model, participate, improve, inspire, progress, sustain, understand, reform, respect.

As a group, our three most meaningful, purposeful, and exciting verbs/phrases are:

_____   _____   _____

2. Whom are you here to help? Every mission implies that someone is helped.

_____

3. Pick the cause or issue that you would like to impact in a positive way through your work.

_____

All together:
The mission of the _____ is to _____ (actions)
_____ (cause), to, for, or with
_____ the group that receives your help.

Adaptation done by Brenda Wittman at Medcenter One Health System from the book *The Path: Developing Your Mission Statement,* by Laurie Beth Jones.

II. Vision Development

Four elements of a vision:

1. It is written down.
2. It is written in present tense as if it were already accomplished.
3. It covers a variety of activities and spans broad timeframes.
4. It includes a balance of addressing the needs of providers, patients, and environment that anchor it to reality.

Dream and don't be inhibited by your reality. Often a vision represents those areas that need improving as well as those areas of service that are to continue as a priority.

Considering your groups desired accomplishments, brainstorm the following question:
What would it be like if this were the best place for us to work and best place for people to seek service?

III. Ask each person to comment on how this experience felt to them.

Write comments down and share them at the partnership workshop.

TABLE THIRTY TWO

Examples of Mission and Vision

*Rehab Services

Mission: Through compassionate partnership with patients, caregivers, and other health care providers, we will provide rehab services to maximize function and quality of life.

Vision:
- Closely connected, continuity of care.
- Availability of necessary equipment.
- Establish/maintain rapport while negotiating rehab goals/treatment plan/safety issues.
- Professional judgment respected and supported by the agency, physicians, insurance companies.
- Support to continue being competent ethical caregivers.
- Treating people with respect as a guest in their homes.

•Home Care Patient Care Team

The **mission** is to promote the optimal level of holistic health for our patients, patient's family and support systems through a holistic focus, excellence in service, nurturing, fostering independence and serving as patient advocates.

VISION
Providers: Having the time for work to be done, the time needed to do paper work. Continuity of patient load. Positive relationships between team members, other teams, management, administration, patients and families. Encouragement and supportive of each other. Need time to accommodate meeting times.

Patients: Regard each patient as a valued individual, a "person." Dignity and respect. Continuity of providers. Availability of someone who knows them and their care when they call. A need to feel "connected" to the agency through personnel they know. Promoting and allowing patients to make their own choices by providing them with education/information. (Acceptance and support of patient's right to choice.)

Table Thirty Two. continued

Environment: Safety, availability, increased communication regarding the home, social, and physical environment.

*Social Work Department

Mission: We exist to promote better mental health by providing holistic care in a safe environment using a team approach in partnership with patient, family and community.

Vision: We envision a commitment to the community in which persons with mental illness are provided the quality of care they need, and in which mental illness no longer carries a social stigma.

**Women's Medical Center

Mission: Comfort, care and commitment to the health of all women.

Vision:
1. We are committed to provide every woman with a positive experience through education, health maintenance, and promotion.
2. As co-workers and providers we respect ourselves, each other, women, and the families we serve.
3. A collaborative team between staff and women with a focus on body, mind, and spirit.
4. We provide a partnership with fellow staff, women, and the community.

**Q&R Clinic - Mandan

Mission: Our family caring for your family.

Vision: To provide compassionate care and guidance for your family and the community.
To fulfill your needs in a comfortable atmosphere.
To have education as an ongoing commitment.

*Reference: Visiting Nurse Services, Grand Rapids, Michigan.
**Reference: Medcenter One Health System, Bismarck, North Dakota.

SECTION II

TELLING OUR STORIES

TABLE THIRTY THREE
ooooooo
"TELLING OUR STORIES"

Purpose:

Telling Our Stories is an interactive exercise by which individuals share their stories with each other. It offers an opportunity to first reflect on our own "stepping stones" or milestones in life. . .and then to share them with others. Telling each other's stories can be a powerful partnering or team building experience.

This exercise is also an effective tool for self-introspection and reflection. This personal timeline offers an opportunity to ask questions about our own journey. We can raise consciousness around our health: BodyMindSpirit.

Supplies Needed:
- Actual small stones or other small objects (e.g., Hershey's Kisses).
- Paper and pencils

Directions:
1. **Individual Reflection** - Each person identifies and writes down major "stepping stones" or milestones in their life that they feel led and/or impacted their life's journey and where they are right now. Offering a specific question may help facilitate the process, e.g. "From birth to now . . . what are the major events/experiences that have shaped where you are now? What have been the "stepping stones" that have led you in your decision to serve in your current role?"
2. **Sharing Stories** - Form small groups. Note: It may not be necessary to form small groups if the original group is already small in size. Ideally, each small group would have no more than 4-6 people.
   - Option A=Each person in the group shares their story with the others using their "stones" as a story telling tool and visual. As the story teller shares each milestone, they place an actual stone/object on the table or in the center of the group while they describe its significance.
   - Option B=If time does not allow each participant to share all milestones. Each person shares two milestones, one that carriers feelings of joy for them and one that evokes feelings of challenge or difficulty.
3. **Key Learnings** - Bring all small groups back together. Have them share their key learnings from doing this exercise. What did they learn about themselves? What did they learn about their peers? In what ways will the things that they learned impact them in their day-to-day work together?

"Telling Our Stories"

Personal Worksheet

In the space below plot the events or milestones of your personal path. You can connect them in any way, such as using peaks and valleys or a spiral. Consider both significant events and people in your life.

Date of Birth   **Present**

Questions for further self-reflection (this is a great tool for journaling and continued introspection):

• What image best describes my milestones? Circles, waves, smooth, straight?

• What was my greatest pain? Greatest joy?

• Do any events evoke feelings for me? If so, what feelings: job, pain, disappointment, excitement?

• When and in what ways has my passion been trying to surface?

• What led me to choose my current profession?

• How do my current roles fulfill my personal mission in life?

• What implications do my significant life events have on my ability to build relationships with others?

• In what way does learning another's story help me to partner with them?

Reference Note: This concept has been used by many people but this version was inspired by experiences with Judy Brown and Beth Jandernoa in a Dialogue Workshop and Sr. Rhea Emner in her RISEN Program.

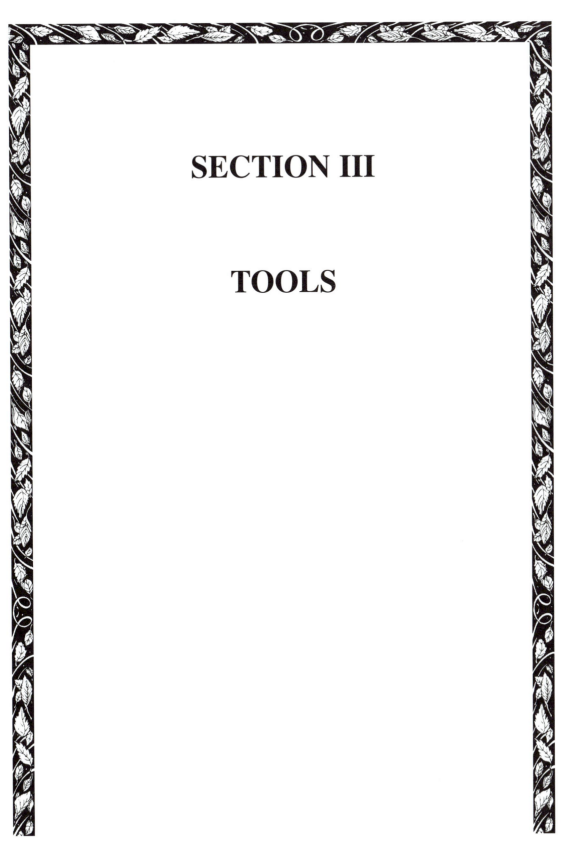

SECTION III

TOOLS

TABLE THIRTY FOUR

SELF-REFLECTION TOOL

BELIEFS THAT SUPPORT AN EMPOWERING OR "POWER RELEASING" PROCESS

Rating Scale: (1 - Not at All; 2 - Little; 3 - Somewhat; 4 - Quite; 5 - Very)

Personhood Issues

I believe that we as providers:

____ • are each a unique whole with an integrated physical, psychological, sociocultural, and spirtual dimension.
____ • influence each other.
____ • will make mistakes.
____ • need others.
____ • have choices.
____ • are accountable for our choices.
____ • have limitations.
____ • have different strengths, expertise, and needs.
____ • are continuous learners.
____ • are continuous teachers.
____ • are unique individuals worthy of respect.
____ • are goal/purpose driven.
____ • strive for mutuality in our many personal, professional roles.
____ • need humor.
____ • need diversity in practice.
____ • understand change is difficult, but a norm.

Interrelationship Issues

____ • I believe that we:
____ • can expect respect, dignity and trust.
____ • need to articulate to another what is needed.
____ • need to articulate what we expect from each other.
____ • need to know it is okay to ask for help.
____ • need to help others and role model to others how to ask for help.
____ • strive to anticipate colleague's needs as well as patient's needs.
____ • need to support the other person's ability to adapt to change.
____ • can expect role modeling from peers.
____ • need open, direct, timely, honest communication and professional exchange.
____ • need an opportunity to have open exchange and give input.
____ • have the right, responsibility, and accountability to give input into decisions that affect us.
____ • need to articulate values, beliefs, and expectations, responsibilities, and accountability to each other.
____ • need to know the strengths/responsibilities and expertise of each track.
____ • need to hold the other tracks/positions accountable for their expertise.
____ • know that each track shares responsibility and accountability for patient care.
____ • recognize that all tracks in nursing need resources.
____ • understand that listening to another does not mean we must agree.
____ • respect diversity of opinions; know it's okay to disagree.
____ • recognize the foundation for a good relationship is trust.
____ • recognize that trust is built on sharing values and beliefs and behaviors that consistently support same.
____ • need to stop dysfunctional communication patterns such as perpetrator, rescuer, and victim.

Table Thirty Four, continued

Process Issues

I believe that an empowering or "power releasing" process:

- ___ • sees the health care team as a whole with members in practice, resource/education, management, and research tracks.
- ___ • is rooted in the core beliefs of the profession.
- ___ • demands a clear vision from all its members of those services of the profession.
- ___ • represents a hope that has always been present in the profession.
- ___ • is an innate component of evolving humanity as well as an evolving profession.
- ___ • is not an organizational chart or governmental phenomena.
- ___ • is not only participatory, but service ownership of all members of the profession.
- ___ • is based on the beliefs of human dignity, respect, collaboration and collegiality of the profession's members.
- ___ • is not a process of power but of strength.
- ___ • is not a motionless theory, but a living continuous process.
- ___ • assures that the process of decision making is not position or track directed, but position/track integrated.
- ___ • assures decision making is driven by CONSENSUS which forms the foundation of collegial relationships.
- ___ • assures the professional, who provides a service that requires sensitivity to the multidimensions of man, will have an environment that treats the provider with the same respect.
- ___ • recognizes that the history and nature of our professional services does not naturally mentor us as risk takers.
- ___ • recognizes that the traditions, rituals, and routines so commonly a part of our practice environment produce barriers for us as we attempt to create safe environments for risk.
- ___ • recognizes that the historical traditions, rituals and routines did not support an environment sensitive to the wholeness of the patient or provider.
- ___ • clarifies that the process of decision making is equally as important as the decision or outcome.
- ___ • assures decisions are never made in a vacuum.
- ___ • holds every person in the group accountable to the outcome of a group decision.
- ___ • understands that all decisions are made on a continuum.
- ___ • understands that the decision making process is not always black or white but always require judgment and decision making.
- ___ • promotes trust, autonomy, choices, alliance, accountability, ownership, integrity, innovation cohesion, consistency, and congruency.
- ___ • makes it safe to take risks.
- ___ • erases guilt, anxiety, fear, paranoia, powerlessness, and secrecy.
- ___ • is the heartbeat, the fuel, the power needed for the transformation process to move from institutional to professional practice.
- ___ • creates empowered professional members.
- ___ • knows that every person will play a significant role in changing the practice culture to one in which caring for one another is as important as caring for patients.

TABLE THIRTY FIVE

SELF-REFLECTION OF LEADERSHIP BEHAVIOR
Below are the characteristics of a leader. Evaluate yourself on a scale of 1-5.
Rating Scale: (1 - Not at All; 2 - Little; 3 - Somewhat; 4 - Quite; 5 - Very)

I personally:

___ • know and cherish the vision of professional practice.

___ • know I am accountable to serve followers.

___ • am seen as a problem solver, not complainer.

___ • use first party, timely, honest communication.

___ • am clear and consistent on my leadership style.

___ • follow-up in timely manner.

___ • can articulate value system and expectations.

___ • am consistent in behaviors that support professional practice and shared governance or empowerment.

___ • understand, value, and use the consensus process.

___ • empower others to own and manage their practice.

___ • create structures/processes that support others in their management of practice.

___ • know empowered practitioners can empower people to heal.

___ • create an environment that motivates, nurtures, and:

--assures equity.

--is safe for change, yet assures continuity.

--clarifies priorities.

--facilitates trust.

--heightens spirit of colleagues.

--promotes autonomy and innovation.

--stimulates risk-taking.

--finds seeds of victory in defeats.

--assures memory so growth occurs from mistakes.

--promotes open, direct communication.

--provides hope.

___ • help colleagues analyze and redesign the unit's practice patterns, rituals, and routines that impact service delivery.

___ • am not turf oriented.

___ • create opportunities for others to experience shifts of consciousness from task to outcome orientation.

___ • consciously ask how each decision made within the group facilitates or impedes the process of delivering patient care.

___ • make decisions based on what will support the best practitioner, not the worst.

___ • share my expertise as mentor, teacher, coach, challenger, counselor, role model, and expert change agent.

__ • help colleagues create the future.

__ • recognize each colleague is an individual and at different levels of professional expertise.

__ • have vision of what each peer can be, their potential.

__ • dialogue with peers about practice issues.

__ • share professional views with peers.

__ • help peers think beyond traditional responses to barriers of professional nursing.

__ • keep peers literate of realities of whole picture (operations, education, practice, research).

__ • connect groups to attain higher systems levels.

__ • provide and share resources to grow as professionals and leaders of professionals.

__ • provide opportunities to develop judgment and decision making abilities of each peer.

__ • understand that professionals need an environment that supports diversity.

__ • value my peers' expertise.

__ • know that rituals and routines can interfere with innovation.

__ • am a good listener, sounding board and filter.

__ • use self-disclosure as means of examples.

__ • support the principles of change.

__ • enhance collaboration with interdisciplinary members of health care team about patient care issues.

__ • enhance feedback loops.

__ • have consistent expectations with all peers regarding professional practice issues.

__ • demonstrate team work, unity, collegiality by communicating with others.

__ • help colleagues see they do not have to adapt to reality, but change it.

__ • help colleagues see that ambiguity, risk and uncertainty could be first step in creating a new reality.

__ • help colleagues become innovators by reversing assumptions.

__ • know the difference between doing things right and doing the right thing.

__ • synchronize efforts and energies to assure consumer's satisfaction and professional's satisfaction.

__ • balance the forces of change and continuity.

TABLE THIRTY SIX

COUNCIL MEMBERS ACCOUNTABILITIES AND EXPECTATIONS

To what degree do you have these key success factors in place? Circle the number that most closely represents your current practice	1 = Not at all	2 = little	3 = somewhat	4 = usually	5 = always
1. Center decision making around what is best for patient and family.	1	2	3	4	5
2. Be clear on scope of practice.	1	2	3	4	5
3. Have open, direct, respectful, and timely communication.	1	2	3	4	5
4 Mentor and be mentored, coach, facilitate, become teacher and learner.	1	2	3	4	5
5. Attend and prepare for partnership council sessions.	1	2	3	4	5
6. Role model core beliefs to colleagues, interdisciplinary team, patients, families and community.	1	2	3	4	5
7. Be receptive to feedback, constructive criticism and value diverse opinions.	1	2	3	4	5
8. Strive to be good listeners.	1	2	3	4	5
9. Discuss practice issues with peers.	1	2	3	4	5
10. Assure that every colleague knows the purpose, structure and process of the partnership council.	1	2	3	4	5
11. Demonstrate ownership of partnership council process.	1	2	3	4	5
12. Communicate what is needed to best fulfill role.	1	2	3	4	5
13. Value expertise of all tracks.	1	2	3	4	5
14. Support each track and every peer in the transformation from an institutional to professional practice.	1	2	3	4	5
15. Know that each colleague is a unique, multi dimensional person who has hopes, goals and dreams.	1	2	3	4	5
16. Understand and use the consensual process consistently.	1	2	3	4	5

TABLE THIRTY SEVEN

PARTNERSHIP COUNCIL SUCCESS FACTORS

To what degree does your council have these key success factors in place? Circle the number that most closely represents current practice **The council structure and processes promote: support and promote:**	1 = not at all	2 = little	3= some what	4 = usually	5 = always

1. Membership that includes all tracks:
    Practitioner/Support staff
    Operations Resources (Manager)
    Practice/Learning Resource
    (CNS/Educator)
    Research Resource
	1	2	3	4	5

2. A consistent place where partnerships are developed and practice issues are addressed.	1	2	3	4	5
3. Membership that reflects composition of unit (e.g., adequate numbers of members representing all role categories.)	1	2	3	4	5
4. Continuous learning.	1	2	3	4	5
5. Decision-making at the level where service is rendered.	1	2	3	4	5
6. Partnering of council members 1:1 with staff.	1	2	3	4	5
7. Linkage with all other shared work team efforts.	1	2	3	4	5
8. Linkage with all other dept./division initiatives/committees.	1	2	3	4	5
9. Linkage with interdisciplinary teams.	1	2	3	4	5
10. Clarity on the purpose of the council as compared with staff meetings, task forces, CQI, TQM, etc.	1	2	3	4	5
11. The use of principles of dialogue, check-in, and consensus.	1	2	3	4	5
12. Utilize agenda/minutes to provide organization and communication.	1	2	3	4	5
13. Leadership by a practitioner who is selected by members.	1	2	3	4	5
14. Meetings that are open to any interested staff.	1	2	3	4	5
15. Meetings that are held on a consistent basis.	1	2	3	4	5
16. Annual goal planning sessions.	1	2	3	4	5
17. Keeping the focus on what is best for the patient.	1	2	3	4	5

Page 265

SECTION IV

TABLE ON
CORE BELIEF REVIEW

TABLE THIRTY EIGHT

CORE BELIEF WORKSHEET

New Core Belief	Meaning/Key Principles	Examples/How I Practice
▸ Quality emerges in environments where individuals share mission, values, and partnerships.	*We believe the patient deserves quality care. When providers are synchronized in regard to mission and principles, and partner together, quality emerges. The culture and environment impact partnerships, patient care experiences and quality outcomes. We are the environment, culture and organization . . . and we create it. Mission and principles provide the foundation for the health care team to: collaborate, develop strong partnership with each other and with patients, and take ownership for quality.*	
▸ Each person has the right to health care which promotes wholeness in body, mind and spirit.	*Each person has the right to receive health care services which focus not only on the physical aspects of health, but also the psychological, sociocultural, and spiritual dimensions. There is a dynamic connection between body, mind and spirit. The patient/family's health needs (not rituals/routines of the health care team) should be the focus of care.*	
▸ Each person is accountable to communicate and integrate his/her contribution to care.	*Every provider is accountable to be clear on their unique services and to provide these services. All providers need to explain their role to patients/families so they can help them understand the unique roles and how they fit together to serve them. If the consumer doesn't know what we do, then how can they value it?*	
▸ Health care is planned, coordinated, and delivered in partnership with the person/family/community.	*This core belief calls for coordination within the health care paradigm and in partnership with the person receiving care. Coordination and partnership parallel with the principles of quality. The provider must be in synch with the person. It calls for all disciplines to be a masters of mutuality which precedes individualization. Mutuality drives the coordination of health care for the whole interdisciplinary team and focuses the necessary care and teaching for the individual's unique needs.*	

Page 268

New Core Belief	Meaning/Key Principles	Examples/How I Practice
❥ New ways of thinking are essential to continually improve health.	*We need to become comfortable with transition from one paradigm to the next. Life is nothing more than a journey from one paradigm to the next. If we can't let go of the old paradigm, there is no journey, it is a continuous ride on the carousel. If we can't let go, then we cannot continuously learn. Staying in an old paradigm can prevent learning and new thinking. The spirit is the potential of every human being. The mind and the spirit in partnership provides unlimited support for transitions. When we hold on to old thinking and do not continuously learn, our spirit, or potential, is trapped within. New thinking is nothing more than new learning. Learning and new thinking have no end, only beginnings. New thinking in the mind unlocks the door to endless possibilities because it frees up the spirit. This core belief brings these realities into our day to day practice*	
❥ Empowerment begins with each person and is enhanced by partnerships and systems supports.	*Empowerment is a state of being in which the person has the power, the authority to act in his/her role to achieve the mission and live the core beliefs. This belief brings a powerful message that we believe each person, whether provider or recipient of care, is accountable for, and has ownership of his/her own life, health, healing, mission, etc. Although empowerment starts within the individual, it is enhanced by relationships with others, the systems, and cultures.*	

SECTION V

PARTNERSHIP COUNCIL LEADERSHIP WORKSHOP

TABLE THIRTY NINE

PARTNERSHIP COUNCIL LEADERSHIP WORKSHOP

Content Outline

I. Welcome/Check-In

II. Living The Principles of Partnership
   a. Personal mission/shared mission
   b. Recommended Videos:
      - Margaret Wheatley - *Leadership And The New Science*
      - Stephen Covey - *Law Of The Harvest*

III. Introduction To The Principles of Dialogue
   a. Exercises to practice dialogue skills

   Lunch

IV. Partnership Council Overview
   a. Purpose
   b. Structure/format
   c. Roles/responsibilities
   d. Core linkages (One-on-One, shared work teams, etc.)
   e. Shared decision making (consensus, dialogue)

V. Panel Presentation/Transformational Stories

VI. Key Learning/Check-Out

TABLE FORTY

EXAMPLES OF LANGUAGE, WORDS AND PROCESSES
THAT ARE BARRIERS OR ENHANCERS
OF EMPOWERING PROCESSES

ENHANCES	INTERFERES
Non-judgmental	Judgmental/Opinionated
Consistent message	Chaos and confusion
How you say it that matters "we" instead of "you"	Communication jams
Consensus and clarity on what we are going One-on-One with.	Negative body language
Consistent looking agenda and minutes.	Confusion on the issues. Not knowing or understanding what they are.
"Did everyone get One-on-One?"	Paper storm - keep it a minimum.
"have we tried…"	"We already know what the answer is."
"We could…"	"You should…"
"Maybe what we need is…"	"I want you to…
"We need to know what you think about…"	"They wanted me to ask…"
"I think…"	"Mandatory . . ."
"I don't know but I'll try to find out."	"They think…"
"[Mary] knows a lot about this. Let's contact her."	"They said…" "She said…"
"What do you think?"	"Why didn't you…"
"How can I help?"	"Low level…"
"What do you need?"	"She's just a staff nurse."
"What can we do about it."	"The institution requires"
"Let's get that on the agenda."	"Some things are a given"
"Let's put our heads together."	"Some things never change."
"Let's see what we can do within the budget."	"This is how we do it here."
	"The budget will never allow this."

TABLE FORTY ONE

WHAT MAKES ONE-ON-ONE WORK?

1. Commitment to and belief in the importance of the process of One-on-One. (How you ask, receive, and give information makes all the difference).
2. Knowing that you are receiving and learning valuable information.
3. Understanding that if one person is not represented, the whole group is deprived.
4. Valuing the process.
5. Feedback that is timely. When there is feedback and evidence of the One-on-One process. We can see that it makes a difference.
6. Timeliness. One-on-One takes time and needs to be done in as timely a manner as possible so feedback can get back.
7. Trust. We need to trust that One-on-One will make the difference and that we will have the opportunity for a One-on-One interaction every month.
8. Tools. Unit leader feedback tools help to narrow, focus, and clarify information sought as well as provide a method for data gathering.
9. Consistency.
10. Appropriate language and communication.
11. Good feelings. Connecting with another individual. Other sources of information.
12. Knowing you're not alone.
13. Relationships. Know, care about and value your colleagues. Make an effort to find out what is important to them, within a professional practice framework as well. What do they like the most about their profession? What is their greatest accomplishment?
14. Understanding that One-on-One is a two-way information, data gathering mission as well as a teaching, learning and sharing session.
15. Giving people time to respond. Sometimes they can't give good answers without thinking things through, especially if they are already occupied with an assignment. They need to have some time to think about what we are asking so they can adequately articulate their true feelings.
16. Clarity.
17. Vision. It is easier to obtain information if your unit has a clear vision of where they are going and everyone knows where that is.
18. Honesty about issues. No secrets. No holding back information as a power or control weapon.

19. Contact at the same time every month is an enhancer.
20. Good listening skills. Being able to "hear" what your colleagues are saying.
21. Being knowledgeable and articulate about the process.
22. Persistence.
23. Humor.
24. Stepping outside of rituals, routines and context.
25. Dealing with what is current instead of what is old history.
26. Alliance.
27. Opportunity to state your beliefs and what you think is right.
28. Validation.
29. Integrity.

TABLE FORTY TWO

Role Play Scene

Some of the One-on-One
Issues we will address include:

Apathy

- Establishing mutuality with peer
- Clarity on purpose of One-on-One/consensus
- Patience and persistence
- Feedback on decisions made based on peer input/collective wisdom

Conflict

- Establishing mutuality with peer
- Clarity on purpose of One-on-One/consensus
- Your clarity on the issue/topic presented
- Advocacy/Inquiry skills

Table Forty Two, continued

Scene One: Apathy

One-on-One Script	**Observations**
Council Member/ Representative - Mary	

Peer - Alice

Mary -
"I need to talk to you real quick about how we do break coverage on our unit."

Alice -
"Oh yeah."

Mary -
"Yes. We are hoping to be more self-facilitating when it comes to break coverage. After all, when it comes to covering our assignments we certainly know more about what's going on then the charge nurse... don't you think?"

Alice -
"I really don't think it matters what I think. You are all going to do what you want to do anyway."

(silence)

Mary -
"Well... that is why I'm talking to you about it."

Alice -
"Yeah... Yeah... Listen... I really have to go now, see you later."

Table Forty Two, continued

Scene Two: Conflict

One-on-One Script   **Observations**

Council Member/
Representative - Sue

Peer - John

Sue -
*"Hi John. Thank-you for finding
some time this evening to talk to me
about the council's One-on-One items.
How much time do you have?"*

John -
*"I asked Gail to cover my assignment
for about 15 minutes."*

Sue -
*"Great... hopefully we'll be able to
get through these in that time. Let me
get your thoughts first on break
coverage for our unit since I know
this is near and dear to your heart.
Remember last month I brought to you
the question if there were any issues
from your perspective related to break
coverage?"*

John -
*"Oh yeah... I remember alright.
Obviously nothing has been resolved
yet... I didn't get a break two nights
this week."*

Sue-
*"Well... I brought your concerns back
to the Council last month. We also heard
feedback from several other staff along
with some suggestions to help ensure
adequate break coverage."*

Table Forty Two, continued

One-on-One Script	**Observations**

One-on-One Script

"One of the suggestions on the table that the Council members thought had a great deal of potential was that we, the staff, would self-facilitate our own break coverage . . . rather than the charge nurse."

John -
"That's never going to work with the staff on this unit!! Half the time we don't see each other and some people around here are so set in their own ways they will never change!!"

Sue-
"So you don't think it will work?"

John -
"No way."

Sue-
"O.K. . . . if that's the way you feel about it . . ."

SECTION VI

COMPETENCY-BASED DEVELOPMENT

BUTTERWORTH HOSPITAL, PATIENT CARE SERVICES

Competency-Based Development-   Partnership Council Coordinator

Name: _____

Director: _____

Self Assessment Code (SAC)

0 = No Experience	2 = Can Perform Independently
1 = Needs Assistance	3 = Able to Resource Others

TABLE FORTY THREE

SAC	Competency & Performance Criteria.	Learning Activity	Validation Options	Validation Method Used Initials & Date — Timeframe:	Comments
	1. Competency Statement: Demonstrates professional accountabilities in role of Council Coordinator.				
	1. Explore role accountabilities and working relationship with other unit leaders in order to develop partnering relationships. A. Director	• Shadow experience and complete learning objectives	SR	month (4 hours)	
		• Complete partnership worksheet.	CW	6 months A) ☐	
		• Attend NAC with Director and complete learning activities.	SR		
	B. Clinical Coordinators	• Meet with each of the dept. CCs and complete learning objectives	CW	2-3 months (20-30 minutes each) B) ☐	
	C. Clinical Nurse Specialist (CNS)	• Shadow experience and complete learning objectives	SR	month (4 hours)	
		• Complete partnership worksheet.	CW	C) ☐	
		• Attend Advanced Practice Committee with CNS and complete learning objectives.	SR	6 months	
	D. Staff Educator (SE)	• Complete learning objectives.		month (2 hours) D) ☐	
	2. Develops partnerships with outside unit resource. a. CPM Staff - kathy or Michelle	• Complete partnership worksheet and learning objectives.	CW	month (1 hour) A) ☐	
	B. Co-Chairs of Central Council	• Complete partnership worksheet and learning objectives.	CW	3 months (1 hour) B) ☐	

Validation Method: VF-Verbalized Report   RD-Return Demonstration   OP-Observed Performance   RP-Role Play

     SR-Self Report   CW-Completed Worksheet

i:\nrslshcbo96blk.doc   © Butterworth Health System   Page 1

Table Forty Three, continued

Competency & Performance Criteria.	Learning Activity	Validation Options	Timeframe	Validation Method Used Initials & Date	Comments
C. Adm Director (if applicable)	• Complete partnership worksheet and learning objectives.	CW	2 months (1 hour)	C) ☐	
D. Director or Quality, Education, Research	• Complete partnership worksheet and learning objectives.	CW	2 months (1 hour)	D) ☐	
E. Unit Medical Director (if applicable) with Unit Director	• Complete partnership worksheet and learning objectives.	CW	2 months (1 hour)	E) ☐	
F. Others(s)	• Complete partnership worksheet and learning objectives.	CW	2 months (1 hour)	F) ☐	
32. Demonstrates continuous learning behaviors. A. Develops awareness of resources for continuous learning.	• Attend Partnership Workshop • Review Resource Book • Attend Leadership Development Series • Attend leadership conferences • Read/discuss leadership journal articles • Read/discuss leadership books	SR	1-2 month (8 hours) as avail. 6 months 6 months	A) ☐	
B. Proactively seeks leadership learning. C. Brings continuous learning needs/ideas to colleagues at leadership meetings council.	• Present information form one of the above learnings at a UBC meeting	SR OP	6 months	B) ☐ C) ☐	
4. Establishes/strengthens the connection of quality and outcomes to council. a. Integrates QI to council.	• Meet with council-based QI coordinator and complete learning objectives.	SR	1-2 month (30 min.)	A) ☐	
B. Verbalizes key quality concerns on department/service area.	• Attend council-based and department QI meeting, multidisciplinary QI as appropriate.	SR	3 months (2-3 hrs.)	B) ☐	
C. Obtains literature reviews when appropriate.	• Obtain literature review.	SR	6 months (30 min.)	C) ☐	
D. Articulates examples of research utilization innovation on unit.	• Discuss research utilization with CNS and/or attend central orientation. (see 1c part of time spent with CNS).	SR	6 months (1 hour)	D) ☐	
E. Articulates purpose of clinical pathways and integration with CPM tools.	• Attend central orientation. Janice Schriefer, Director - Outcome Management Program. • Attend one Clinical Path meeting	SR	3 months (1 hour) 3-6 month (1 hour)	E) ☐	

Validation Method: SR-Self Report   VF-Verbalized Report   RD-Return Demonstration   OP-Observed Performance   RP-Role Play

CW-Completed Worksheet

© Butterworth Health System

i:\nrslshvcbo96blk.doc

Page 2

Competency & Performance Criteria	Learning Activity	Validation Options	Validation Method Used Timeframe	Initials & Date	Comments
5. Demonstrates clarity on a mission/vision/goals from a personal organizational/divisional/ department perspective.					
A. Articulates organizational/divisional/department goals.	• Write a personal mission statement. • Locate and review organization/ division/department goals.	SR	month	A) ☐	
B. In collaboration with Unit Director, coordinates annual department goal setting session in the Spring for effective date of July 1.	• Review goal setting section in the Resource Book.	SR	3months	B) ☐	
C. Writes measurable goals consistent with organizational/divisional mission/vision/goals with councils.	• Plan calendar for periodic goals review (tool).	OP	6 months or sooner if session scheduled	C) ☐	
D. Writes action plans for goals, include timelines and work distribution teams of council.	• Read ch. 3 & 4 of Reilly "Behavioral Objectives" (available in Health Sciences Library).	OP		D) ☐	
E. Conducts periodic goal review to assure on-going progress toward goals.		SR		E) ☐	
6. Coordinates review/revision Council Bylaws in collaboration with Director annually in the spring from effective date of July 1 (Spring).	• Review Resource Book	OP	6 months or sooner if needed	6) ☐	
7. Facilitates consensual validation process of guidelines.	• Complete one consensual validation of a guideline. • Review consensual validation process at council meeting.	SR OP	4 months 4 months	7) ☐	

Validation Method: SR= Self Report   VF=Verbalized Report   RD=Return Demonstration   OP=Observed Performance   RP=Role Play

CW = Completed Worksheet

i:\nrslsh\cbo96blk.doc   © Butterworth Health System   **Page 3**

Page 284

Table Forty Three, continued

Competency & Performance Criteria	Learning Activity	Options	Validation Method Used — Initials & Date (Timeframe:)	Comments

2. Competency Statement: Demonstrates effective leadership of council meetings and processes, and in daily activities.

Competency & Performance Criteria	Learning Activity	Options	Initials & Date	Comments
1. Prepares and utilizes resources for council meetings/processes.				
A. Signs out meeting rooms.	• Attend 1-2 other departments, council meetings and complete learning objectives.	OP	6 months (2 hours) — A) ☐	
B. Articulates process for meeting minutes (typing, distribution, format, timelines, Resource Book, etc.)	• Reviews Resource Book.	SR	month — B) ☐	
C. Verbalizes process for copy machine/ copy center.	• Complete copy center request.	SR	month — C) ☐	
D. Identifies support personnel available and process for quick meeting minutes turn around.	• Contact secretarial support.	SR	month — D) ☐	
E. Verbalizes how to use interdepartmental mail.		SR	month — E) ☐	
2. Uses effective leader/facilitator and change agent skills.				
A. Reviews the agenda at start of meeting.	• Review techniques with Director, practice at council meetings and have ongoing feedback with Director and council.	OP	4 months — A) ☐	
B. Links other department/service area activities/ committees into councils. 1) Identify purpose of each. 2) Establish/strengthen a good process for linkage with each unit committee leader.	• Contact/connect with each department committee leader.	OP	4 months — B) ☐	
C. Uses effective communication techniques with council and on department/service area. 1) Conflict resolution. 2) Group dynamics skills.	• Review techniques with Director, practice at council, and have ongoing feedback with Director and staff. • Psych CNS can be useful resource here		4 months — C) ☐	

Validation Method:

SR= Self Report   VF=Verbalized Report   RD=Return Demonstration   OP=Observed Performance   RP=Role Play

CW = Completed Worksheet

© Butterworth Health System

Page 4

i:\nrslsh\cbo96blk.doc

Page 285

Competency & Performance Criteria	Learning Activity	Validation Options	Validation Method Used — Initials & Date (Timeframe:)	Comments
D. Role models hospitality to guests who attend. 1) Contact guests ahead of time for clarity on objectives.	• Review techniques with Director, practice at council, and have ongoing feedback with Director and staff.		D) □ 4 months	
E. Summarizes and assures clarity at the end of meeting re: specific 1:1 issues (e.g., agenda items/meeting).		OP	E) □ 4 months	
F. Sets the agenda for the next Council meeting at the end of the meeting.		OP	F) □ 4 months	
G. Evaluates the meeting with all council members before adjourning.		OP	G) □ 4 month	
3. Assures Council decision-making represents all staff.	• Review techniques with Director, practice at council, and have ongoing feedback with Director and staff. • Review resource book.	OP		
A. Seek 1:1 feedback on decision-making issues.			A) □ 4 months	
B. Determine if adequate staff representation is present.			B) □ 4 months	
C. Hold council members accountable to have their peer feedback/input represented even when they can't attend the meeting.			C) □ 4 months	
4. Uses appropriate group process methods to facilitate open exchange and input from all members.		OR VF		
A. Nominal Group Technique (NGT)	• Practice at Council meeting, review with Director. • Review Resource Book. • New Facilitator Workshop.		A) □ 4 months	
B. Rank ordering	• Practice at Council meeting, review with Director. • Review Resource Book. • New Facilitator Workshop.		B) □ 4 months	
C. Structured Discussions	• Practice at Council meeting, review with Director. • Review Resource Book. • New Facilitator Workshop.		C) □ 4 months	

Page 286

Competency & Performance Criteria	Learning Activity	Validation Options	Validation Method Used Initials & Date Timeframe:	Comments
D. 7-step agenda	• Practice at Council meeting, review with Director. • Review Resource Book. • New Facilitator Workshop.		month D) □	
E. Consensus F. Dialogue	• Discuss with PPC Chairpersons. • Discuss with CPM Coordinators.		month E) □ 4 months F) □	

Validation Method:

SR= Self Report

VF=Verbalized Report
CW = Completed Worksheet

RD=Return Demonstration

OP=Observed Performance

RP=Role Play

© Butterworth Health System

Page 6

i:\nrslsh\cbo96blk.doc

TABLE FORTY FOUR

Council Coordinator Partnership Worksheet

This partnership worksheet is designed to be used in an interactive discussion during which each person will address each question as they begin building the foundation for their partnership.

	Council Coordinator	Partner/Role _____
1. What you can expect from me:		
2. What I need from you:		
3. Describe your role as it relates to the core beliefs.		
4. Describe your role as it relates to the council.		
5. How can we assure we stay connected?		

Person attended with _____

	Clinical Resource Committee	Nursing Advisory Council	Quality Improvement	Advanced Practice
1. State the purpose and membership of the council/committee.				
2. Describe typical agenda items.				
3. Contrast purpose of the council/committee with CPC.				
4. Describe ways the council/committee and CPC are connected.				
5. Identify how committee/ council connects with the work of PCS.				
6. Discuss learnings from the meeting that helped you to gain a broader perspective on issues as a whole.				

TABLE FORTY FIVE

SECTION VII

CELEBRATION/
ADVANCEMENT
SESSIONS
(GOAL SETTING)

TABLE FORTY SIX

Example of Preparation Packet

TO: Partnership Council Members
FROM: Carol and Darlene
DATE: May 25, 1997
RE: Annual Goal Setting Retreat

Our goal setting retreat is quickly approaching! The retreat will be held on Thursday, May 29, 1997 from 4:00 p.m. to 8:00 p.m. at John Ball Park. Plan to meet by the pond near the shelter. Bring a blanket (if you prefer back support feel free to bring a low beach chair or backrest) and your own beverage. Boxed lunches will be provided.

Attached are several handouts, some which require completion prior to attending the retreat. Below is a list of the handouts and what needs to be done with each:

- **Peer Feedback Sheet**
  Obtain feedback from your peers on potential goals for our unit in the coming year, include your own thoughts as well, bring them with you to the dialogue for reference. It is important that we remember the peers we represent.

- **Self-Evaluation Tool**
  Please evaluate yourself on leadership behaviors expected of council members, this is for self-reflection and will not need to be shared.

- **Dialogue Introspection**
  Please read and bring to the retreat.

- **Partnership Council Success Factor Assessment**
  Please complete as soon as possible and turn in to my mailbox by Thursday (5/29) morning.

We are looking forward to spending time together strengthening our relationships and planning for the future of our unit. You will be contacted to determine your sandwich preference. If for some reason you are unable to attend, please contact me as soon as possible at extension 1439.

See you in the park!

GOAL SETTING SESSION PEER FEEDBACK SHEET

Please consult with each peer you represent and seek their thoughts on what things on 7 North could be improved or worked on in the coming year. Think about things we can do as a unit to strengthen our practice, relationships, and services. Please include your own thoughts in the space provided.

Peer:_____
Comments:

Peer:_____
Comments:

Peer:_____
Comments:

Peer:_____
Comments:

Peer:_____
Comments:

Peer:_____
Comments:

SELF-REFLECTION OF LEADERSHIP BEHAVIOR

Below are the characteristics of a leader. Evaluate yourself on a scale of 1-5.
Rating Scale: (1 - Not at All; 2 - Little; 3 - Somewhat; 4 - Quite; 5 - Very)

I personally:
__ • know and cherish the vision of professional practice.
__ • know I am accountable to serve followers.
__ • am seen as a problem solver, not complainer.
__ • use first party, timely, honest communication.
__ • am clear and consistent on my leadership style.
__ • follow-up in timely manner.
__ • can articulate value system and expectations.
__ • am consistent in behaviors that support professional practice and shared governance or empowerment.
__ • understand, value, and use the consensus process.
__ • empower others to own and manage their practice.
__ • create structures/processes that support others in their management of practice.
__ • know empowered practitioners can empower people to heal.
__ • create an environment that motivates, nurtures, and:
    --assures equity.
    --is safe for change, yet assures continuity.
    --clarifies priorities.
    --facilitates trust.
    --heightens spirit of colleagues.
    --promotes autonomy and innovation.
    --stimulates risk-taking.
    --finds seeds of victory in defeats.
    --assures memory so growth occurs from mistakes.
    --promotes open, direct communication.
    --provides hope.
__ • help colleagues analyze and redesign the unit's practice patterns, rituals, and routines that impact service delivery.
__ • am not turf oriented.
__ • create opportunities for others to experience shifts of consciousness from task to outcome orientation.
__ • consciously ask how each decision made within the group facilitates or impedes the process of delivering patient care.
__ • make decisions based on what will support the best practitioner, not the worst.
__ • share my expertise as mentor, teacher, coach, challenger, counselor, role model, and expert change agent.

__ • help colleagues create the future.

__ • recognize each colleague is an individual and at different levels of professional expertise.

__ • have vision of what each peer can be, their potential.

__ • dialogue with peers about practice issues.

__ • share professional views with peers.

__ • help peers think beyond traditional responses to barriers of professional nursing.

__ • keep peers literate of realities of whole picture (operations, education, practice, research).

__ • connect groups to attain higher systems levels.

__ • provide and share resources to grow as professionals and leaders of professionals.

__ • provide opportunities to develop judgment and decision making abilities of each peer.

__ • understand that professionals need an environment that supports diversity.

__ • value my peers' expertise.

__ • know that rituals and routines can interfere with innovation.

__ • am a good listener, sounding board and filter.

__ • use self-disclosure as means of examples.

__ • support the principles of change.

__ • enhance collaboration with interdisciplinary members of health care team about patient care issues.

__ • enhance feedback loops.

__ • have consistent expectations with all peers regarding professional practice issues.

__ • demonstrate team work, unity, collegiality by communicating with others.

__ • help colleagues see they do not have to adapt to reality, but change it.

__ • help colleagues see that ambiguity, risk and uncertainty could be first step in creating a new reality.

__ • help colleagues become innovators by reversing assumptions.

__ • know the difference between doing things right and doing the right thing.

__ • synchronize efforts and energies to assure consumer's satisfaction and professional's satisfaction.

__ • balance the forces of change and continuity.

DIALOGUE INTROSPECTION
Dialogue is a process that enhances the emergence of truth.

What is Dialogue?	**Thoughts, Realizations, Wonderings. Learnings (FACILITATOR HINTS)**

What is Dialogue?

How is dialogue different from other forms of conversation?
> Debate - "To beat down."
> Deliberate - "To weigh out."
> Discussion - "To break apart."

Most of our meetings are like ping pong matches in which the participants bat their opinion around the room or like merging traffic in which there is little listening, just waiting for an opening to get one's opinion inserted. Discussion is not bad. It is often how we make decisions and get things done.

Dialogue: "A flow of meaning."
Dialogue is another form of conversation in which we genuinely inquire into ways of thinking that we take for granted. It is not about trying to come to consensus or make a decision, but rather to explore and reflect, to listen to everyone's thinking as just as valid as my own, to be willing to examine my own thinking and be influenced by the thinking of others.

Examples of distinctions between dialogue and discussion:

Discussion	**Dialogue**
Defend	Explore
Certainty	Uncertainty
Competence	Vulnerability
Know	Learn
Separation	Connection
Stating	Uncovering
Expert	Beginner
Opinion	Truth
Judging	Searching
Dependent/ Independent	Interdependent

Share some of these guidelines.

Guidelines for the emergence of dialogue:
a. Leave our roles and positions outside.
b. Display and genuinely questions our assumptions and those of others.
c. Suspend certainty and judgment.
d. Slow down, leave space between comments.
e. Have a willingness to be surprised and influenced by another.
f. Not here to fix, manage, or process.
g. No hidden agendas or perplexed outcomes.
h. Allow for silence.
i. Speak from "I" and listen to the "WE."
j. Allow multiple perspectives to surface without needing to resolve them.
k. Consider others' perspectives/opinions as just as valid as your own.

Note: This two page handout can be used by participants as a format to facilitate dialogue in their settings.

Table Forty Six, continued

Dialogue Introspection. Page Two

A Process for Dialogue to Emerge	Thoughts, Realizations, Wonderings. Learnings (FACILITATOR HINTS)
1. Developing the Practice Field. The purpose of the practice field is to establish an environment where the conditions are prime for dialogue to emerge. A place where participants can practice the art of dialogue. It is really a list of considerations for the group that addresses how they wish to be together. Sample practice field: a. Keep confidentiality. b. Speak from "I." c. Listen deeply to others and yourself. d. No side conversations or interruptions. e. No assuming-check each other for understanding. f. No agendas, no leaders, no judgments. g. Value each person's contribution. Additions from group:	1. *Share purpose and examples. Ask for additions from the group. They can record them on their individual dialogue introspection sheets.* 2. *There will be a question provided for each person to answer during Check-In.*
2. Check-In. A "Check-In" is an invitation for each individual in the group to share his/her thinking. It is a way for other group members to practice listening skills and gain insights. Check-In sets the tone for being together in a different way.	3. *Starting the Dialogue.* *Before we begin, it might be helpful to realize that what we are about to engage in may feel awkward because the pace is different. Sometimes there are moments of silence which we are not used to in the fast pace of our regular meetings.*
3. Dialogue Question, Statement, or Quote. Facilitator will read the question, statement, or quote and offer a moment of silence for participants to reflect.	4. *Introduce the Question.* *To stimulate our thinking for the dialogue I(we) would like to first share the following questions, give you time to reflect, and then provide an opportunity for you to share your thinking with the person next to you.*
4. Dialogue Experience. Invite anyone to begin speaking as they feel moved to do so.	5. *After hearing the question, take a few minutes to think about your own questions and thinking with regard to this issue. Think even deeper and ask yourself what is behind that thinking? The question is:*
5. Debrief on Dialogue Experience. a. Participants to write key learnings on 3x5 card and give to facilitator. b. Invite participants to share their experiences and learnings with the group.	6. *As facilitator, feel free to share any realizations, observations, energies, and/or noticings you have about the dialogue experience.*
6. Closing Poem.	*Thank everyone for participating. Note that speaking is not the sole indicator of participation. Many people participated by listening and experiencing internal dialogue, all of which are contributed to the experience and wisdom gained.*

Dialogue is a time to practice relationship building skills of intention, listening, advocacy, inquiry, and silence.

Table Forty Six, continued

PARTNERSHIP COUNCIL SUCCESS FACTORS

To what degree does your council have these key success factors in place? Circle the number that most closely represents current practice. **The council structure and processes support and promote:**	1=not at all	2=little	3= some what	4= usually	5= always
1) A consistent place where partnerships are developed and practice issues are addressed.	1	2	3	4	5
2) Continuous learning.	1	2	3	4	5
3) Decision-making at the level where service is rendered.	1	2	3	4	5
4) Partnering of council members 1:1 with unit staff.	1	2	3	4	5
5) Linkage with all other unit initiatives/committees.	1	2	3	4	5
6) Linkage with all other department/division initiatives/committees.	1	2	3	4	5
7) Linkage with interdisciplinary teams.	1	2	3	4	5
8) Clarity on the purpose of the council as compared with staff meetings, task forces, CQI, TQM etc.	1	2	3	4	5
9) The use of dialogue and consensus.	1	2	3	4	5
10) Utilize agenda/minutes to provide organization and communication.	1	2	3	4	5
11) Membership that includes all tracks: Practitioner/Support Staff Operations Resources (Manager) Practice/Learning Resource (CNS/Educator) Research Resource	1	2	3	4	5
12) Membership that reflects composition of unit (e.g., adequate numbers of members representing all job categories).	1	2	3	4	5
13) Leadership by a practitioner who is selected by members.	1	2	3	4	5
14) Meetings that are open to any interested staff.	1	2	3	4	5
15) Meetings that are held on a consistent basis.	1	2	3	4	5
16) Annual goal planning sessions.	1	2	3	4	5
17) Keeping the focus on what is best for the patient.	1	2	3	4	5

Page 298

Goal Setting Retreat Agenda
May 29, 1997

4:00 P	Warm-up: Check-In	15 min
4:15 P	Assign timekeeper, Review of minutes Review of agenda	5 min
4:20 P	Celebration Evaluate 96-97 Goals	30 min
4:50 P	Discuss self-evaluation	10 min
5:00 P	Review results of UBC evaluation	15 min
5:15 P	Dinner	30 min
5:45 P	Future Trends	10 min
5:55 P	Meditation: Review peer feedback and own goals	5 min
6:00 P	Dialogue Review - set practice field	10 min
6:10 P	Reading and reflection	5 min
6:15 P	Dialogue	60 min
7:15 P	Closing - Reading, check-out	15 min
7:30 P	Summarize key themes (complete key learning card)	10 min
7:40 P	Next steps	10 min

TABLE FORTY SEVEN

SAMPLES OF GOAL SETTING

Butterworth Hospital
Partnership Council
May 29, 1997

Meeting Started: 1600   Meeting Ended: 2000   Leader: Carol/Darlene
Recorder: Jeanne

Present: Carol, Darlene, Melinda, Gail, Marti, Chad, Mary, Dorothy, Beth, Wendy, Jeanne,
Deb, Cindi, Kathy, Deb, Lisa, Brenda, Jeanne, Wendy, Sheila

Absent: Ruth, Karen

TOPIC	DISCUSSION	ACTION PLAN
1. Warm Up		
2. Minutes/Agenda Review	Approved	
3. Celebration of Accomplishments	• Kitchenette • Chart racks in desk (clipboards) • Teams together-changing how we're doing things • Clinical Pathway-LOS, outcomes good • New thermometers, equipment • Staffing on Monday, Thursday (7-3) improved • Call lights improving-PSS 90% good/excellent • Excellent support staff, all staff • More members on Partnership Council-all roles represented • Strong ECA team • Good new staff-active participation • Difference in meetings from others-how team interacts • Ability to be a part of council	

Table Forty Seven, continued

TOPIC	DISCUSSION	ACTION PLAN
4. Review of 96-97 Goals	Family centered (partnerships) CQI team • more interdisciplinary interaction • keep working on integrating multidisciplinary team Positive affirmation • team coming together, increased accountability, integration, people taking initiative, ECA contributions, seeing patients/families as individuals Continue dialogue-use it more with all staff	
5. Future Trends	Marti shared perspectives on future trends based on the impact of managed care.	
6. Dialogue	An hour was spent exploring the future of the unit.	
7. 97-98 Goals	Themes that emerged during the dialogue were: 1. Environmental issues (i.e., supplies, physical aspects of unit) 2. Multidisciplinary partnership - trial with MSW/Nurse/Physician community mental health model 3. Team Spirit-connectiveness-with other shifts, hope for the future 4. Explore eldercare issues 5. Continue dialogue	Will discuss strategies to accomplish these goals at the next meeting. Please share with your peers.

Table Forty Seven, continued

Summary of Key Learning Cards:

- If we share more, we will care better. If we lean on one another, we will become strong together. Together we can care the most.
- Team Spirit-One goal taking care of our patient needs. That is what it's all about.
- Respect and dignity when they are present keep people connected.
- Spirit of the team.
- Know myself better.
- We are a family who needs and cares for each other - no one outside our "Butterworth family" can ever truly understand the unique experiences we have had together. We should never forget how important the "family" feeling is and how lucky we are to have it.
- The team seems to have progressed incredibly in building unity-the desire now for next step is to invite others to join; to make an effort to allow others to feel a sense of belonging and ownership with the care given on our unit.
- Spirituality is key to quality care, team spirit, and partnerships. It starts with each person's own journey and willingness to believe the best of others and be vulnerable.
- Working here makes me realize how great it is. I have had other jobs and friends with their jobs where there is not a "family" or "spiritual" atmosphere like here. This makes it better to work here and I feel better as a person.
- I appreciate the way we all care for one another.
- Balance as a person will enhance patients, families, and staff. Excited about opportunity to educate residents - introduce them to benefits for all from Interdisciplinary care. Silence was good.
- It was a good learning experience. I gained new insights on how important it is to work closely with others. I enjoyed learning about other people's view of the unit.
- I learned how important dialogue is to team partnership.
- Working together to make things better. That's Empowerment.
- Use dialogue and everything around you will become clear.
- Partnerships will emerge as we learn each other's stories - our peers and our patients.
- Increase knowledge in specialized area - urology, geriatrics. So much of what we are doing here brings the family (at home) and the family (at work) together they can't be separate - treating patients as family, co-workers as family.

<u>Table Forty Seven, continued</u>

- Individual and team esteem creates quality outcomes for our customers and ourselves.
- If I were in this bed, unable to move, what would I need...Is there anything else I can get you to make you more comfortable?
- Respect leads to big think.
- Spirit of the team can only make a day and increase quality of care.

Next Meeting: Thursday, June 26,1997   1600-1700

Respectfully Submitted,

Jeanne

TABLE FORTY EIGHT

ADDITIONAL SAMPLES OF MINUTES AND PLANS

1997 Goals - Post Anesthesia Care Unit

Partnership Goals

a. Linkage with OR anesthesia to increase collaboration
Sue, Carol R., and Carol P. will work on setting up monthly meeting
with Dr. J. who is our PACU Representative to the Anes group-
*goal to reduce # of phone calls needed to send pts. to floor on sup-
plemental 02

b. Increase linkage to CPM office for support and education
Kathy Wyngarden will attend Partnership Council mtgs.
Explore value of monthly leadership mtg
Cathy W., Lorraine, Carol, & Bev

c. Increase communication from Partnership Council - Peers
Set up new list for unit reps. (Cathy & Lorraine)

d. Increase open/direct communication between staff/anes/management
Bev and Candi to organize - explore new ways to facilitate this goal

e. Gather information and share knowledge with other units as needed
Kathy will attend OR UBC mtgs/prn
Lorraine will attend BOC mtgs./prn
Work with other units as needed

f. Develop LPN role
Bev, Irene, Dawn, Karen and Lorraine

I. Operational

a. Call room - library - conference room
Carol R. to explore with Kathy (Director) whether 3rd iso room
could be converted for this purpose

b. Music/head sets for PACU pts
Cathy W. to look into cost and infection control issues

c. Resolve problem of lack of pillows/IV poles
Candy/Mae/Cathy W.

d. Explore possibility/feasibility of doors in outside corridor (hall) to
block access to hallway in front of PACU

Table Forty Eight, continued

     e.   Less confusion in admitting families to PACU
Carol R. will inform FWR person that PACU staff will tell them the "bay number" when calling for families in the PACU

     f.   Handle "hold" pts. more efficiently
Set up "unit" on peds side of PACU and discharge pts. to this unit. Staff with a float or LPN

     g.   Work on plan for admitting pts to PACU from the OR in a more organized manner
Brainstorm in UBC

II. Quality Care

     a.   Promote quiet environment in PACU
all staff need to be involved and remind each other

III. Educational

     a.   Increase knowledge of use of alternative therapies
educational committee

TABLE FORTY NINE

Endoscopy Goal Setting Session
March 26, 1997

Meeting Started: 1705   Meeting Ended: 1845

Present: Joan-Presenter   Deb-Presenter
           Jean-Timer   Kathy-Director

Marsha, LPN	Diane, RN	Lisa, RN-NRC
Terri, RN-CC	Jody, RN-NRC	Alice, RN
Tone, RN	Terry, RN	Melissa, Transporter
Elaine, RN	Jodi, US/UA	Kim, Endo Tech.

Excused: Michelle, Endo Tech   Absent: Karen, RN

Item	Discussion	Action
Agenda	Shown at this time was a 16 minute video recommended by Michelle. This video about growth and rebuilding following destruction and despair was thought provoking. A brief discussion followed regarding how this applies to life and goals.	
Review of 1996-1997 Endoscopy Goal Statements	There was a group consensus that all five goals were partially or fully met. Those partially met goals were ongoing goals for our department: • Increase knowledge and technical skills. (Met and ongoing) • Successful transition to moving unit to 5W and return redesign. (Met and ongoing) • Endoscopy documentation to be consistent with hospital standards. (Met and ongoing) • Creative staffing as allowed by departmental FTEs. (Met and ongoing) • Improve socialization. (Partially met)	
New Goals set for 1997-1998	Kathy suggested each new goal have its own committee members. This idea was accepted by all staff.	
1. Improve morale	• Treat each other with respect • Teamwork • Improve MD behavior toward staff	Organization of morale shared work team: • Alice, Terri, Joan, Michelle • Resolve (employee assistance program) will be coming to talk to Endo staff.

Page 306

Table Forty Nine, continued

Item	Discussion	Action
2. Successful transition to new Endoscopy Department.	Tentative move - April 17th Physicians will be asked if they would like to be included on this committee. Weekly meetings will be held until the move. The first meeting will be held on April 1, 1997, during work hours when time allows.	Organization of transition shared work team. Diane Deb Elaine Kim Melissa Jodi Marsha
3. Call time	• Weekend coverage • Rotation • Terri presented information obtained from the physicians at the last interdisciplinary meeting regarding "call"	Explore different options to even out call rotation. Status: Awaiting QI information regarding weekend call cases. A Call Time committee was formed: Kim Beth Alice Elaine Jean Marsha
4. Continuing Education		An Education shared work team. was formed: Michelle Karen Swanee Jean Train all RNs for equipment assisting for ERCPs. Education: RNs to new scope machine and equipment cleaning process.
Future Committee Reports	All committee reports will be given on a monthly basis at staff meeting or PRN.	
	The 1997-1998 goal setting statements were accomplished successfully.	

Respectfully submitted,

Deb
Co-Coordinator

TABLE FIFTY
Example of Organization-Wide Goals

Organizational CPM/Professional Practice Initiative Timeline

INITIATIVE	FY'96 Theme: PARTNERSHIPS	FY'97 Theme: MUTUALITY
DOCUMENTATION TOOLS	Improve various documentation competencies. 2 Housewide audits completed and results shared w/UBCs and PC. Complete 2 Clinical Practice Guideline (CPG) validations. Complete implementation of all documentation tools housewide except in ED.	Connect ED w/documentation system. Conduct 2 housewide documentation audits; Fall audit 90% compliance. Select computer documentation vendor and design automation documentation system processes. Initiate education of automated documentation fundamentals. Complete validation of 3 CPGs. Education Records evolve into Outcome Records.
PARTNERSHIPS	Complete new care delivery systems on 2 units. Promote NM/UBC Chair partnerships. Strengthen PC officers, PPC and CNE partnerships. Pt./Family participates on 1 UBC. Physician participates/has close working relationship w/2 UBCs. Improve CNA/tech preceptor program to facilitate retention of high quality nurse extenders.	Complete new care delivery systems on 4 units. Pt./Family participates on PC and 3 UBCs. Physician participates/has close working relationship w/4 UBCs. Obtain unit specific summaries which record CNA/tech preceptor program improvements and to track achievements/improvements.
PC & UBC STRUCTURE/ PROCESS/ OUTCOME	Ongoing Leadership Workshops. Continue to refine process of goal development, follow through and evaluation. Increase incorporation of Core Beliefs and value equation as measurement standards of "worth." PPC consultations w/UBCs 2-3x/yr. Increase amount of lateral involvement on units. Continue Leadership Skill Building Series.	Continue Leadership Workshops. Continue Leadership Skill Building Series. Increase lateral involvement in unit initiatives. Incorporate affiliates representation on PC. Cooperate w/CPMRC's consortium-wide study, "Impact of CPM Implementation."
PROFESSIONAL GROWTH	Estimate needed resources for ongoing professional development. Design and implement professional development offering thru Education Resources. Presentations at CPM National Conferences and other professional seminars/conferences. Professional nursing presentations to the community and schools of nursing by staff.	Presentations at National CPM Conference and other professional seminars/conferences. Staff actively involved w/planning and preparation for JCAHO survey. Promote novice to expert initiatives. Staff skill development in promotion of mutuality. Promote opportunities for nursing to participate in the creation of and to understand the new IL Nurse Practice Act.
PROFESSIONAL PRACTICE PROCESSES	Conduct housewide delegation workshop to standardize foundation of understanding among RNs. Obtain summaries of unit specific progress on delegation and track achievements/improvements. Provide a variety of opportunities which clarify nurses understanding, articulation and demonstration of their scope of practice. Implement housewide professional exchange report. Conduct housewide 2 staff/patient/family interviews.	Support piloting of various peer review approaches. Enhance staff interviewing and Plan of Care competencies. Enhance opportunities and evidence of mutuality w/patients and families. Continue collection of unit specific progress on delegation to track achievements/improvements. Continue various opportunities for scope of practice clarity.
RESEARCH/ SCHOLARSHIP	Introduce concept of clinical scholarship. Explore and identify clinical scholarship opportunities. Host annual Research Conference.	6 units will be involved w/clinical scholarship initiatives. Host annual Research Conference.

Table Fifty, continued

INITIATIVE	FY'98 Theme: COORDINATOR OF CARE
DOCUMENTATION TOOLS	Connect flow of nursing-gathered patient data within MHS and its affiliates. Begin implementation of automated documentation system. Complete validation of 3 CPGs.
PARTNERSHIPS	Complete new care delivery systems on 4 units. Pt. Family participates on PC and 5 UBCs. Physician participates/has close working relationship w/6 UBCs. Obtain unit specific summaries of CNA/tech preceptor programs to track achievements/improvements.
PC & UBC STRUCTURE/ PROCESS/ OUTCOME	100% lateral involvement demonstrated on 15 units; no unit reports <75% involvement.
PROFESSIONAL GROWTH	Presentations at National CPM Conference and other professional seminars/conferences. Staff participate w/CPMRC's implementation team. Staff skill development in fulfilling role as coordinator of care.
PROFESSIONAL PRACTICE PROCESSES	Support continues and approaches to peer review are demonstrated in increased numbers. Enhance staff's demonstrated competency re: coordinator of care.
RESEARCH/ SCHOLARSHIP	12 units will be involved w/clinical scholarship initiatives. Host annual Research Conference.

Reference: Cathy Schwartz, Memorial Medical Center, Springfield, Illinois

APPENDIX B

Clinical Practice Model Resource Center (CPMRC)
Grand Rapids, Michigan

Mission:
Enhance partnering relationships and world linkages for generation of collective knowledge and wisdom that continually improves the structure, process and outcomes of professional service and community health.

Bonnie Wesorick, RN, MSN
Founder

Laurie Shiparski, RN, BSN, MS
Professional Practice Specialist

Diane Hanson, RN, BSN, MM
Practice Guidelines Specialist

Ellen Hale, RN, MSN
Informatics Specialist

Darlene Josephs, CPS
Operations Administrator

Linda DeLeeuw
Administrative Secretary

Connie Lindsey
Administrative Secretary

Marie Kegel
Administrative Secretary

Researchers:
Karen Grigsby, RN, PhD
Donna Westmoreland, RN, PhD
University of Nebraska Medial Center
College of Nursing, Omaha, Nebraska

Additional partners include a diverse interdisciplinary resource team.

CPM Associate Consortium

Mission:
Collectively create professional practice and learning environments that empower each partner to provide their unique healing contribution.

Mary Koloroutis, RN, MS
Abbott Northwestern Hospital
Minneapolis, MN

ALEGENT HEALTH SYSTEM:
Pom Gaines, RN
Judy Riggert, RN, MA
Alegent Health Bergan Mercy Medical
Center
Omaha, NE

Debbie Cohen, RN
Debbie Tiffey, RN
Alegent Health Community Memorial
Missouri Valley, IA

Cynthia Lesch-Busse, RN, BSN
Alegent Health Immanuel Medical Center
Omaha, NE

Connie Peters, RN, BA
Alegent Health Memorial Hospital
Schuyler, NE

Kathy West, RN, BSN
Alegent Health Mercy Hospital
Corning, IA

Cindy Kallsen, RN, BSN
Alegent Health Mercy Hospital
Council Bluffs, IA

Toni Regni, RN
Alegent Health Midlands Hospital
Papillion, NE

Betty Jo Balzar, RN, MSN
Appleton Medical Center
Appleton, WI

BUTTERWORTH HEALTH SYSTEM:
Michelle Troseth, RN, MSN
Bonnie Wesorick, RN, MSN
Senior Advisor for Professional Practice
Kathy Wyngarden, RN, MSN
Butterworth Hospital
Grand Rapids, MI

Pat Duthie, RN, BSN
Christie Peck, RN, BA
Community Resource Center
Grand Rapids, MI

Visiting Nurse Services
Grand Rapids, MI

Mary Gray, RN, MSN
Centura Health-St. Mary-Corwin Medical
Center
Pueblo, CO

Deb Masich, BSN, CCRN
Columbia Rose Medical Center
Denver, CO

Dee Blakey, RN, BSN
Flagstaff Medical Center
Flagstaff, AZ

Brenda Srof, RN, MSN
Goshen College
Goshen, IN

Ellen Stuart, RN, MSN
Grand Rapids Community College
Grand Rapids, MI

HARRIS METHODIST
HEALTH SYSTEM:
Diane Thomas, RN, MSN, CETN
Harris Continued Care Hospital
Bedford, TX

Marilyn Knight, RN, MSN
Harris Home Health
Fort Worth, TX

Kathy Ratliff, RN, ADN
Harris Methodist Erath
Stephenville, TX

Nancy Pittman, RN, MS, CNA
Harris Methodist Fort Worth
Forth Worth, TX

Kelly Smith, RN
Harris Methodist - HEB Hospital
Bedford, TX

Rochelle Jee, RN, BSN
Harris Methodist Southwest/Northwest
Fort Worth. TX

Markeeta Edwards, RN, BSN
Harris Methodist - Walls Regional
Clebume, TX

Marsha Vanderveen, RNC, MS
Holland Community Hospital and Home
Health Care
Holland, MI

Barbara Scarpelli, RN, BSN
Hotel Dieu Grace Hospital
Windsor, Ontario, Canada

Sue Caulfield, RN,C, MS
Diana Cave, RN, MSN
Sandy Heresa, RN, MSN, OCN
Kaiser Sunnyside Hospital
Clackamas, OR

Kim Dixon, RN, BSN
Liberty Hospital
Liberty, MO

Karen Kline, RN, MScN
Katherine McIndoe, RN, MSN
Lions Gate Hospital
N. Vancouver, British Columbia, Canada

Katy Badovinac, RN
Mary Dean, RN
Mary Kaurich, RN
Jan Waterman, RN
Macomb Hospital Center
Warren, MI

Linda Barnes, RN, BS
Magic Valley Regional Medical Center
Twin Falls, ID

Barbara Yingling, RN, BSN, MAED, C
Massillon Community Hospital
Massillon, OH

Shirley Hamann, RN, MSN, ONC
Medcenter One Health System
Bismarck, ND

Cathy Schwartz, RN, MS
Memorial Medical Center
Springfield, IL

Pat Nakoneczny, RN, BSN
Northern Michigan Hospital
Petoskey, MI

Debra Skidmore, RN, BSN
Phoenix Children's Hospital
Phoenix, AZ

Kathleen Henderson, CNS
Saint Joseph Health Center
Kansas City, MO

Glenda Skaggs, RN, BSN
St. Catherine Hospital
Garden City, KS

Deb Tracy, RN, BSN, CCRN
St. Jude Medical Center
Fullerton, CA

Sue Chase-Cantarini, RN, MS
St. Mark's Hospital
Salt Lake City, UT

Betty Jo Balzar, RN, MSN
Theda dark Medical Center
Neenah,WI

Margret Comack, BN, MEd
Toronto East General Hospital
Toronto, Ontario, Canada

Lanyce Keel, RN, MA
University of Nebraska Medical Center
Omaha, NE

Rani Srivastava, RN, MScN
Wellesley Central Hospital
Toronto, Ontario, Canada

Chrystle Whitaker, RN
Wesley Medical Center
Wichita, KS

Chris Shaw, RN, BSN
West Allis Memorial Hospital
West Allis, WI

APPENDIX C

Margie Bosscher, RN
Margie is a 20 year staff nurse. She has participated with CPM for eight years as Partnership Council Coordinator, Central Council Co-Coordinator, and partner in implementation to practice at several Consortium hospitals.

Jeanette Brooks, LPN
An 18 year practitioner, Jeanette has had many years of experience in developing partnerships and being a member of a Partnership Council. She has gone to other units to speak on how partnerships have worked for her and also has talked to orientees about partnership assignments. She has been a presenter in workshops and at the CPM International Conference to share her learning and experience on this topic. She also has shared her experience with partnerships by participating in a video so other units could view it.

Deb Chapman, PCA
Deb is a Patient Care Associate and part of the non-licensed support staff at the hospital where she has served for two (2) years. She is a member of the Partnership Council. She has been a presenter at leadership workshops and also at the CPM International Conference to share her learning and experience as support staff on the Partnership Council.

Tracy Christopherson, RRT
Tracy is a 13 year Respiratory Care practitioner. She has been a pioneer for interdisciplinary involvement in Partnership Councils. She has been a council coordinator and is presently a member of her department's Partnership Council. She has presented nationally on Partnership Councils and also travels to sites currently using councils to offer support and share learnings.

Jan Falk, RN
Jan is a 25 year practitioner and has had many years of experience as coordinator and member of a Partnership Council. Because she values partnerships, she has been a presenter at workshops and national and international conferences to share her learning and experiences.

Carol Glass, RN
Carol is a 26 year practitioner. She is co-chair of the Central Partnership Council and her unit Partnership Councils. She is a leader and mentor

throughout the hospital system on partnerships and councils. She has presented at workshops and national conferences and also travels to health care sites to share her learnings.

Carol Geurink, RPh
Carol is in her 16th year as a Pharmacist. She is currently a member of a unit-based Partnership Council. She brings her expertise in pharmaceutical care and drug utilization to this group. She continues to expand her partnering relationships based on the wisdom and guidance provided through the Partnership Council.

Joseph Moore, MD
Joe is an Obstetrician who practiced for 26 years and is new to CPM and Partnership Councils. However, over the past eight years, he has been actively involved in community health and works collaboratively with nurses, community health workers and community members in the development of programming responsive to community identified need. This collaborative approach and the methods employed in achieving desired goals parallels the work being done in the Partnership Councils. His involvement now exemplifies a desire to have physicians connect in partnership within clinical health care teams.

Martha (Marti) E. Rheault, RN
Marti has been a Registered Nurse for over 12 years. She has had the opportunity to develop partnerships both professionally and personally. She strives to integrate partnership into practice so that "we-they" thinking can be replaced with "us" thinking. Marti represents the resource track at her unit Partnership Council, and has shared her experiences with this role through presentations to new council members from her own institution as well as from other Consortium sites.

Deborah Ritz-Holland, RN, BSN, OCN
Debbie is an 11 year practitioner. She has been involved in developing partnerships not only on her Oncology unit, but also has had the opportunity to partner with other members of the healthcare team and throughout the Consortium. She was a CPM Co-coordinator on the Oncology unit for approximately three years and has since become the coordinator for the Outpatient Oncology Clinic. She realizes the importance and value of these partnerships. She shares and continues her participation and growth within these realms by her personal commitments to herself and others.

Jeanne Roode, RN, MSN, CNA
Jeanne has been a Nurse Manager for the past 15 years and has provided leadership in the implementation of a clinical practice model at her organization. She has been a member of Partnership Councils for over eight years and provides consultative services to client hospitals throughout the U.S. and Canada on the role of the Operations Resource (Manager). She presents nationally on topics related to establishing partnerships and creating empowering work environments.

Kristin Root, BSW, SW
Kristin has been a Medical Social Worker at Butterworth Hospital for seven years. As a current member of the Orthopedic unit's Partnership Council, she has worked closely with an interdisciplinary team to develop partnerships on the unit as well as within the Medical Social Work Department. In addition to traveling to Consortium sites, Kristin has shared her learning and experiences on this topic at workshops and national conferences.

John Silowsky, RN
John is a nine year practitioner. He has been a Council Coordinator for his department for four years and continues to mentor others in his Critical Care department on the work of partnership. He has presented nationally on Partnership Councils and shared mission and visions. He has facilitated dialogue and continues to integrate this technique into the functioning of his Partnership Council. He also travels to new sites implementing practice councils to offer support and share learnings.

Darren VandeZande, RN, BSN
Darren has been a practitioner on an Orthopedic unit for seven years and has forwarded much effort in developing and mentoring others in the development of partnerships during this time. Over the past five years he has been a member of his unit's Partnership Council and as a Clinical Coordinator, continues to be a leader and facilitator for partnership on his unit as well as being actively involved in various other hospital-wide multidisciplinary initiatives.

Marcia Veenstra, RN, BSN
Marcia is a 30 year practitioner. She has practiced in multiple settings from OB to ICU to Long Term Care. She has been a Council Coordinator for many years and co-Chair of the Centralized Partnership Council. She travels to Consortium sites to share her leadership with those beginning the journey. She has been a presenter in workshops and national conferences. She believes she continues to learn from the wisdom shared by others and hopes to contribute to your partnership journey.

Bibliography

Ackoff, R. (1986). <u>Management in small doses.</u> New York: John Wiley & Sons.

Barker, J. (1992). <u>Future edge: Discovering the new paradigms of success.</u> New York: William Morrow & Co.

Block, P. (1993). <u>Stewardship: Choosing service over self-interest.</u> San Francisco: Berrett-Koehler Publishers.

Bridges, W. (1991). <u>Managing transitions. Making the most of change.</u> Reading, MA: Addison-Wesley Publication Co.

<u>Character sketches from the pages of stricpture illusted in the world of nature.</u> Volume I. (May, 1986). Institute in Basic Youth Conflicts, Inc. Oak Brook, Illinois.

Covey, S., Men-ill, A. and Men-ill, R. (1994). <u>First things first: To live. to love. to learn, to leave a legacy.</u> New York: Simon & Schuster.

Covey, S. (1992). <u>Principle-centered leadership</u>. New York: Simon & Schuster.

Covey, S. (1988) <u>The law of the harvest.</u> (Video) Seven habits of highly effective people video illustrations. Pueblo, UT: Covey Leadership Center, Inc.

Dass, R. (1992). <u>Path of service: Here and now in 90's.</u> (Cassette Recording). Boulder, CO: Sounds True.

DePree, M. (1989). <u>Leadership is an art.</u> New York: Dell Publishing.

Ferguson, M. (1980). <u>The aquarian conspiracy.</u> New York: G.P. Putman & Sons.

Fox, E. (1941). <u>Find and use your inner power.</u> San Francisco: Harper Collins Publishers.

Ghoshal, S. and Bartlett, C. (1997). <u>The individual corporation: A fundamentally new approach to management.</u> New York: HarperCollins Publishers, Inc.

Issacs W. (April, 1993). "Dialogue: The power of collective thinking." The Systems Thinker. 4(3), p. 1-5.

Jandernoa, B. and Gillespie, G. (June, 1997). "Leadership in the new milsnnium." Presented at the International Dialogue Gathering, Allendale, MI.

Jones, L.B. (1996). The path: Creating your mission statement for work and for life. New York, NY: Hyperion.

Jones, M. (1995). Creating an imaginative life. Berkeley: Conari Press.

Kaiser, L.(1994). Creating the future of health care. (Cassette Recording). Front Royal, VA: National Cassette Services, Inc.

Kelley, R. (1992). The power of followership: How to create leaders people want to follow and followers who lead themselves. New York: Currency/Doubleday.

Kornfield, J., & Feldman, C. (1991). Stories of the spirit, stories of the icart: Parables of the spiritual path from around the world. San Francisco: HarperCollins Publishers, Inc.

Lambert, L., Walker, D., Zimmerman, D. P., Cooper, J. E., Lambert, M. D., Gardner, M. E., and Slack, P.J. (1995). The constructivist leader. New fork: Teachers College Press.

Merton, T. (1961). New seeds of contemplation. New York: New directions Publishing.

Nouwen, H. (1974). Out of solitude. Notre Dame, IN: Ave Maria Press.

Palmer, Parker, J. (October, 1990) Leading from within. Reflections on spirituality and leadership. Indianapolis, IN: Campus Ministries. (Available from Potter's House Book Service, 1658 Columbia Road NW, Washington, DC, 20009.)

Peck, M. S. (1987) The different drum: Community making and peace. New York: Simon & Schuster, Inc.

Quinn, D. (1993). Ishmael. New York: Bantan Hard Cover.

Quorum Health Resources (1992). <u>Leading process improvement teams:</u> <u>A guidebook.</u> (Available from Quorum Health Resources Inc. 105 Continental Place, Bretwood, TN, 37027.)

Remen,R.N. (1996). <u>Kitchen table wisdom: Stories that heal.</u> New York: Riverhead Books.

Roach, M.S. (1997). <u>Caring from the heart: The convergence of caring</u> <u>and sprituality.</u> NJ: Paulist Press.

Rost, J.C. (1991). <u>Leadership for the twenty-first century.</u> Connecticut: Greenwood Publishing Group.

Schrage, M. (1990). <u>No more team! Mastering the dynamics of creative</u> <u>collaboration.</u> New York: Currency/Doubleday.

Senge, P. (1991). <u>The fifth discipline: The art and practice of the learn-</u> <u>ing organization.</u> New York: Currency/Doubleday.

Senge, P., Roberts, C., Ross, R., Smith, B., and Kleiner, A. (1994). <u>The</u> <u>fifth discipline fieldbook.</u> New York: Currency/Doubleday.

Shiparski, L. (1997). <u>Change is life. Poems of personal transformation in</u> <u>the work place.</u> Michigan: Practice Field Publishing.

Teresa, Mother. (1996). <u>Meditations from a simple path.</u> New York: Ballantine Books.

Underwood, P. (1997) On the nature of clan mothers. <u>At The Crossroads.</u> Issue Six, p. 22-23.

Wesorick, B. (1995). <u>The closing and opening of a millennium: A jour-</u> <u>ney from old to new thinking.</u> Michigan: Practice Field Publishing.

Wesorick, B. (1996). <u>The closing and opening of a millennium: A jour-</u> <u>ney from old to new relationships in the work setting.</u> Michigan: Practice Field Publishing.

Wesorick, B., Shiparski, L. (1997). <u>Can the human being thrive in the</u> <u>work place? Dialogue as a strategy of hope.</u> Michigan: Practice Field Publishing.

Wheatley, M. (1992). <u>Leadership and the new science: Learning about organization from an orderly universe.</u> San Francisco: Berrett-Koehler Publisher.

Wheatley, M. (1993). <u>Leadership and the new science.</u> (Video). Carlsbad, CA: CRM Films.

Wheatley, M. and Kellner-Rogers, M. (1996). <u>A simpler way.</u> San Francisco: Berrett-Koehler Publishers.

Whyte, D. (1995). <u>The intelligent organization.</u> (Cassette Recording). Langley, WA: Many Rivers Press.

Williamson, M. (1993). <u>A return to love.</u> New York: Harper Paperbacks.

Zigler, Z. (1988). <u>Goals.</u> (Cassette Recording). Carrollton, TX: Zig Zigler Corporation.

Send any comments or inquiries regarding this journey to:
CPM Resource Center
600 28th St., S.W.
Grand Rapids, MI 49509
616/530-9206
616/530-9245 FAX
info@cpmrc.com

Glossary

Analysis - Separating the whole into parts.

Balance - A harmony of relationships within self and with others necessary to achieve mission.

BodyMindSpirit - The essence of a human being.

Consensus - Bringing the voices of many to uncover options, expose collective wisdom and move collectively in action.

Continuous Learning - The ability to experience each moment as a learner and teacher for the ongoing growth of self and others.

Culture - An invisible field. The presence of the unseen souls of the many who walk or have walked there unfolding the story of a people.

Debate - To beat down.

Deliberate - To weigh out.

Dialogue - Collective exploration in which truth and meaning emerge among participants.

Discuss - To shake apart, examine pro's and con's.

Equal Accountability - A relationship between members of a group driven by ownership of mission, not power-over or fear.

Evaluation - Noticing the synchronization of processes that demonstrate outcomes, learning, celebrations, things that work, and things that do not work.

Field - A space of potential connection and explanation.

Followership - Collaboration in effort toward achieving a mission.

Healthy Culture - The connection of the unseen souls carrying out important work.

Intention - A personal choice to connect with another at a deeper level of humanness.

Intimacy - The act of opening yourself to others by sharing your true feelings.

Key Learning - Awareness of an insight, realization, "aha", or discovery that deepens understanding.

Low Morale - The absence of the soul's expression and the inability to connect work with purpose and meaning.

Mission - A call to live out something that matters or is meaningful.

Non-Shared Decision Making Field - Examples include: debate, deliberation voting, and discussion which are often used to analyze issues but have outcomes of win lose. Individual preferences and analysis of the pros and cons are the goal. These methods do not have the intention of seeking deeper meaning or shared agreement.

One-on-One - A partnering relationship between a Partnership Council member and a designated peer; the manner or process in which every person is connected to the whole.

Partnership Council - An infrastructure that creates a place to develop and enhance relationships and have meaningful conversations in order to tap into the collective wisdom necessary to achieve the shared mission and vision.

Point of Care - Processes, outcomes, and interactions occurring between care providers and the consumers of health care.

Potential - An inherent capacity within oneself and others to continuously learn, grow, and create.

Scope of Practice Process - A continuous learning process that has system supports to bring interdisciplinary colleagues together in order to clarify scope of service and integrate those services at the point of care.

Shared Decision - Each person realizes their accountability to outcomes in light of their unique responsibilities.

Shared Decision Making - Making decisions together in ways that tap individual and group wisdom. The long term goal is to increase our shared understanding and move in action collectively.

Shared Decision Making Field - Consensus and dialogue are required to develop shared understanding around complex issues. Synthesis, or connecting a whole from its parts is the goal in this field. Shared agreement is an outcome of consensus and shared understanding an outcome of dialogue.

Shared Leadership - Brings forward the capacity of every member to partner and achieve the shared purpose.

Shared Work - Each person's accountability to create a healthy work culture.

Shared Work Team - A group gathered to collectively address a specific issue necessary to create, maintain or expand a healthy work place.

Soul - The essence, the spirit of life, the center of humanness, joy, and creativity.

Synthesis - Forming the whole from parts.

Tracks - A term used to describe the basic roles associated with expertise necessary to accomplish the nature of work. Example: practitioner, manager/operations resource, educator/learning resource, or educator.

Trust - A sense of synchrony on important issues or things that matter.

Unhealthy Culture - The disconnection of the unseen souls carrying out important work.

Vision - What it would look like if we fully lived our mission and purpose.

Voting - Expressing one's personal preference.

Vulnerability - The willingness to look at oneself, know oneself and connect with others as you are, not as you think others desire you to be or you are supposed to be.

Index

Special acknowledgment and appreciation to the following colleagues whose feedback enhanced this book.

Betty Jo Balzar	Elaine Keller
Linda Barnes	Connie McAllister
Dee Blakey	Katherine McIndoe
Mike Bosscher	MJ. Peterson
Sue Chase-Cantarini	Kathy Ratliff
Kim Dixon	Carol Roberts
Peggy Flores	Carol Robinson
Mary Gray	Barbara Scarpelli
Karen Grigsby	Cathy Schwartz
Carol Guler	Chris Shaw
Ellen Hale	Glenda Skaggs
Carmen Hall	Rani Srivastava
Shirley Hamann	Luella Theurer
Diane Hanson	Diane Thomas
Darlene Josephs	Donna Westmoreland
Lanyce Keel	

A special thank you to Linda DeLeeuw who coordinated this entire effort including typing and manuscript layout.